NEW JERSEY ARTS

NEW JERSEY ARTS

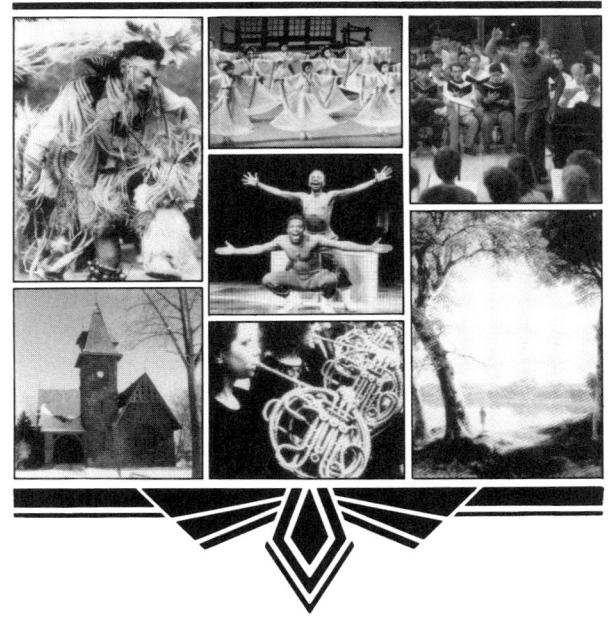

Patricia Herold

RUTGERS UNIVERSITY PRESS
NEW BRUNSWICK AND LONDON

Library of Congress Cataloging-in-Publication Data
Herold, Patricia, 1953–
New Jersey arts / Patricia Herold.
p. cm.
ISBN 0-8135-1553-X (cloth)   ISBN 0-8135-1554-8 (pbk.)
1. Arts—New Jersey—Directories.   2. Arts facilities—New Jersey—Directories.   3. Art commissions—New Jersey—Directories.   I. Title.
NX110.H47   1990
700'.25'749—dc20   89-49082

British Cataloging-in-Publication information available

Copyright © 1990 by Patricia Herold
All rights reserved
Manufactured in the United States of America

For Peter and Catherine

Contents

How to Use This Book   ix
Key to Symbols and Abbreviations   xv

Visual Arts   1

Centers   41

Dance   69

Music   87

Theater   117

Festivals   139

Education and the Arts   155

Appendixes   179

New Jersey County and Area Arts Agencies   181

Grantmakers   185

How to Use This Book

In the last decade, New Jersey's arts world became one of the richest and fastest growing in the United States. In 1989, New Jersey spent more public money than any state in the country, except New York, on the arts. For fiscal year 1990, it ranked third in the nation, despite a nearly two-million-dollar budget cut for the New Jersey State Council on the Arts. But beyond government statistics, a look through this book should prove the point.

Here you'll find information on one of the world's finest collections of Tibetan art, on a small theater company that revives long-forgotten eighteenth-century plays, and on one of this country's most distinguished chamber music ensembles, which rose from obscurity to national recognition in less than a decade.

You'll learn about the stunning success of New Jersey's foremost symphony orchestra and its new, young conductor; about a program that offers playwriting workshops to juvenile offenders; and about the history of some of the world's leading choirs.

And you'll discover the art in Xerox prints and soup tureens.

In short, you'll see that challenging, entertaining, high-caliber arts experiences do not require a journey to New York or Philadelphia.

New Jersey Arts is designed to help you find the best art, music, stage performances, screenings, and poetry readings not only in your area but also throughout the state. It will tell you about art exhibits, mime performances, and jazz festivals that are worth a trip north, south, east, or west. This book offers up-to-date information on hundreds of organizations, events, and people in the visual arts, dance, theater, music, film, and poetry—from Hoboken to Cape May, from Long Beach Island to the Delaware Water Gap. It is meant to serve as a handbook for both the dilettante and the devotee. Those who simply enjoy the arts will discover here a host of ways to spend an evening or weekend. Those who love a particular art form will find information on where and how to pursue that passion.

Do you like to combine art with nature? This guide will show you where to find sculpture and classical music in informal, outdoor settings. Do you know someone with a physical or mental disability? The book includes information on theaters, museums, and other arts orga-

HOW TO USE THIS BOOK

nizations that offer special programs for the mentally and physically disabled. Do you have school-age children? Each entry includes a section on educational programs and events, listing hundreds of classes, lectures, workshops, and apprenticeships for young people and adults, from preschoolers to senior citizens.

To help you make the most of this information, the book is divided into seven major sections: Visual Arts, Centers, Dance, Music, Theater, Festivals, and Education and the Arts. Film and video organizations are included in the Visual Arts section. Major festivals, such as the New Jersey Shakespeare Festival, really institutions rather than a short-lived series of performances, are listed under Music or Theater, as the case may be. There is a small subsection, at the end of the Centers section, devoted to the state's poetry centers and organizations that sponsor readings. Within the sections, arts organizations are listed alphabetically.

In the arts, as in all enterprises, different things matter to different people. You may choose, for instance, to visit a museum because it is located ten miles from your home. Or you may elect to attend performances only at New Jersey's most highly regarded theaters or by its most outstanding classical music ensembles. One way to determine whether an organization suits your particular needs and tastes is to pay attention to the symbols (see Key to Symbols) to the right of each listing. They are designed to help you distinguish among organizations not only in terms of collections or repertoire (information supplied within the listing itself), but also in terms of physical assets and particular appeal. For instance, is a museum surrounded by hiking trails? Does it have a backyard rose garden? Or a sculpture garden? Does it offer programs for young people, the visually impaired, or working artists? Does it operate a museum shop? Another aid to selection is the acronyms to the right of each listing for information on whether the organization has earned awards and/or commendations from the governor or the New Jersey State Council on the Arts.

Two symbols deserve special explanation. First, a word about the fee symbol. In the Visual Arts, Dance, Music, Theater, and Festivals sections, the symbol for fee appears when an organization generally charges an admission fee or requests a donation. Fees to the public range anywhere from a nominal charge of one dollar at some museums to fifteen dollars or more for theater or concert tickets. (Keep in mind that a museum with free admission may charge a fee for special programs, such as studio art courses.) The Education and the Arts section is a little bit different. It lists two kinds of organizations: arts schools that present on-site performances to the public and arts organizations that take educationally oriented performances into schools, community centers, churches, and so on. School and community-center performances, while free to the audience, usually are not free to the school or center. In both cases, where a fee is charged, the symbol for fee appears.

In the Theater section, a symbol indicates whether an organization is an Equity theater, in which case it hires a certain percentage of Actors Equity union actors and stage managers and adheres to other industry standards.

Each organization's entry includes the following: Vital Statistics—name, address, telephone number, and days and normal hours of operation (most institutions are closed on holidays; always call ahead), where applicable; Special Programs and Events (arranged alphabetically)—annual or regularly scheduled events and programs of special interest; and Educational Programs and Events (arranged alphabetically)—classes, workshops, lectures, apprenticeships, and other educational opportunities for children and adults. The remainder of the entry takes a look at the people, programs, and achievements that distinguish the organization.

Entries give the locations where performances or exhibits are regularly held. In the Music and Theater sections, the approximate number of seats in the primary performance facilities is noted. Where the administrative and box office telephone numbers differ, both are given.

Of course, every effort has been made to present the most up-to-date, accurate information possible. However, if you plan to visit a museum, for instance, or attend an event sponsored annually by a chamber music ensemble, it is always advisable to call ahead. Hours, programs, and art exhibitions and displays do change.

At the back of the book are two appendixes, one listing foundations and corporations that make grants to New Jersey artists and arts organizations; the other, New Jersey arts agencies that channel state and county money to local organizations and individuals and provide important arts resources and information to the arts world and the public.

It may help the reader to know that the arts world tends to divide organizations into two categories: presenters and producers. Presenters do what the word implies: they present art programs—concerts, plays, sculpture exhibits, poetry readings, and other events—to the public. Producers create those concerts and plays, choosing the musicians and actors, selecting the script or musical pieces, rehearsing them, and developing a play or concert. This book lists both producers and presenters, but it does not separate them. Instead, it places each organization, whether producer or presenter, under whichever heading

HOW TO USE THIS BOOK

(Theater, Music, etc.) best defines its mission and activities. As it happens, most (but not all) presenters can be found in the multi-disciplinary Centers section. Producers are generally found in other sections. However, there are exceptions. If, for instance, a presenter offers mainly musical programs, that organization will be listed under Music.

Also, keep in mind that this book is intended to serve as a guide and sampler, not a catalog. *New Jersey Arts* by no means mentions all the worthy organizations in the state, but does list many of the most prominent and interesting.

In general but with some exceptions, this book covers nonprofit, professional arts organizations and institutions. Of course, New Jersey has a rich tradition of amateur community theater and music groups, which play a vital role in the cultural life of their communities. If you are interested in listings of these groups, the New Jersey State Council on the Arts or your local arts agency can provide them.

Be aware that most New Jersey libraries, county colleges, and state and private colleges and universities sponsor a wide range of arts programs and events, serving as performing arts centers in their own right. The state's two major universities—Rutgers, The State University, and Princeton University—have been listed as Centers. But others—notably Montclair State College and William Paterson College in Wayne—also provide an array of arts programs and performances to the public. Most museums also serve as performing arts centers, often offering theater, music, and dance events and/or series. And house and historical museums, generally not covered here, also maintain art collections.

In preparing this book, I collected and compiled lists, sent out questionnaires, conducted interviews, confirmed facts, and updated information as close to press time as possible. Naturally, organizations whose staff did not provide information are not listed. Almost every organization in this book displays one or more of the following characteristics:

It demonstrates statewide or regional impact and/or appeal.
It features an interesting or innovative program, collection, or personality.
It reflects a national, regional, or statewide trend.
It serves as a good example of a type of organization that thrives in the state where listing all such organizations would be impossible.

In the body of each entry you'll find not only facts about the size of the organization and the number and scope of its offerings, but also information on its history and artistic philosophy. Is it an experimental theater, regularly performing new plays and setting classics in unusual

HOW TO USE THIS BOOK

locales? Or a traditional one, dedicated to performing revivals of proven Broadway hits? Each listing provides a glimpse of the character of an organization.

Although numbers—whether of seats in a house, productions, performances, or performers—can be deceptive, the "statistics" included in this book are meant to help you sense what kind of arts experience to expect at a given theater or museum.

As you consult this book, you are sure to notice how many of the organizations listed were founded after 1980. The fact is that the New Jersey arts world, as mentioned earlier, experienced tremendous growth in the last decade. The eighties brought increased professionalism and self-confidence to New Jersey artists and arts organizations. Numerous new arts organizations were founded, and a number of them, such as the New Jersey Chamber Music Society, became success stories in just a few years. In 1984, 602 individual artists sought state fellowships; by 1989, that number had more than doubled. All told, the number of "arts experiences" enjoyed by audiences in New Jersey museums, theaters, concert halls, centers, schools, and other venues grew from 12.7 million in 1987 to an estimated 14 million in 1989.

Much of this new vitality was due to an almost unparalleled commitment to the arts on the part of our state government. Governor Thomas H. Kean was an ardent supporter of the arts, and the programs and budget of the state's arts council, founded in 1966, expanded during his tenure. The new administration of James Florio, however, with a budget crisis pending, has proposed a major cut in the state's arts appropriations.

Although some believe public interest in the arts will grow in the 1990s, government support is likely to flag. During the 1980s, development dollars boosted the economy, and this meant more corporate and individual contributions to the arts and bigger arts audiences. The healthy economy also attracted new audiences. No longer considered a "bedroom" state sandwiched between Philadelphia and New York, New Jersey became a major national employment center. More and more New Jerseyeans now live *and* work in their state; having dispensed with a commute, they probably have more time and inclination to seek cultural enrichment in their home state.

Just as major corporations moved from New York in search of less expensive and more livable quarters for employees during the late seventies and eighties, so did artists. In particular, Hudson River communities such as Jersey City and Hoboken attracted a large number of New York refugees—painters, sculptors, musicians, and actors—who are

HOW TO USE THIS BOOK

now active in New Jersey. They founded galleries, music ensembles, arts service organizations, and theater groups. Many have continued to work both in Manhattan and New Jersey, enriching cultural offerings on both sides of the river. How and whether the state's artists and arts organizations will survive the budget crunch is an overriding issue for the coming years.

Of course, New Jersey's cultural traditions and achievements stretch far back beyond the 1980s to its first human settlements. This state has given birth to many prominent artists and arts institutions and innovations. The film industry was born here, in the Thomas Edison studio known as Black Maria. A pioneer of modern dance, Ruth St. Denis, was born in Somerville. Paul Robeson, one of the greatest singers the country has known, was born and educated here. When he was not busy with his medical practice, William Carlos Williams wrote poems in Rutherford. The Newark Museum stood in the forefront of early public arts education. And the Princeton University Art Museum is one of the oldest university arts institutions in the nation.

To reflect this rich artistic heritage, the book includes Arts notes about New Jersey arts organizations or industries and character/career sketches of music, art, and theater personalities. Also scattered throughout the text are Arts lists which provide information on everything from arts publications to university and corporate galleries. Arts quotes are personal reflections on life in the arts from conductors, art historians, directors, singers, and other artists.

I want to thank the many, many people who helped me to complete my task by offering their time, information, insights, and encouragement.

In preparing this book, I found myself regretting that space limitations prevented me from offering more information and telling more stories about New Jersey's arts organizations, history, and personalities. I hope *New Jersey Arts* leaves you equally hungry for more. You are sure to discover, as I did, that New Jersey's arts world is surprisingly diverse and rich, and that it lends itself to almost endless exploration.

Key to Symbols and Abbreviations

	Actors' Equity Association theater.
	This organization charges a fee or requests a suggested donation.
	Special programs or facilities for the disabled.
	This organization offers an outdoor attraction.
	This organization has a gallery or museum shop.
	Special programs for working artists.
	Special programs for young people.
AFG	Artistic Focus Grant recipient—The New Jersey State Council on the Arts determined this organization was capable of achieving national prominence and gave it funding aimed at helping it do so.
DAO	Distinguished Arts Organization—The New Jersey State Council on the Arts determined that this organization exhibited both artistic excellence and sound management practices.
GAA	This organization received a Governor's Arts Award for contributions in its field.
MIO	This organization was awarded Major Impact Status by the New Jersey State Council on the Arts, on the basis of high artistic and management standards. Only Major Impact Status organizations qualify for Artistic Focus funding.
RCAE	The New Jersey State Council on the Arts designated this organization a Regional Center of Artistic Excellence.
SCAE	The New Jersey State Council on the Arts designated this organization a State Center of Artistic Excellence.

NEW JERSEY ARTS

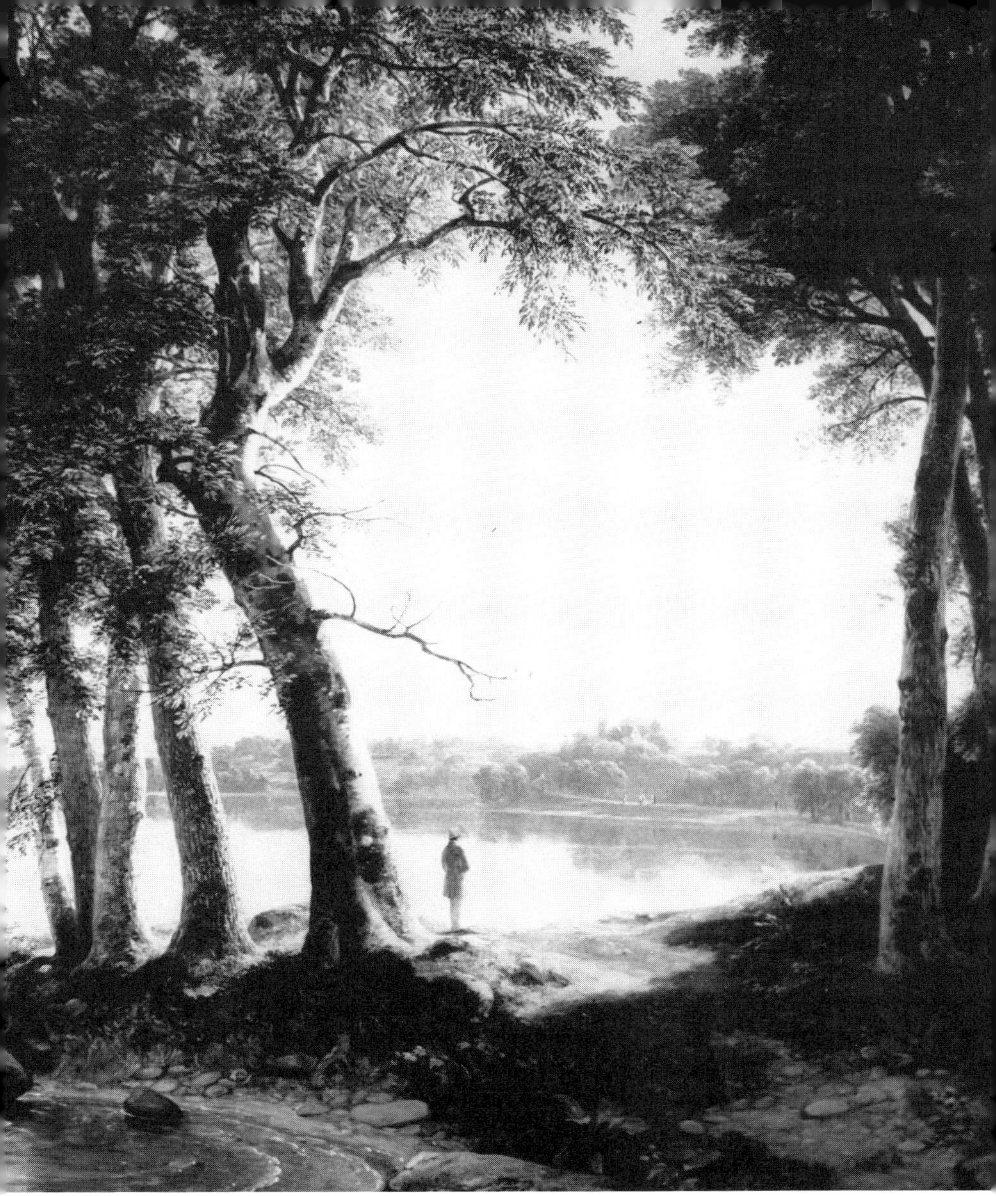

VISUAL ARTS

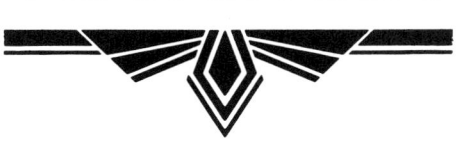

Overleaf: Asher B. Durand, whose *Early Morning at Cold Spring* is in the Montclair Art Museum permanent collection, pioneered a style of painting that became the hallmark of the Hudson River School.

VISUAL ARTS

African Art Museum of the S.M.A. Fathers
23 Bliss Avenue, Tenafly 07670   201-567-0450
Hours: 10 AM–5 PM, every day except Sunday.

The African Art Museum is operated under the auspices of the Society of African Missions, a missionary order of the Catholic Church, founded in France in 1856. The society still conducts missionary work in West Africa and maintains several parishes in the United States, including one in Newark.

The museum is the only one in the state devoted to art from Africa. Its collection, assembled by Catholic missionaries, includes traditional African art representing some one hundred different cultures and twenty countries, from masks and sculpture to woodcuts, instruments, textiles, and totems in ivory and metal. Many works are from West and East Africa.

The museum, which opened in 1980, mounts at least one major exhibit each year, usually assembled from its permanent collection and/or metropolitan New York–New Jersey area collectors. Recent shows have included "Values in African Art and Culture," an examination of how human values are taught through art, and "Mask of Liberia," a survey of Liberian masks. In 1989–1990 the museum sponsored a documentary film series called "Africa's Heritage and History."

Special Programs and Events: ☐ Appearances by African dance groups; occasional.

Educational Programs and Events: ☐ Lectures. ☐ Slide presentations and workshops on African art for children from pre-kindergarten through high school. ☐ Teacher workshops on African Studies.

Aljira   A Center for Contemporary Art
Two Washington Place, Newark 07102   201-643-6877
Hours: Noon–6 PM, Wednesday through Sunday.

Founded by a group of working artists in 1983, Aljira shows the work of minority New Jersey artists, predominantly from the Newark area. The name Aljira is taken from the word meaning "dreamtime" in Australian aborigine, and it was chosen to conjure up the sense of timelessness associated with creative endeavors. The gallery, located in a Newark loft space, showcases established and emerging artists and emphasizes a multicultural approach to social and artistic issues.

VISUAL ARTS

In keeping with its emphasis on minority issues, Aljira frequently explores the phenomenon of diaspora, the separation of people from their homeland and native culture. In 1988, it presented "Art from the African Diaspora." Another recent exhibition showcased the work of twenty-five Nigerian artists. In 1989, Aljira presented a show called "Diary of a Neighborhood: African-American Barbershops and Beauty Salons as Cultural Institutions," which examined the meaning of contemporary hairstyles and the barber and beauty shop as a reflection of the character of a community. A barber chair, slides of beauty salons in one artist's neighborhood, and a mural illustrating various hairstyles were all part of the program. Aljira usually presents between four to six exhibits annually, changing shows every four to eight weeks.

Special Programs and Events: ☐ Jazz, poetry readings, and other performances in connection with exhibits.

Educational Programs and Events: ☐ Occasional lectures and slide talks in connection with exhibits and/or the issue of diaspora.

Animal Art Museum

St. Hubert's Giralda, 575 Woodland Avenue, Madison 07940
201-377-5541
Hours: 11 AM–4 PM, Wednesday, Friday, and Saturday.

The Animal Art Museum is New Jersey's only nonprofit gallery devoted to animal art. It contains the collection of Geraldine R. Dodge, the Rockefeller heiress, dog breeder, and philanthropist, whose love of animals led her to assemble a large assortment of paintings and sculpture featuring horses, dogs, cats, and other domestic, farm, and hunt animals. Mrs. Dodge was especially fond of the work of Rosa Bonheur; two of her works are on display here. Located on the grounds of the former Dodge estate, the gallery is operated under the auspices of the St. Hubert's Giralda Animal Welfare Center and Shelter.

Upon Mrs. Dodge's death in 1973, the bulk of her animal art collection was auctioned by Sotheby Parke Bernet to provide an endowment for the animal welfare center and shelter. A recent sale to benefit the center disposed of many additional works, including one of the highlights of the collection, Rosa Bonheur's *Horse Fair*. Only a small portion of Mrs. Dodge's collection remains; those pieces are on display in the attic gallery. The assortment includes eighteenth- and nineteenth-century animal bronzes, oils, and lithographs and numerous watercolors by the

VISUAL ARTS

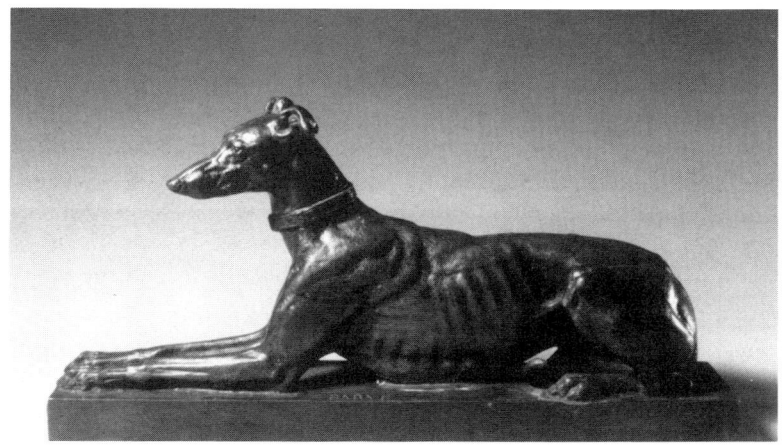

Geraldine Rockefeller Dodge, of New York and Madison, assembled a vast collection of animal art, which included numerous European bronzes. This nineteenth-century piece, *Greyhound*, was created by Antoine Louis Barye.

portraitist Ward Binks, who drew many dogs belonging to the British royal family and was commissioned to capture the likenesses of Mrs. Dodge's pets.

Special Event: ☐ Juried contemporary animal art show, exhibition, and sale held in the fall.

Art Center of Northern New Jersey (see Centers)

Art Center of Trenton (see Artworks)

Artworks
The Visual Arts School of Princeton and Trenton

Offices: Artworks/Princeton, 45 Stockton Street, Princeton 08540
609-921-9173
Gallery, studio space, and offices at: Artworks/Trenton, The Art Center of Trenton, 19 Everett Alley, Trenton 08611   609-394-9436
Hours: 11 AM–5 PM, Tuesday through Saturday.

Founded as the Princeton Art Association in 1964, Artworks is now a gallery/school that offers exhibits featuring New Jersey artists and more

VISUAL ARTS

than thirty-five studio and art history and appreciation classes. The gallery is located in an 8,000-square-foot Trenton warehouse. Recent shows have included "Figurative Inquiry," made up of contemporary works in a variety of media by seven New Jersey artists, including Jacob Landau and Mel Leipzig; "On the Wall, Off the Wall: Recent Sculpture," showcasing works by six New Jersey artists; and "Delaware Valley Landscape Painters," featuring works by nineteenth- and twentieth-century regional painters. Artworks presents six or seven exhibits annually, changing shows every two months. Most are mounted in its main gallery; some community-oriented exhibits are hung in a hall gallery.

Special Programs and Events: □ Art camp for children, ages seven to eleven. □ Classes to prepare people with disabilities to take regular art classes; occasional. □ Classes for disabled children and adults; occasional. □ Museum trips. □ Studios for rent. □ Studio tours.

Educational Programs and Events: □ After-school classes for teenagers. □ After-work classes for adults. □ Classes and workshops in Chinese painting and calligraphy, watercolor, sculpture, figure studies, enamel, weaving, design, and art history for young people and adults. □ Lunchtime talks by artists during exhibits. □ "Picture This" and "Cartoon Capers": painting, sculpture, collage, fiber, and cartoon art classes for children. □ Summer classes for children and adults. □ Working artist lectures.

Atlantic City Arts Center

Garden Pier, New Jersey Avenue and the Boardwalk, Atlantic City 08401   609-347-5844
Hours: 9 AM–4 PM, every day but Christmas.

This thirty-six-year-old center with a view of the Atlantic Ocean presents twelve exhibits a year, showing works by various artists, many from Atlantic City and New Jersey. The year-round schedule of changing exhibits in the center's two galleries includes an annual "Black Art Exhibition: Paintings and Sculpture" and a "Hispanic Art Exhibition." One recent show titled "Fragments of Atlantic City: Lest We Forget" featured watercolors reflecting on the contrast between the resort's past and present.

Special Programs and Events: □ Boardwalk Art Show; annually in June and September. □ Statewide juried art show; annually in April. □ Winter holiday and membership shows.

VISUAL ARTS

Ben Shahn: In the Name of Justice

"I began to believe that art did, after all, have a mission . . . its mission was to tell what I felt, to say what I thought to be my own declaration. . . . Pictures would be my manifesto." This statement by the artist is from the afterword to *For the Sake of a Single Verse*, by Rainer Maria Rilke, illustrated by Ben Shahn (1898–1969).

One of this country's most successful social realists, Shahn believed that art had a mission, and he painted political statements. His best-known work is a series of twenty-three paintings inspired by the controversial trial of Sacco and Vanzetti. Trained as a lithographer, Shahn achieved a distinct graphic quality in his works, and he rendered stark portraits with jagged, bold, precise lines. A painting of Mao Tse-tung shows the Chinese leader on his back, spewing a cartoon-like balloon of indecipherable symbols and squiggles.

Born in Lithuania, Shahn lived in Brooklyn before moving to Roosevelt, New Jersey. During the 1930s he painted WPA murals in New Jersey, New York, and Washington, D.C. He also designed sets for two ballets by Jerome Robbins and for an e. e. cummings play. His *Tom Mooney Handcuffed* (1932–1933), a portrait of the labor leader sentenced to death for participating in a bombing, is in the collection of the New Jersey State Museum. Shahn's work is also in the collection of the Newark Museum. The Ben Shahn Galleries at William Paterson College in Wayne was named in his honor. Jonathan Shahn, Ben Shahn's son, still lives in Roosevelt. He has exhibited internationally, and recently was featured in a one-man show at the Rider College Art Gallery.

Ben Shahn Galleries

William Paterson College of New Jersey, 300 Pompton Road, Wayne 07470   201-595-2654 or 201-595-2467
Hours: 9:30 AM–5 PM, Monday through Friday; call for evening hours.

Named for the twentieth-century New Jersey–based social realist, the Ben Shahn Galleries was founded in 1979, as a teaching institution associated with the William Paterson College art department. The gallery mounts twelve exhibits during the academic year, usually presenting a new one every six weeks, and displays contemporary art by New York and New Jersey artists, often showing works by emerging Soho and East Village artists. It also takes a special interest in New Jersey art and architectural heritage and history; recent exhibits have included "Public

VISUAL ARTS

Connoisseurs' Collections

Great art resides not only in New Jersey museums but in private collections as well. Occasionally collectors are willing to let the public peek at their prize paintings and sculptures. Such was the case in 1972, when the New Jersey State Museum sponsored "Festival '72," an exhibition of decorative and fine arts from New Jersey private collections. A wealth of paintings by important artists were shown, including two Monets and a Degas from the collection of former Senator H.O.H. Frelinghuysen, and works by Gauguin, Van Gogh, and Renoir from the collection of magazine publisher Malcolm S. Forbes. In 1988, the museum presented "Chairman's Choice: A Miscellany of American Paintings from the Forbes Magazine Collection," which included paintings by numerous well-known artists such as Edward Hopper, Winslow Homer, and Andy Warhol.

Art in New Jersey: The American Renaissance," "Nineteenth-Century Maritime New Jersey," and "The Nineteenth-Century Paintings of New Jersey Landscapes."

Special Program: □ "Art at Lunch": lunchtime art-history lectures and slide shows by William Paterson faculty members and docents, from 11:30 AM to 12:15 PM, during the fall and spring semesters; visitors bring lunch, the gallery provides coffee and tea.

Educational Programs and Events: □ Gallery tours. □ Slide lectures for special groups.

Bergen Museum of Art and Science (DAO 1989) $ 🏛 ♿

Ridgewood and Farview Avenues, Paramus 07652   201-265-1248
Hours: 10 AM–5 PM, Tuesday through Saturday; 1–5 PM, Sunday.

Created in 1956 by scientists, artists, and educators, the Bergen Museum originally concentrated on artwork and scientific exhibits of interest to Bergen County residents. Since then it has adopted a broader scope, aimed at a regional and statewide audience. Though the museum concentrated for many years on the relationship between art and science, it is in the process of reevaluating this emphasis. In addition to its science collection, the Bergen Museum maintains a small permanent collection of twentieth-century art, including works by Warhol, Chagall, Picasso, and Calder.

VISUAL ARTS

Special Programs and Events: ◻ Culture, history, and art exhibit; annual. ◻ Concert series. ◻ Mastodon Concerts (named for Hackensack Mastodon, whose remains were unearthed near the museum in 1963).

Educational Programs and Events: ◻ Arts and crafts classes for children and adults. ◻ Children's lectures, seminars, and demonstrations based on current exhibitions.

Blackwell Street Center for the Arts Inc.

32-34 West Blackwell Street, Dover 07801   201-328-9628
Hours: 11 AM–5 PM and 6–9 PM, Wednesday; 11 AM–5 PM, Saturday and Sunday; first Friday of the month openings 7:30–10 PM.

This gallery space located in the back of a renovated downtown building shows the work of emerging and established area artists. The center was founded in 1983 by a dozen artists with studios in the Dover area. Most exhibits feature the work of members, who must submit work to a jury to qualify for admission. Frequently member artists show works inspired by a common theme: recent shows have included "Gardens" and "Windows." The gallery exhibits works in all media, sometimes mixing media within a single show.

Special Programs and Events: ◻ Juried show; annual. ◻ Student show open to Morris County high school students; annual.

Educational Programs: ◻ Art workshops.

Campbell Museum

Campbell Place, Camden 08103   609-342-6440
Hours: 9 AM–4:30 PM, Monday through Friday.

The Campbell Museum is the only museum in the country—and perhaps in the world—dedicated to the art of serving soup. It exhibits soup-related objects, including tureens, ladles, and bowls made of silver, porcelain, and other materials. The museum's collection concentrates on tureens from the eighteenth and nineteenth centuries, when tureen artistry was at its height. Plain and fancy, bizarre and fanciful, some of the vessels on exhibit are fashioned in the shapes of animals, fruits, or vegetables; others are painted with elaborate scenes or heavily engraved.

Special Programs and Events: ◻ *Artistry in Tureens,* a film outlining the history and technique behind the creation of soup tureens; shown by

VISUAL ARTS

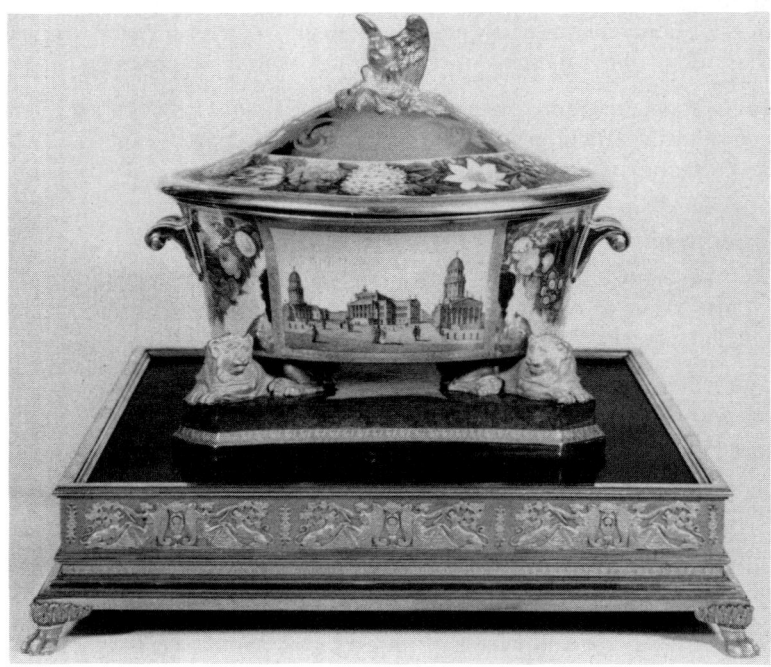

Designed to serve both functional and aesthetic purposes, soup tureens such as this nineteenth-century German porcelain one are displayed at the Campbell Soup Tureen Collection, Campbell Museum, Camden.

appointment. □ Christmas exhibition. □ Occasional contemporary soup tureen competitions.

Center for the Arts in Southern New Jersey
5 Greentree Centre, Route 73, Marlton 08053   609-985-1009
Hours: 9:30 AM–3:30 PM, Monday through Friday.

Founded in 1980, the Center for the Arts in Southern New Jersey was designed to provide a showcase and arts education facility for southern New Jersey visual artists, performing artists, art groups, and audiences. Its gallery frequently features works by South Jersey artists; recent shows have included works by Mel Leipzig of Trenton and by Southern New Jersey and Delaware photographers. The Center makes an effort to reach the disabled and others who may otherwise not have the opportunity to be involved with art. It has hosted the annual juried show by

VISUAL ARTS

Visibility, the New Jersey organization for disabled visual artists. It presents a new exhibit every month.

Special Programs and Events: ☐ Classes for the blind and visually impaired. ☐ Outreach program bringing art to the emotionally and physically handicapped. ☐ Tours to major museums.

Educational Programs and Events: ☐ Enrichment/enjoyment courses in calligraphy, fiber arts, printmaking, music appreciation. ☐ Studio art for children and young people. ☐ Workshops with working artists for adults and children.

City Without Walls (DAO 1988, 1989)

One Gateway Center, Ground Level, Newark 07102   201-622-1188
Hours: 10 AM–6 PM, Monday through Friday.

City Without Walls has long been a gallery with a conscience. Recent shows have addressed the issue of housing and homelessness and examined the similarities between the AIDS epidemic and a turn-of-the-century tuberculosis plague. Founded in 1975, City Without Walls now has three hundred members and is both a showcase for emerging artists and a platform for commentary on urban issues. The gallery exhibits change almost monthly; at least ten are mounted each year, the majority containing works by members. It may be the only gallery in the state that invites visitors to enjoy an exhibit twenty-four hours a day, since the space is lighted round-the-clock and is visible from the street through large windows.

Special Programs and Events: ☐ Black History Month show; annual. ☐ New Members Show; annual. ☐ Performing art events; occasional. ☐ Small Works "Metro" Show: Restricted to works no larger than 12 inches in any dimension, this exhibit opens at City Without Walls, then travels throughout the state and metropolitan area; annual.

Drew University Photography Gallery

University Center 104, Drew University, Madison 07940
201-408-3456
Hours: 12:30–2 PM and 7:30–10:30 PM, Monday through Friday.

The Drew University Photography Gallery exhibits only fine art photography and photojournalism, regularly presenting works by nationally and internationally known photographers. Founded in 1973 by Drew professor of philosophy and photography-club advisor John Copeland, the gallery offers one-man or -woman shows, featuring the work of such contemporary photographers as portraitist Arnold Newman and Philippe Halsman, who has numerous *Life* magazine covers (mostly of celebrity subjects) to his credit. It presents five major shows annually, from September through April, borrowed mainly from Manhattan galleries such as the Witkin and Sidney Janis. In addition, the gallery sponsors a yearly student/faculty show in April.

Special Program: ☐ Opening night slide/lecture by exhibiting photographer.

Extension Gallery/Johnson Atelier
Technical Institute of Sculpture
60 Ward Avenue Extension, Mercerville 08619   609-890-7777
Gallery hours: 10 AM—4 PM, Monday through Thursday. Atelier open by appointment.

The brainchild of Johnson & Johnson heir and sculptor J. Seward Johnson, Jr., the atelier was founded in 1974. Johnson wanted more control over the production of his own lifelike cast-bronze sculptures, and he envisioned a school/workshop where students, technicians, and sculptors might work together to produce a work of sculpture that was technically, as well as artistically, excellent. The Johnson Atelier operates on the principle that a technical apprenticeship benefits student and professional artist alike. Here modern sculptures—many of monumental proportions—have been cast and fabricated for some of the world's most prominent artists, from New Jersey sculptor George Segal to Marisol. Today the atelier draws students from all over the world. Exhibits at the gallery change monthly.

Special Program: ☐ Atelier tours—visitors can watch sculptures molded into final form in aluminum, cast iron, or bronze at this state-of-the-art casting facility; by appointment.

First Mountain Crafters Inc.
650 Prospect Avenue, West Orange 97952   201-577-0179
Gallery: Essex Green Shopping Plaza, Prospect Avenue, West Orange
Hours: 10 AM—5:30 PM, Monday through Saturday.

First Mountain Crafters, founded in 1956, operates a craft gallery and provides information and services for craftspeople throughout the state. Crafts by member artists are always on display at the gallery, and the group sponsors occasional group shows and special exhibits, sometimes featuring guest artists or themes; recently a show examined the role of the cat as an art object. Workshops, taught in crafts studios

VISUAL ARTS

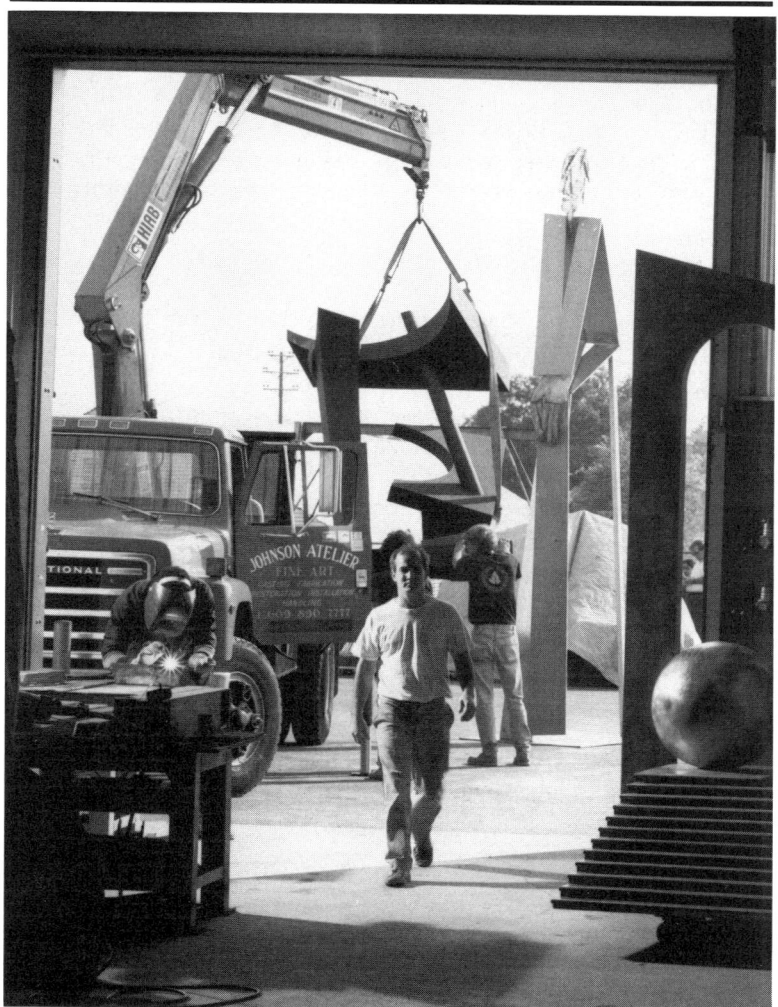

Staff workers help load a newly cast sculpture at the Johnson Atelier, a foundry and technical institute whose Extension Gallery is open to the public. Photo: Philip Smith.

VISUAL ARTS

ARTS PUBLICATIONS

Arts Management Collection
New Jersey State Council on the Arts
  Four North Broad Street, CN306, Trenton 08625   609-292-6130
  List of books and periodicals on arts management, fundraising, grants, and other topics available at participating county libraries

Art Matters
  Art Matters Inc., 2213 Walnut Street, Philadelphia 19103
  215-564-2340
  Monthly newspaper covering the visual arts in the Philadelphia metropolitan area

Arts-in-Education
  Arts Council of the Essex Area, Montclair State College, Valley Road, Upper Montclair 07043   201-744-1717
  Resource directory published every two years, giving information

by master craftspeople, both members and guest artists, are open to the public.
Educational Programs and Events: ☐ Craft lecture series. ☐ Craft workshops. ☐ Outreach craft lectures and demonstrations.

Hunterdon Art Center (DAO 1987) $ ♿ 🎭 🏛 //
7 Center Street, Clinton 08809   201-735-8415
Hours: Noon–4:30 PM, Tuesday through Friday; 1–5 PM, Saturday and Sunday.

Known for its collection of prints by nationally and internationally acclaimed artists such as Salvador Dali, Fairfield Porter, and Grace Albee, the Hunterdon Art Center sponsors the oldest annual print exhibition in New Jersey. Traditionally this juried show, which attracts hundreds of entries, has been assembled by print curator Anne Steele Marsh, who founded it in 1957. The center itself was founded in 1952, and it occupies the central scenic attraction in picturesque Clinton Village: an old gristmill that sits astride waterfalls on the Raritan River. Newly renovated and expanded, the center now acts as a regional cultural center for exurbia, presenting not only visual arts exhibits, but also music, film, and theater programs and productions. Exhibits, many of which draw on the permanent collection, change every six weeks. Recent visual arts shows have included "Small Towns and Villages" and "Cele-

VISUAL ARTS

on an array of artists and organizations serving New Jersey students and teachers

Directory of Visual Art Organizations in New Jersey
Federated Art Associations of New Jersey, P.O. Box 2195, Westfield 07091   201-232-7623

Discover Hidden Treasures
Guide to the Museums of New Jersey
Museums Council of New Jersey, Ben Shahn Center, William Paterson College, Wayne 07470   201-595-2676
A listing of New Jersey museums of all descriptions

New Jersey Poetry Resource Book
The Poetry Center, Passaic County Community College, College Boulevard, Paterson 07509   201-684-6555

---

bration of the Horse." The Hunterdon Art Center is on the National Register of Historic Places.

Special Programs and Events: ☐ National Print Show; annual in March or April. ☐ Summer program for disabled students.

Educational Programs and Events: ☐ Classes in painting, drawing, watercolor, photography, calligraphy, and crafts. ☐ Lectures and workshops in fine and performing arts.

The International Center for Japonisme
The Jane Voorhees Zimmerli Art Museum
Rutgers, The State University of New Jersey, New Brunswick 08903
201-932-7237
Hours: Same as Jane Voorhees Zimmerli Art Museum.

Rutgers was the first American college to welcome a group of Japanese exchange students. Since then, it has demonstrated a special affinity for Japan, and its Jane Voorhees Zimmerli Museum has assembled a large collection of Japanese and Japanese-influenced artwork. In the 1980s, Zimmerli director Phillip Dennis Cate decided that the rising international profile of Japan warranted a more formal expression of the link with Rutgers. As a result, The International Center for Japonisme was founded in 1986 under museum auspices. The center organizes exhibits, symposia, lectures, and conferences on the Japanese influence

VISUAL ARTS

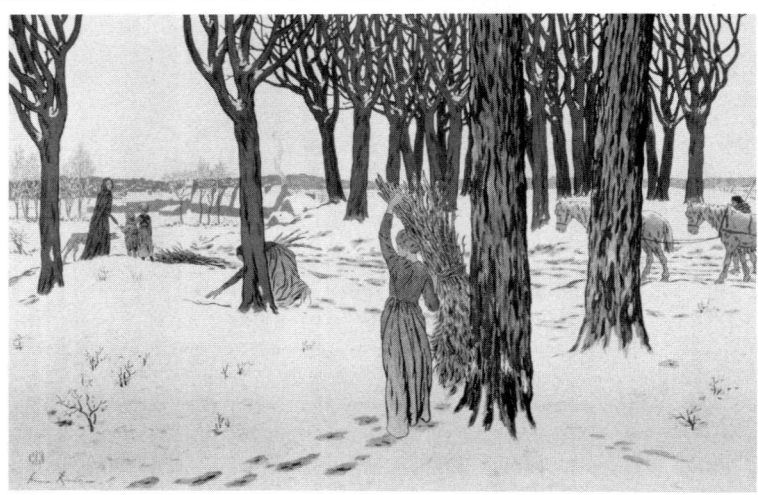

L'Hiver, an 1896 ten-color lithograph by Henri Rivière, is one of the works in the Japonisme collection at the Jane Voorhees Zimmerli Art Museum, Rutgers, The State University, New Brunswick. The collection documents the Japanese influence on turn-of-the-century French artists.

on Western culture and promotes communication between Japan and the West, not only in art but in politics and economics as well.

A number of Institute exhibits have traveled to Japan, including "Floating World: The Japanese Spirit in Turn-of-the-Century French Art." One hundred wood block prints owned by one of Rutger's first exchange students, industrialist Matsukata Kojiro, were shown in a 1988 exhibit called "Masterpieces from the Tokyo National Museum: The Matsukata Collection of Ukiyo-E Prints." The Center does not maintain its own gallery; exhibits are mounted at the Zimmerli.

Educational Programs: ☐ Conferences and seminars on the Japanese influence on Western culture, past and present.

Jane Voorhees Zimmerli Art Museum
Rutgers, The State University of New Jersey, George and Hamilton Streets, New Brunswick 08903   201-932-7237
Hours: 10 AM–4:30 PM, Monday, Tuesday, Thursday, Friday; Noon–5 PM, Saturday and Sunday; closed Saturdays in summer.

VISUAL ARTS

Built in 1983 and named for the mother of Rutgers alumnus and philanthropist Alan Voorhees, the Zimmerli Museum evolved from the much smaller University Art Gallery. The museum's greatest strength lies in its large collection of graphic arts from the fifteenth century to the present. It houses prints from many cultures, including nineteenth- and twentieth-century American and European works. Some of its finest pieces are turn-of-the-century French color prints and posters. The Zimmerli also has built a teaching collection around American contemporary prints, collected from a variety of printmaking studios nationwide. Proofs and blocks illustrating the printing process are also part of that collection.

The Rutgers Collection of Children's Literature contains original illustrations of contemporary children's books; a permanent exhibit demonstrates how a book is assembled and produced. The museum also owns the personal collections of George Overbury "Pop" Hart, a prominent Fort Lee artist, and New Jersey children's book illustrator Roger Duvoisin and is the headquarters for the International Center for Japonisme (see above). The Zimmerli presents approximately ten exhibits annually, the majority curated by the museum staff.

Special Program: ☐ Youth Art Day, an annual March showcase for art by New Jersey youngsters.

Educational Programs: ☐ Classes for young people on Saturdays during September through June. ☐ Outreach programs related to permanent and special exhibitions.

Jersey City Museum (DAO 1987, 1989)

472 Jersey Avenue, Jersey City 07302   201-547-4514
Hours: 10:30 AM–8 PM, Wednesday; 10:30 AM–5 PM, Thursday through Saturday; closed Saturdays during the summer and on public holidays.

Views of Manhattan from the Jersey waterfront have long been popular subjects for artists. The Jersey City Museum collection features numerous paintings of New York City from the "other" side of the Hudson, from the nineteenth century to the present.

Founded in 1901, the Jersey City Museum closed its doors due to financial difficulties in 1955. Since reopening in 1975, it has become a force among New Jersey museums, especially in the field of contemporary art, emphasizing works by Hudson County and other New Jersey resi-

VISUAL ARTS

Gaetano Federici: Monuments to the Sacred . . . and the Profane

The son of an Italian mason, Gaetano Federici (1880–1964) brought an artist's hand to the family tradition of working with mortar and stone. In his Paterson studio he produced sculptures and bas-reliefs for churches, graveyards, and public buildings. His statues honored prominent New Jersey and Paterson personalities: mayors, assemblymen, and philanthropists.

Federici sculptures lent dignity and importance to family mausoleums in the Mt. Nebo Cemetery and Laurel Grove Memorial Park in Totowa and in Woodlawn Cemetery in the Bronx, a favorite burying ground of the rich and famous. Some of his religious works were commissioned as decorations for public buildings, such as St. Barnabas Hospital in Newark and St. Michael's Church in Paterson.

But, on occasion the sculptor produced a lighter kind of art. In 1942, he made bas-relief portraits of comedian Lou Costello, a Paterson native who found success in Hollywood, and of Mark Twain. Still surprising, however, is the most profane of all his works, executed shortly before his death: an elegant, irreverent bas-relief picturing a nymphlike female water skier skimming topless across the water.

Many Federici sculptures can be seen in their original locations, and the Lambert Castle Museum of the Passaic County Historical Society in Paterson maintains a collection of the artist's works.

---

dents. The museum, located above the Jersey City Public Library, showcases works by Jersey City artists past and present, and its permanent collection includes etchings by August Will and works by other visual artists who thrived during that city's turn-of-the-century heyday. The museum also highlights works by minority artists. It presents four or five major exhibits annually, eight or nine one-person shows, and changing exhibits from its permanent collection.

Special Programs and Events: □ Black History Month family and school programs. □ Slide registry for New Jersey artists, curators, architects, etc. □ Exhibit drawn from works of artists represented in a slide registry of more than four hundred contemporary New Jersey artists.

Educational Programs and Events: □ In-school and museum bilingual workshops and lectures for Jersey City school children in connection with exhibits. □ Portable programs: slide lectures in schools, hospitals and community centers.

VISUAL ARTS

Macculloch Hall Historical Museum $ 🎟
45 Macculloch Avenue, Morristown 07960   201-538-2404
Hours: 2–4:30 PM, Thursdays and Sundays from April through late November, or by appointment.

Nineteenth-century political cartoonist Thomas Nast created the elephant and the donkey as symbols of the Republican and Democratic parties. He also invented the modern-day image of Santa Claus as a fat, rosy-cheeked, and jolly gentleman. Nast lived in Morristown, and Macculloch Hall, headquarters for the Morristown Historical Society, maintains an extensive collection of his works. Some portion of this collection is on view at all times.

Macculloch Hall dates back to sometime between 1810 and 1814, when it was built as a home for the Macculloch family, members of which had emigrated from Scotland in 1809. Prominent Morristown residents lived in the house until it was purchased by W. Parsons Todd, mayor of Morristown, who turned the Federal-style house into a museum in 1954. It is on the National Register of Historic Places.

Special Program: ☐ Rose Day, annual June exhibition of flower paintings by local artists with an occasional display of old-fashioned roses in the house gardens.

Mediamix, Inc. $ 🎬
P.O. Box 1623, New Brunswick 08903   201-249-9623 or 201-249-1375
Hours: Friday and Sunday night film screenings. Media arts exhibitions and conferences at changing locations in the New Brunswick/Central New Jersey area.
Main screening facility: Voorhees Hall (300 seats), Rutgers, New Brunswick; Milledoler 100 (150 seats), Rutgers, New Brunswick.

Mediamix provides education and entertainment for experimental, independent filmmakers and their audiences. It offers symposia on such subjects as technology and aesthetics, women in media, and small format production and screenings of documentary, feature, and abstract films, including works by members as well as films and videos by well-known and little-known independent filmmakers.

Founded in 1985 by filmmakers Albert G. Nigrin, Jim Vassanella, and Walter Blakely, Mediamix is both a membership and a presenting organization; it provides information and support services for media artists

VISUAL ARTS

A Very Public Art: New Jersey's Post Office and Courthouse Murals

Serving as decorative backdrops for the public's business, murals are everywhere in New Jersey—in post offices, courthouses, and city halls.

Perhaps the best of them can be seen at the Hudson County Courthouse. Public patronage of the arts triumphed there in the early years of the twentieth century, when the Hudson County Board of Freeholders decided to build a monument to justice and Jersey City. Architect Hugh Roberts designed a vast building whose interior, with its towering domed ceiling, ample lunettes, and niches, demanded something more than mere decoration. For this task, Roberts commissioned some of the finest muralists in America: Edwin H. Blashfield, America's "dean" of mural painting, who had executed works in important buildings across the country, including the Waldorf Astoria Hotel in New York City, Francis D. Millet, George W. Maynard, Howard Pyle, Kenyon Cox, Charles Y. Turner, and Henry O. Walker. They painted classical scenes illustrating moral and social virtues such as Courage and Justice.

Years later, the Federal WPA project set painters to work in public buildings throughout the country. In New Jersey, these more utilitarian murals still can be seen in post offices in Princeton, Cranford, and Kearney; in Caldwell, Plainfield, Mt. Holly, and Clifton; in Jersey City; and in Newark. Despite their humbler origins, some WPA murals tackle lofty themes; at the Morristown Courthouse a series of paintings illustrates The Historical and Social Development of the Law.

Ben Shahn, later recognized as one of this country's most talented social realists, served as Diego Rivera's apprentice on murals at Rockefeller Center in New York City. He also painted a mural at an elementary school in Roosevelt, New Jersey, where he lived.

---

and independent producers and shows films to the general public. In conjunction with Rutgers University's media services department, Mediamix sponsors the Rutgers University Film Co-op, which presents experimental, documentary, and feature films at various New Brunswick locations. Screenings include both classics and little-known works, from Billy Wilder's *Sunset Boulevard* to shorts produced by Mediamix members.

Special Programs and Events: □ "Art in Motion," experimental and documentary film and video screenings in a café setting. □ Media arts conference; annual. □ Media arts exhibition; annual. □ Mediamix Me-

VISUAL ARTS

dia Arts Festival; annual (22 Friday nights between September and April; see Festivals). ◻ Summer film series in June and July. ◻ Sunday night free screening series in cooperation with Rutgers University Film Co-op at Kilmer Library on Kilmer Campus in Piscataway. ◻ Super Mediamix U.S. 8 Millimeter Contest and Film Festival; annual (see Festivals).

Educational Programs and Events: ◻ Film workshops and symposia on technical and aesthetic skills and issues, led by media experts.

Mid-Atlantic Center for the Arts (see Centers)

Middlesex County Cultural and Heritage Commission
(see Agencies Appendix)

The Monmouth Museum $ 🏛 👥
Brookdale Community College Campus, off Newman Springs Road, P.O. Box 359, Lincroft 07738   201-747-2266
Hours: 10 AM–4:30 PM, Tuesday through Saturday; 1–5 PM, Sunday.

Founded by the Junior League of Monmouth County, the Monmouth Museum has no permanent collection. Lacking the funds to purchase major collections and works, the museum borrows for its shows. The museum director and exhibition committee recently mounted "Portrait of a Period: The Playground on the New Jersey Shore," which consisted of paintings, objects, and costumes from the period 1865–1910. Another show curated by the museum staff was "The Western Experience," which borrowed nineteenth- and twentieth-century artworks from prominent arts institutions such as the Metropolitan Museum of Art and The Smithsonian. The museum, which staged its first show in 1965, also hosts traveling exhibitions from major museums, collections, and institutions, such as "Masterpieces of American Folk Art" and "Indian Art of the Americas." It presents four to six shows each year and is accredited by the American Association of Museums.

Educational Programs and Events: ◻ Children's Wing and Junior Gallery tours. ◻ Museum tours in New York, Philadelphia, and Europe.

The Montclair Art Museum (DAO 1987, 1988, 1990; MIO/AFG) $ 🎭 🏛 👥
Three South Mountain Avenue, Montclair 07042   201-746-5555
Hours: 10 AM–5 PM, Tuesday, Wednesday, Friday, Saturday;

VISUAL ARTS

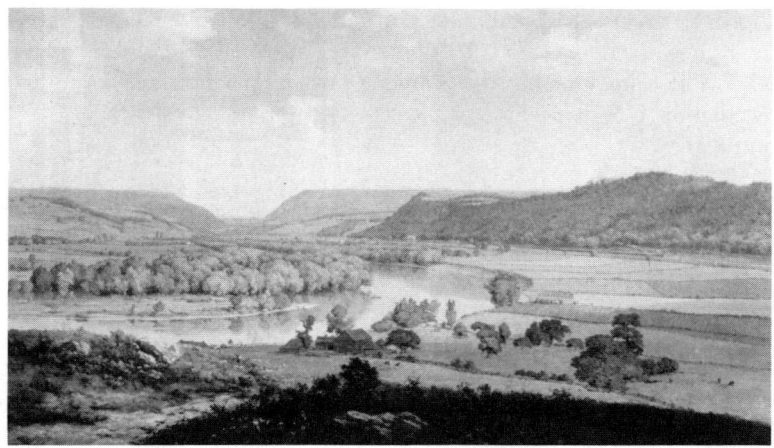

The 1859 painting *Delaware Water Gap* is part of the large collection of works by nineteenth-century artist and Montclair resident George Inness at the Montclair Art Museum.

2–5 PM, Thursday (except for second and fourth Thursdays, 2–9 PM); 2–5 PM, Sunday; Call for summer hours.

Known for its fine collection of American art, the Montclair Art Museum was conceived in 1909, when prominent collector and Montclair resident William T. Evans offered to donate paintings to the town, provided officials would build a museum to house them. The museum opened in 1914, displaying fifty-four American paintings and a number of Native American pieces donated by another Montclair resident, Annie Valentine Rand. Today, it maintains a wide-ranging American collection that features works by artists such as Edward Hopper, John Singer Sargent, Mary Cassatt, Winslow Homer, and Andrew Wyeth and many early portraits. It houses a large collection of landscape paintings by the late nineteenth-century artist George Inness, a Montclair resident. Recently the museum has been developing its collection of contemporary American art.

The Montclair Art Museum generally offers fifteen special exhibits annually, originating half and borrowing half. Exhibits on loan have included collections of movie posters, carousel animals, and French impressionist paintings. Staff-curated exhibits such as "Song of the Loom:

VISUAL ARTS

New Traditions in Navajo Weaving" have traveled to other states. The museum maintains some three thousand Native American works. The Rand Society, created under the auspices of the museum, researches and exhibits works by Native American artists. The museum grounds form a small arboretum, where visitors can take a brochure-guided walking tour of labeled specimen trees and shrubs. The Montclair Art Museum is accredited by the American Association of Museums.

Special Programs and Events: ☐ Concerts. ☐ Film series; annual. ☐ Lecture series. ☐ Slide rental collection available to the public.

Educational Programs and Events: ☐ Art classes in drawing and painting for adults and children. ☐ Teachers' workshops in which art and social studies enrichment outreach programs tackle topics such as "Math in Art; Art in Math" and "Art Reflects Change," a program including a teacher workshop and in-school activities based on nineteenth- and twentieth-century landscape paintings in the museum's collection.

Morris Museum $ ♿ ⚥

Six Normandy Heights Road, Morristown 07960   201-538-0454
Hours: 10 AM–5 PM, Monday through Saturday; 1–5 PM, Sunday.

The Morris Museum is a family-oriented museum located in a Georgian mansion built in 1907 by prominent Morristown resident Peter H. B. Frelinghuysen as the centerpiece of his 150-acre cattle-breeding establishment, Twin Oak Farms. Today, the museum contains seven major collections: Fine Arts, Geology, Natural Science, Anthropology, Archaeology, History, and Decorative Arts. Its small fine arts collection contains early twentieth-century and contemporary American paintings, drawings, and prints. The museum often presents special visiting exhibits, and will offer more after a major addition is completed. Recent shows have included "The Civil War: Rare Large Format Albumen Prints" and "The Soaring Spirit: Contemporary Native American Arts." The Morris Museum is accredited by the American Association of Museums.

Special Programs and Events: ☐ Children's theater. ☐ Classical music concerts. ☐ Dance programs. ☐ "Special Event Days," family-oriented lectures, workshops, tours, demonstrations, and exhibits on a particular theme, often inspired by a major exhibit.

Educational Programs and Events: ☐ Classes and workshops for children and adults. ☐ School loan program to provide exhibits that travel to area schools.

VISUAL ARTS

"We All Held the Hands of Those Born in the 1700s"

New Jersey has a rich folk art tradition. One of the most well-received folk artists was Henry Thomas Gulick (1872–1964), a hard-working farmer and Monmouth County resident who turned to painting when he was in his seventies. Gulick's family had lived in Monmouth County since colonial times, and no doubt he felt that the land connected him to his ancestors. Gulick chose subjects that had changed very little over the centuries: farmhouses, stables, country roads, orchards, homestead rooms, and fields full of livestock. As he reportedly said and as his paintings show, "We all held the hands of those born in the 1700s."

As a working farmer, Gulick did not find time for art until he retired. But then he tried to paint nearly every day. Domestic details captivated him, and he painstakingly recreated the colors and patterns of wallpaper in his front hall, plants in a sunny window, an oriental rug in the dining room, and apple baskets on the barn floor. Gulick's humble pictures depict a tranquil, orderly world in which man has successfully tamed nature.

The artist enjoyed the height of his fame in his eighties and nineties, when he exhibited his works at the Montclair Museum of Art and Seton Hall University. Asked how he managed to lead so long a life, Gulick had this matter-of-fact reply, according to Barbara Kaufman Cate, a personal acquaintance and associate professor of art history at Seton Hall: "To my Maker. Each person is born like a top; some are wound tightly for a long spin." The Montclair Art Museum, Newark Museum, and Monmouth County Historical Society own Gulick works.

Museum of American Glass (see Wheaton Village, Visual Arts)

New Jersey Center for Visual Arts
Palmer Gallery
68 Elm Street, Summit 07901   201-273-9121
Hours: Palmer Gallery—Noon–4 PM, Monday through Friday;
2–4 PM, Saturday and Sunday.

Founded by a group of artists in 1933 under the name Summit Art Center, The New Jersey Center for Visual Arts dedicates itself to art classes and contemporary art exhibits. It was the first institution in New Jersey to offer arts symposia to secondary school teachers; one recent printmaking symposium featured a lecture by Frank Stella. One of the

VISUAL ARTS

largest arts schools in New Jersey, in 1988 the center enrolled 875 students. The center's Palmer Gallery presents five major exhibits each year, supplemented by one-person and group shows featuring works by New Jersey artists. A smaller Members' Gallery hosts rotating shows by member artists. In 1988, the center presented a retrospective exhibit of New Jersey sculptor George Segal's works. The school is accredited by the American Association of Museums.

Special Programs and Events: ☐ Corporate gallery exhibits. ☐ Faculty exhibition; annual. ☐ Film showings. ☐ Jazz concerts. ☐ Members' exhibition; annual. ☐ National juried show; annual. ☐ Statewide tours.

Educational Programs and Events: ☐ Visual arts classes for adults and children. ☐ Workshops, demonstrations, and art appreciation lectures.

New Jersey Designer Craftsmen, Inc. (DAO 1990)

17 Livingston Avenue, New Brunswick 08901   201-246-4066
Hours for The Gallery: 10 AM–4 PM, Wednesday and Thursday; 10 AM–8 PM, Friday and Saturday. Works also on display at Allaire Village, Allaire State Park, Allaire, and the New Jersey State Museum Shop, Trenton.

Founded in 1950, New Jersey Designer Craftsmen is probably the oldest and largest craft organization in the state. It represents craftspeople who work in both contemporary and traditional media, from potters and weavers to quilters and fabric artists. The organization promotes crafts throughout New Jersey, publishing a newsletter and calendar listing craft fairs, sales, and festivals and sharing information on prominent and emerging craft artists, grants, workshops, and other craft-related matters. The New Jersey Designer Craftsmen's craft map is a guide to more than sixty crafts organizations statewide. It is a resident member of the New Brunswick Cultural Center, where its gallery is located.

Special Programs and Events: ☐ "Crafts Weekend," a juried "fine craft fair" held annually at locations around the state. ☐ Slide file available for the use of museums, galleries, corporations, and art centers.

Educational Program: ☐ Information on statewide craft workshops, master classes, and demonstrations for craftspeople and the public.

VISUAL ARTS

Gustav Stickley: The Fine Art of Craft

Today's New Jersey would be anathema to Gustav Stickley (1858–1942), a man attracted to the state by its turn-of-the-century farms and fields.

Stickley built a utopian getaway on the side of a hill in Parsippany-Troy Hills in 1908. From there and from his showroom and offices in Manhattan, this furniture maker, philosopher, architect, and designer disseminated his ideas on art, craft, and life. In *The Craftsman* magazine and in the houses and furniture he designed, Stickley advocated a return to simplicity and integrity. He believed that natural colors and materials such as oak, copper, and fieldstone needed no embellishment.

With his insistence on purity and beauty in domestic objects, Stickley moved into the forefront of the turn-of-the-century American arts and crafts movement. He envisioned Craftsman Farms, his Parsippany-Troy Hills retreat, as a school for boys dedicated to "craftsman" principles. The dream never materialized.

Yet, Stickley's house speaks for him to this day. Still standing on its twenty-six-acre property, it exemplifies his belief that architecture and interior design should encourage a moral way of life. The building's humble, cabin-like appearance emphasizes the natural, not the superficial or ornamental. Inside, on each of five copper hearths is emblazoned an aphorism illustrating the designer's convictions. "The life is so short, the craft so long to lern [sic]," laments one; "By hammer and hand do all things stand," affirms another.

Recently under threat of development as a townhouse community, Craftsman Farms instead has become The Center for the Study of the American Arts and Crafts. The State of New Jersey has awarded money from its Green Acres Fund for the purchase and preservation of the property by the Township of Parsippany-Troy Hills, and the Craftsman Farms Foundation has been formed to renovate the house and open it to the public.

New Jersey Historical Society $ 🏛 ♿

230 Broadway, Newark 07104   201-483-3939
Hours: 10 AM–4 PM, Wednesday through Friday and third Saturday.

A treasure trove of Garden State art and artifacts, the New Jersey Historical Society's museum documents the state's past with paintings, drawings, etchings, engravings, and a particularly large collection of daguerreotypes, photographs, and slides of important and ordinary New Jersey people, places, things, and events. The society, founded in

1845, presents rotating exhibits from its permanent collection, showing decorative and fine artworks, manuscripts, maps, and other objects that illuminate the state's political, economic, and cultural development. Its fine arts collection is extensive, encompassing portraits and landscapes from the eighteenth century to the present.

Special Program: □ Tours of New Jersey historical sites.

Educational Programs and Events: □ Jersey Journeys, a program on New Jersey history for fourth graders. □ Lectures on New Jersey historical sites and history through the twentieth century. □ School tours of exhibits. □ Slide lectures and discussions such as "Windshield Wonders," an examination of New Jersey's roadside architecture.

New Jersey State Museum
Division of the Department of State
205 West State Street, CN-530, Trenton 08625   609-292-6308
Hours: 9 AM–4:45 PM, Tuesday through Saturday;
Noon–5 PM, Sunday.

Anyone who doubts that New Jersey possesses a rich artistic life all its own should stroll through the New Jersey State Museum, where hundreds of paintings, photographs, and prints document the achievements, past and present, of the state's native sons and daughters. Established in 1895 by the state legislature, the New Jersey State Mu-

> "We claim them all. . . . We can be proud that an artist lived here for a few years or a few months, that he taught here briefly or only that he had the grace to be born in the state or die in it."—Selden Rodman, in his introduction to the catalogue for the 1965 New Jersey State Museum show "New Jersey and The Artist."

seum has occupied its present building near the State House complex since 1965. It maintains collections in fine arts, archaeology/ethnology, decorative arts, and natural history. In addition to featuring works by major artists from within the state, the museum owns works by nationally and internationally known artists from outside New Jersey, such as Georgia O'Keeffe and Louise Nevelson. In some cases, paintings by out-of-state artists feature New Jersey subjects; for instance, the

VISUAL ARTS

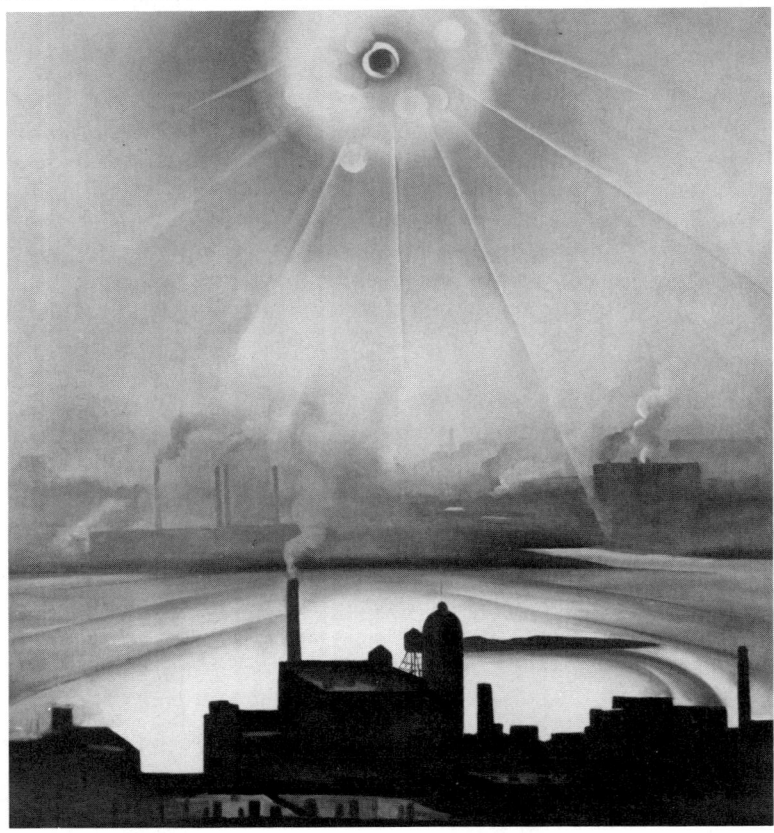

Georgia O'Keeffe's *East River from the Shelton* is one of the works by internationally known artists included in the American collection of the New Jersey State Museum.

museum owns *Houses in Port Monmouth, New Jersey* and *Sea Bright* by Louis Comfort Tiffany, who spent summers at the Jersey shore.

The museum's American Art Collection contains artwork by some of the country's most prominent eighteenth-, nineteenth-, and twentieth-century artists, many of them New Jersey residents, from landscape painters George Inness and Asher B. Durand to social realist Ben Shahn, modernist John Marin, and sculptor George Segal. Its deco-

VISUAL ARTS

rative arts collection provides insight into the social and cultural development of the state, from pre-Revolutionary days to the present, and its miscellaneous arts collections include a large assortment of works by Lewis Wickes Hine, who photographed historic glass works (New Jersey was once known as the "glass state") in Millville and Bridgeton.

The State Museum's annual series, "Contemporary Arts: The New Jersey Context," highlights contemporary works by local and regional potters, painters, sculptors, and craftspeople. The museum also presents numerous other exhibits, some from the permanent collection, others organized by major museums. Recent examples include: "Chairman's Choice: A Miscellany of American Paintings from the Forbes Magazine Collection" and "After Eden: American Landscape 1875–1925." An outdoor sculpture collection includes pieces by Alexander Calder and George Rickey. The State Museum takes its collections to the people; it sponsors outreach exhibits and lectures at schools, community centers, and libraries across the state such as "The Twentieth Century American Art Collection of the New Jersey State Museum" and "Art and Interpretation." The New Jersey State Museum is accredited by the American Association of Museums.

Special Programs and Events: □ Children's theater productions. □ Dance programs. □ Fine-Art Film Series with essays on artists such as Rembrandt and Michelangelo. □ Music programs, including "Brown Bag" outdoor summer concert series.

Educational Programs and Events: □ The museum's bureau of education presents numerous and ever-changing programs and events for adults and children, including: □ Collection loan service providing exhibits from major collections to schools and nonprofit groups. □ Cultural History and Fine Arts Lecture Series on such topics as American Crazy Quilts and Oriental Designs for Late Victorian Home Decoration. □ Film loan service to schools and nonprofit groups from 1,200 titles on subjects within the museum's areas of interest. □ Traveling exhibits and lectures.

Newark MediaWorks

P.O. Box 1716, Newark 07101, or 60 Union Street, No. 3N, Newark 07105   201-690-5474

Newark MediaWorks was founded in 1979 as a forum for media artists, teachers, and audiences. This statewide organization presents film and

B.J.O. Nordfeldt: Making the Best of Both Worlds

Compared by his biographer Van Deren Coke to Cézanne and Gauguin, Swedish-born B.J.O. Nordfeldt (1878–1955) brought his talents to New Jersey late in life.

After many productive years in the bustling arts community of Santa Fe, the artist moved in 1944 to a quiet farm on the outskirts of Lambertville, on the Delaware River. He sought both solitude and proximity to New York, and the combination seemed to work well; during these Lambertville years Nordfeldt produced some of his most critically acclaimed paintings.

An artist whose realistic style grew more and more abstract with the years, Nordfeldt was captivated by the sea. A few of his works depicted landscapes around Lambertville. But the West, particularly the Pacific Ocean, remained a favorite subject. In *Shell, Blue Gull, Net, Shore,* and *Birds,* he captured the mood of the seashore with color and rendered sea life in bold, geometric shapes.

Nordfeldt's paintings have found their way into the collections of some of the world's most prestigious museums. *Movement* and *Plate of Fruit* are owned by the Metropolitan Museum of Art. The Corcoran Gallery and Hirschhorn Museum of the Smithsonian Institution in Washington, D.C., also own a number of his works. So do the Montclair Art Museum, the Newark Museum, the Mercer County Community College Library Gallery, and the Jane Voorhees Zimmerli Art Museum. Both the Zimmerli and the New Jersey State Museum have sponsored exhibitions of his work.

---

video screenings to the public as well as training and development programs for media artists. While it concentrates on the film and video, MediaWorks also sponsors programs in radio, photography, and computer art. Its annual Video and Film Festival screens films and videos by New Jersey artists, from full-length feature films by directors such as John Sayles (his *Matewan* was the first place prize winner in 1988) to shorter features, documentaries, and public affairs spots by less well-known filmmakers.

Special Programs and Events: ☐ Café Cinema features weekly screenings of recent independently produced films in a café setting. ☐ New Jersey Video and Film Festival; annual (see Festivals).

Educational Programs and Events: ☐ Internship program for students committed to careers in media. ☐ Master classes on technical/aesthetic

VISUAL ARTS

subjects. □ Media arts classes at all levels on production, editing, and other technical subjects. □ New Jersey Media Artists Network, which meets quarterly to discuss media issues. □ Symposia on media issues for professional media artists.

The Newark Museum (RCAE 1990, DAO 1988, MIO/AFG, GAA)
49 Washington Street, P.O. Box 540, Newark 07101   201-596-6550
Hours: Noon–4:45 PM, every day except Monday.

New Jersey's largest museum was originally located in the Newark Public Library. Founded in 1909 by John Cotton Dana, who took a strong interest in arts education and American contemporary artists, the Newark Museum recently has attracted regional and national attention with the dramatic renovation of its south wing, designed by Princeton based, post-modern architect Michael Graves. Despite these physical changes, however, an early collection remains among its most distinguished: an assembly of Tibetan art objects and artifacts that is one of the world's largest. Many objects were donated just after the turn of the century by missionary doctor Albert L. Shelton; others were acquired in later years by the museum, which eventually concentrated on objects from the medieval period. Complementing the Tibetan collection are other strong Asian art collections, including Indian, Japanese, Chinese, and Korean paintings, prints, sculptures, and screens. The Newark Museum maintains an extensive collection of American paintings, sculpture, and folk art, especially works by prominent nineteenth- and twentieth-century painters. A highlight of the twentieth-century collection is Joseph Stella's five-painting work, *The Voice of the City of New York Interpreted*. Collections of artworks by African-American and New Jersey artists are growing. The new wing, which opened to acclaim in 1989, includes an education center with a three-hundred-seat auditorium. A sculpture garden is located behind the museum. The Newark Museum is accredited by the American Association of Museums.

Special Programs and Events: □ Newark Black Film Festival (see Festivals). □ Lending collection of fifteen thousand objects for exhibit or educational purposes.

Educational Programs and Events: □ Arts workshop studios. □ Children's theater and music programs. □ Classes in painting, sculpture, calligraphy for professional artists and craftspeople, children, and adults. □ Education center. □ Junior Gallery. □ Library.

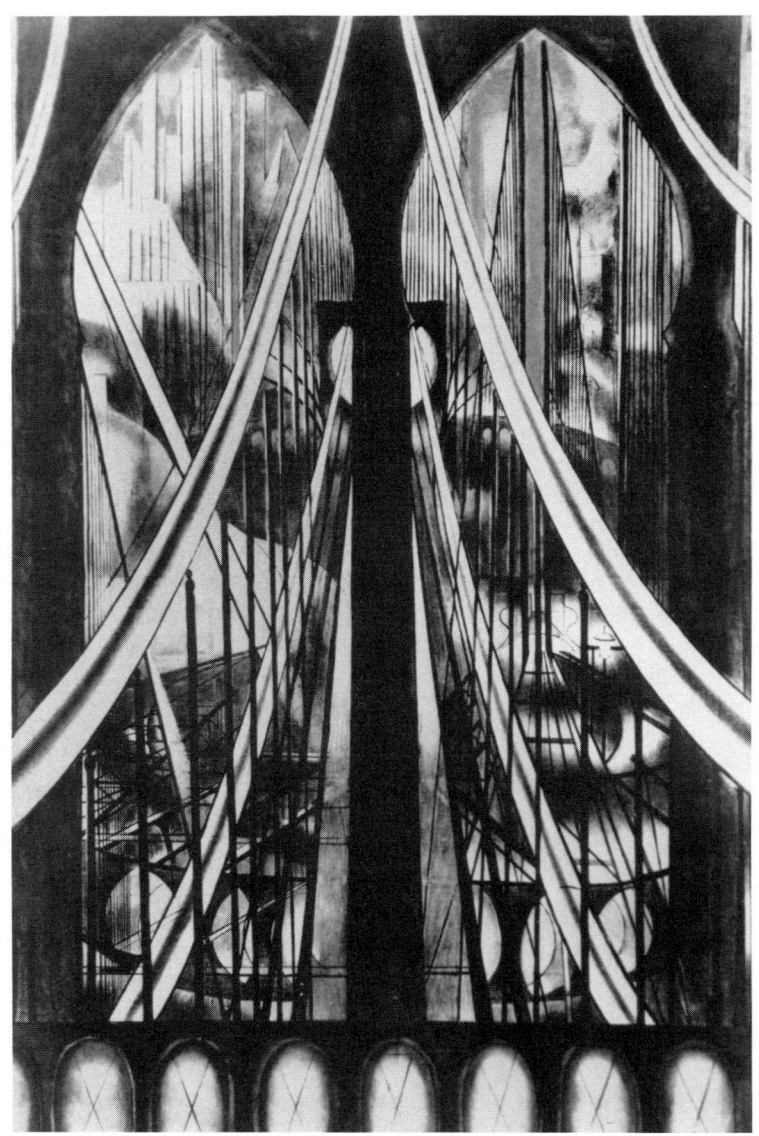

The Voice of the City of New York Interpreted: The Bridge (1920–1922), part of a five-painting work by Joseph Stella, is one of the most significant recent acquisitions by the Newark Museum (Purchase 1937 Felix Fuld Bequest Fund).

VISUAL ARTS

The Noyes Museum $ 🀲 ◨
Lily Lake Road, P.O. Box 489, Oceanville 08231   609-652-8848
Hours: 11 AM–4 PM, Wednesday through Sunday; tours by appointment.

Overlooking Lily Lake, the cedar-sided, angular Noyes Museum is southern New Jersey's only fine arts museum. Founded by local philanthropists who collected folk art, decoys, and antiques, the museum has recently concentrated on contemporary American art, particularly works by New Jersey artists. Its permanent collection includes painting, sculpture, prints, and photography. In keeping with its near-shore location (it is next to the Edwin B. Forsythe National Wildlife Refuge), the museum also maintains a decoy gallery that contains its collection of North American decoys and sponsors exhibitions by prominent American and New Jersey carvers. There is a decoy carver in residence, who demonstrates his art every day (when the museum is open) at 2 PM. The Noyes Museum sponsors arts-oriented panel discussions and lectures by exhibiting artists. Some are of special interest to working artists: for instance, "Public Art Commissions from the Artist's Point of View." The museum presents seven or eight exhibits annually.

Special Program: ☐ Contemporary music concert series, accompanied by discussions with the composers, in association with the Composers Guild of New Jersey (see Music).

Educational Programs and Events: ☐ Meet the Artist Days featuring discussions with artists in connection with exhibits. ☐ Panel discussions on exhibits and arts issues.

Peters Valley Craftsmen, Inc. (DAO 1990) 🀲 ▦ ◨ 🀲
Route 615, Layton, NJ 07851   201-948-5200
Hours: 2–4 PM, every day, June 1 through August 31; guided tours Saturday and Sunday at 2 PM; self-guiding tour brochure available.

The Peters Valley contemporary crafts center is located in the town of Bevans, which dates back to 1823. At one time, this village, located in the Kittatinny Mountains, was considered the ideal setting for a Williamsburg-North. But local artists lobbied to turn Bevans into a crafts center instead. Today, it is a crafts education compound that attracts instructors and resident artists from across the country. Since 1970, Peters Valley has provided studio space for working artists and artisans, and it includes a gallery; ceramic, blacksmith, jewelry, photo, textile, and wood studios; and a kiln.

VISUAL ARTS

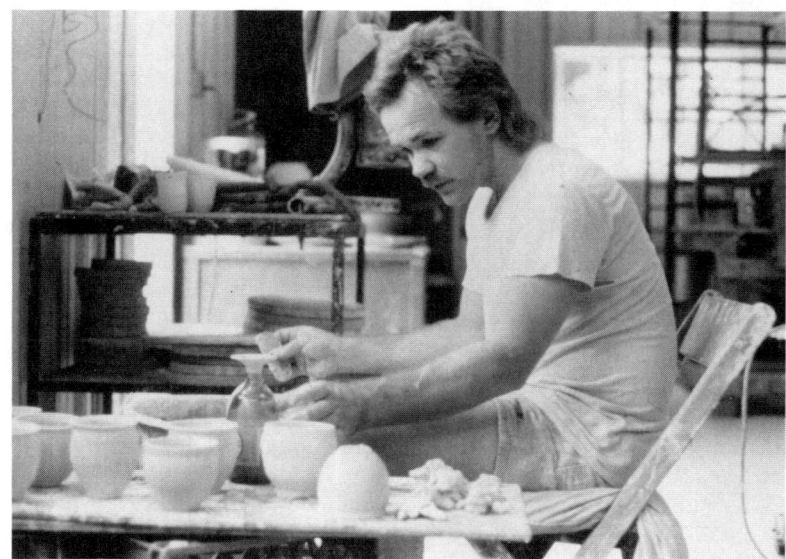

Artisans—from potters to metalsmiths—create, display, and sell their wares at Peters Valley, a crafts compound located in the nineteenth-century village of Bevans.

Special Program: ☐ Peters Valley Summer Craft Fair, featuring juried exhibitions; July (see Festivals).

Educational Program: ☐ Children's program, "Craftsmen At Work," during which professional craftspeople give lectures and demonstrations in area schools and in May at Peters Valley. ☐ Summer workshops in blacksmithing, ceramics, fine metals, photography, textiles, and woodworking.

Princeton University, The Art Museum

Princeton University, Princeton 08544   609-258-3788
Hours: 10 AM–5 PM, Tuesday through Saturday; 1–5 PM, Sunday. Regularly scheduled group tour Saturdays at 2 PM.

The Art Museum at Princeton was built on collections donated by Princeton graduates. Beginning in the 1890s with the porcelain and pottery donations of alumnus William Cowper Prime, the museum has

VISUAL ARTS

received rich and varied collections of all sorts, from African masks to Italian drawings and prints, Roman glass and mosaics, and Chinese scrolls, screens, and snuff bottles. Founded in 1890 and first housed in a stolid Romanesque revival structure, the museum moved to a new home in 1966. In 1989, it completed a new wing that includes a contemporary art gallery, two temporary exhibition galleries, a photography study center, and conservation studios.

The museum maintains particularly fine Far Eastern, Pre-Columbian, prints and drawings, and photography collections as well as a growing contemporary collection that includes works by Pablo Picasso, Jasper Johns, and Milton Avery. It houses a wide range of European paintings, sculpture, and prints, including works by such European masters as Degas, Monet, Rodin, Toulouse-Lautrec, and Gauguin.

A teaching museum, its main season is during the academic year, from September through May, although it is open throughout the summer. It generally presents about four special exhibits annually, including a major exhibit each fall and spring. Often loan exhibits are supplemented by works from the permanent collection. In 1989, the museum developed a touring show, "Central European Drawings: 1680–1800: A Selection from American Collections"; at Princeton, an adjacent gallery showcased additional related works from the museum's permanent collection.

Educational Programs and Events: ☐ Gallery talks for children and adults. ☐ School outreach program including slide/lectures before school tours of the museum.

Princeton University, The John B. Putnam, Jr. Memorial Sculpture Collection 🏛
The Art Museum
Princeton University, Princeton 08540   609-452-3787
Hours: All day, every day.

One of this country's largest outdoor university sculpture collections, The John B. Putnam, Jr., Memorial Collection contains twentieth-century works by internationally known artists such as Louise Nevelson and Alexander Calder. Made possible by a $1 million gift from an anonymous donor, it honors John B. Putnam, Jr., class of 1945, who died in World War II. The collection was assembled under the aegis of the Art Museum over a twenty-year period beginning in 1968, and it

VISUAL ARTS

includes abstract and representational pieces, scattered across the tree-lined campus.

Special Program: ☐ Sculpture Run, a sculpture-to-sculpture athletic/aesthetic "marathon" with mini-lectures on each work; spring.

Printmaking Council of New Jersey (DAO 1987)
440 River Road, Somerville 08870   201-725-2110
Gallery hours: 10 AM–3 PM, Tuesday through Friday;
1–4 PM, Saturday.

New Jersey's only organization devoted exclusively to printmaking, the council was founded in 1973 to support artists creating all kinds of prints, from Xeroxes and silkscreens to photographs and etchings. The council sponsors mainly contemporary shows and occasionally historical shows; a recent exhibit, "Master Prints," presented works from the Albion College (Michigan) collection, including prints by Rembrandt and Chagall. The Printmaking Council also offers numerous classes in all phases and kinds of printmaking, such as Japanese Hanga printing.

Special Programs and Events: ☐ Gallery Exhibit for Special Artists; annual. ☐ Members show; annual. ☐ National Print Exhibition; annual.

Educational Programs: ☐ Classes and workshops in papermaking and intaglio, silkscreen, lithography, photography, and other printing techniques. ☐ Roving Press Program, on-site workshops with a small etching press for corporate and school groups.

Rutgers University Film Co-op (see MediaMix)

Stedman Art Gallery
Fine Arts Center, Rutgers, The State University, Camden 08102
609-757-6245
Hours: 10 AM–4 PM, Monday through Saturday; 5–8 PM, Tuesday and Wednesday.

Located on the Camden campus of Rutgers, The State University, the Stedman Art Gallery concentrates on exhibits with an educational emphasis. "Mathematical Visions," a show assembled from the permanent collection, examined how mathematical theory and imagery such as symmetry and grids influence art. "From Site to Sight: Anthropology, Photography and the Power of Imagery," which was organized by Harvard University's Peabody Museum, was a multidisciplinary show that

VISUAL ARTS

Pivotal New Jersey Landscape Artists

In 1836, Maplewood resident Asher B. Durand (1796–1886), a successful engraver, took up painting. He first concentrated on portraits, then turned to landscapes. He worked outdoors and demonstrated an unusual talent for capturing depth and natural light; in fact, he was one of the first landscape artists to paint in the Hudson River School manner.

Montclair native George Inness (1825–1894), employed elements of Durand's style. But a journey to France—and exposure to the inventive Barbizon School—left him with a far freer, more interpretive brush. With his misty, almost surreal landscapes, he moved American landscape painting toward a more fluid, impressionistic style. Today he is considered one of the country's foremost landscape artists.

While Inness frequently painted scenes of Montclair and the Delaware Water Gap, Durand preferred settings in the Adirondacks or the Berkshires.

Works by both artists are in the collections of the Montclair Art Museum, the Newark Museum, the New Jersey State Museum, and the Metropolitan Museum of Art.

---

explored the role of photographic images in the study of anthropology and included a film series featuring such films as *Nanook of the North* and *The Gods Must Be Crazy*.

The staff annually curates eight exhibits and hosts one traveling exhibit, mostly of works by contemporary artists. The museum generally offers at least one interdisciplinary show each year. One show always draws on the permanent collection, which consists largely of works by contemporary American artists. The biennial "Works on Paper" show originated the year the gallery was founded and draws some three thousand entries from across the country.

Special Programs and Events: ☐ City of Camden Art Exhibition; annual. ☐ Southern New Jersey Artist Invitational Show; annual.

Educational Programs and Events: ☐ Lectures and symposia. ☐ Museum Education Enrichment Program of gallery tours and discussion groups for schoolchildren.

VISUAL ARTS

COLLEGE AND UNIVERSITY GALLERIES

Ben Shahn Galleries, William Paterson College, Wayne
Broadway Gallery, Passaic County Community College, Paterson
Caldwell College Art Gallery, Caldwell
Centenary Gallery, Centenary College, Hackettstown
Courtney Art Gallery, Jersey City State College, Jersey City
Edward Williams Gallery, Fairleigh Dickinson University, Hackensack
Elizabeth P. Korn Gallery, Drew University, Madison
Gallery One, Montclair State College, Upper Montclair
Georgian Court College Gallery, Lakewood
Holman Hall Art Gallery, Trenton State College
James Howe Gallery, Kean College, Union
Kean College Gallery, Union
Maples Gallery, Fairleigh Dickinson University, Madison
Mercer County Community College Library Gallery, Mercer County College, Trenton
Ocean County College Fine Arts Center Gallery, Toms River
Rider College Art Gallery, Lawrenceville
Ramapo College Art Galleries, Mahwah
Robeson Gallery, Rutgers, The State University, Newark
Sherman H. Masten Learning Resource Center Gallery, County College of Morris, Randolph
South and West Galleries, Downtown Arts Building, Rutgers, The State University, New Brunswick
St. Peters College Art Gallery, Jersey City
Stedman Art Gallery, Rutgers, The State University, Camden
The Gallery at Raritan Valley Community College, North Branch
Tomasulo Gallery, Union College, Cranford
Troast Memorial Gallery, Seton Hall University, South Orange
Walters Hall Gallery, Rutgers, The State University, New Brunswick

Thomas A. Edison Media Arts Consortium $ 🎞 ♿

c/o The Thomas Edison National Historic Site, Main Street and Lakeside Avenue, West Orange 07052   201-736-0796

The Media Arts Consortium is named for New Jersey resident Thomas Edison, who developed the first motion picture studio in an awkward shed called Black Maria. The organization promotes film and filmmakers, administering the well-known Black Maria Film and Video Festival, one of the largest of its kind in the country. Recent festival win-

VISUAL ARTS

CORPORATE GALLERIES
Bristol-Meyers/Squibb Corporation Gallery, Princeton
Chubb Corporation, Warren Township
Dow Jones & Company, Princeton
Educational Testing Service: Henry Chauncey Conference Center, Princeton
Peat, Marwick and Maine Collection, Montvale
Nabisco Brands Gallery, East Hanover
Schering Plough Corporation Gallery, Madison

---

ners have included *Breakfast Messages,* about a café love affair, and *Station,* about the Erie-Lackawanna Railroad line.

The consortium's professional film-editing machine is available on site to working New Jersey artists for a modest fee.

Special Programs and Events: ☐ Black Maria Film and Video Festival; annual (see Festivals). ☐ Distinctive Filmmaking Showcase, a retrospective of a major film artist's work or exploitation of a genre such as World War II animation; annual. ☐ New Jersey Guest Artists Showcase in mid-May. ☐ New Jersey Young Film and Videomakers Festival in May.

Wheaton Village (DAO 1989) $ ☐ ∅ ☐
Museum of American Glass
Wade Boulevard, Millville 08332   609-825-6800
Hours: 10 AM–5 PM, every day, April through December and Wednesday through Sunday in January, February, March.

New Jersey was once known as the "Glass State" (a fantastic piece of New Jersey glass, as tall as a man, was exhibited at the St. Louis World's Fair), and Wheaton Village's Glass Museum is located in the heart of what was glass-manufacturing country. In addition to reviewing the history of glass, visitors can watch gaffers create reproductions and contemporary pieces in the adjacent glass factory. There are more than seven thousand objects in the museum, which examines the practical and aesthetic side of glass objects, exhibiting everything from paperweights to stained glass and simple jars. To help keep the art of glassmaking alive, the Creative Glass Center of America, also located at Wharton, offers fellowships to contemporary glass artists based on an international competition.

VISUAL ARTS

Special Programs and Events: □ Craft, paperweight, and pottery shops specializing in pieces by New Jersey artists and artisans. □ Christmas Exhibit. □ Glass Lovers Weekend, a conference featuring lectures and demonstrations of interest to collectors, scholars, and working artists, in alternate odd years. □ South Jersey Woodcarvers Show.

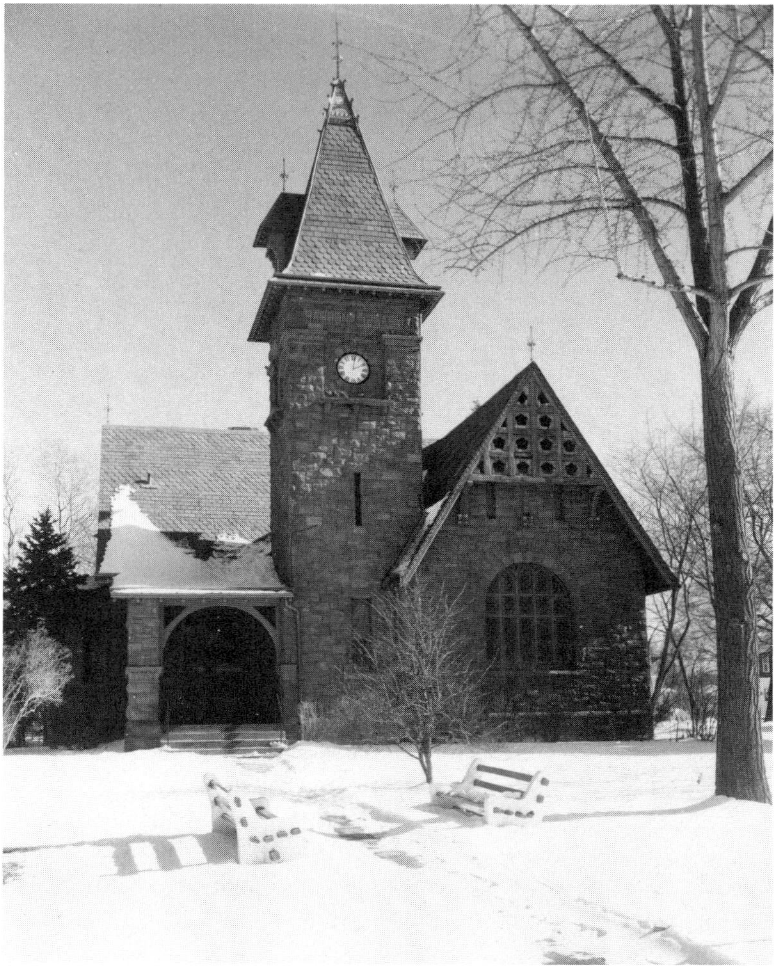

CENTERS

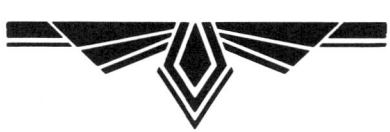

Overleaf: The Barron Arts Center, housed in a picturesque former library built in 1877, offers a year-round schedule of visual arts, music, and poetry programs.

CENTERS

Appel Farm Arts and Music Center $ & ♿
P.O. Box 770, Elmer 08318   609-358-2472
Performance sites: on-site theater (300 seats), outdoor stage, and off-site appearances in community centers, nursing homes, and parks.

The Appel Farm fine and performing arts program and year-round cultural center is located on a 176-acre working farm. Its international staff consists of professional artists and arts educators who promote three endeavors: the arts, farming, and community living. A multidisciplinary organization, Appel Farm was founded in 1960. Pigs, organic vegetables, homemade bread, and ice cream are just part of the experience here for youngsters from all over the world who take classes in drama, music, dance, art, photography, media arts, and creative writing.

Appel Farm also functions as a performing arts center; its calendar includes at least one performing arts event each month from performances by musicians, such as Herbie Mann and the Carolyn Dorfman Dance Company, to chamber music concerts and productions by area performing arts companies; the Delaware Valley Opera Company recently presented Mozart's opera *Cosi Fan Tutte* here.

Special Programs and Events: ☐ Artist-in-residence program, which includes workshops conducted by artists living at the center. ☐ Performing arts series of performances of work by visiting artists and companies; September through June. ☐ Performing arts series for children; September through June. ☐ Sharing the Arts, an outreach program taking the arts into homes for the disabled and senior citizens. ☐ Summer camp; annual. ☐ Summer community concert series; free.

Arts Center of Northern New Jersey $ ♿
250 Center Street, New Milford 07646   201-599-2992
Gallery hours: 9 AM–5 PM, Monday through Friday.
Performance site: Benjamin Franklin Middle School, Teaneck

A combination visual-art school and small-scale cultural center, the Arts Center of Northern New Jersey offers year-round classes in the visual arts, including drawing, painting, and photography for adults, teenagers, and children. In addition, there are classes in poetry, cartooning, and acting. The art center gallery presents monthly exhibits, many by affiliated professional printmakers, painters, sculptors, photographers, and watercolorists.

Special Programs and Events: ☐ Juried art show; annual. ☐ Occasional jazz and classical concerts.

CENTERS

"In the early days, the Township of Freehold gave the organization a $1 per year lease on a piece of land near Turkey Swamp Park. Efforts were begun to build an outdoor stage for summer productions and at the same time a season of shows was planned. There was no parking at the site so the audience had to be bussed in along with chairs to sit on. Mosquitoes also came along for the culture. Costs were higher than anticipated. By the time the summer was over the whole affair was referred to as the "Turkey Swamp Fiasco.""—Lew Williams, Battleground Arts Center

Barron Arts Center
582 Rahway Avenue, Woodbridge 07095   201-634-0413
Gallery hours: 11 AM—4 PM, Monday through Friday. 2—4 PM, Sunday.
Performance site: at the center gallery (100 seats).

Housed in a former library built in 1877, the Barron Arts Center presents seven or eight art exhibits and eight concerts annually, in addition to a monthly poetry-reading series. The center, a Romanesque Revival building with vaulted ceilings and stained glass windows, is operated under the auspices of the Woodbridge Township Cultural Arts Commission. The building is on the National Register of Historic Places.

Special Programs and Events: ☐ First Fridays Concert Series consisting of performances of country, jazz, classical, and popular music. ☐ PoetsWednesday; monthly.

Battleground Arts Center $ ∅ ⚹
P.O. Box 678, 35 West Main Street, Freehold 07728   201-462-8811
Performance sites: Battlefield State Park and in churches, schools, and temples throughout western Monmouth County.

In 1973, the Battleground Arts Center was founded with sixty dollars collected from area residents who were interested in promoting the arts. Since then, it has expanded, and it now sponsors a wide variety of arts programs and performances. The center emphasizes music and theater; it presents an annual youth theater subscription series, as well as seven to ten concerts and special events annually. Summer shows include a folk festival and one or two other musical performances.

Special Programs and Events: ☐ Folk Festival; annual. ☐ *Program Clearinghouse,* providing information on arts programs for local organizations. ☐ Weekly cable television show on the western Monmouth County arts scene. ☐ Youth Theatre productions in fall and winter.

Educational Programs and Events: ☐ Fall and winter children's theater workshops for young people, ages nine to fourteen. ☐ Pre-school performance series for ages three to six. ☐ Summer Drama Day Camp for ages nine to fourteen. ☐ Center orchestras.

Center for the Arts in Southern New Jersey (see Visual Arts)

Count Basie Theatre

Monmouth County Arts Council, 99 Monmouth Street, Red Bank 07701   201-842-9002
Performance site: at the theater (1,400 seats).

The Count Basie Theatre, a performing arts center, is owned and operated by the Monmouth County Arts Council. An art gallery and art studios adjacent to the theater are also part of the arts complex where the council offers programs in all disciplines (about one hundred and fifty events annually). The New Jersey Symphony Orchestra presents an annual series at the theater, as does the Garden State Ballet, which is in residence. The council maintains a year-round multi-disciplinary season that includes a jazz series and occasional play and poetry readings. The Count Basie Theatre lobby is the setting for a musical cabaret that features free performances by local performers.

Special Event: ☐ Arts Fair; spring.

Educational Program: ☐ Outreach substance-abuse-prevention program promoting the performing arts as a positive substitute for drugs; in connection with Monmouth County schools.

Friday Evening Club

80 Miller Road, Morristown 07960   201-538-6413
Performance sites: Morris Knolls High School (1,200 seats) in Denville and the Morristown High School Auditorium (850 seats).

If the Friday Evening Club's name sounds archaic, it is no accident; the club was founded by the mayor of Morristown in 1900. In those days, Friday evening lectures by prominent citizens formed a large part of its program. The club was disbanded in the mid-1940s, but was reorga-

CENTERS

nized in 1979 as a performing arts center without a permanent home. It presents between twenty and thirty events in dance, theater, music, and other performance arts annually in two Morris County auditoriums. The organization's two series, one in Morristown, the other in Denville, offer celebrated performers and ensembles such as Victor Borge, Marcel Marceau, and the Vienna Boys Choir. The season runs from September through May. The Friday Evening Club recently inaugurated an Arts for the Handicapped program that offers free transportation and tickets to the disabled.

Educational Event: □ Pre-performance lectures.

Garden State Arts Center $|&|♣

P.O. Box 116, Holmdel 07733   201-442-9200 or 201-888-5000 (for festival and free program information).
Performance site: in the center's amphitheater (with a capacity of 5,300 under the roof and 5,500 on the lawn).

Star rock, pop, and classical performers—from Ringo Starr and Bob Dylan to Itzhak Perlman—constitute the central attractions at the Garden State Arts Center, which contains the state's largest covered amphitheater, set on Telegraph Hill Park's four hundred acres. Beyond the amphitheater are nature trails and fitness courses. Operated since 1968 by the state's Garden State Parkway/New Jersey Highway Authority, the center has been selected as the site for the New Jersey Vietnam Veterans War Memorial Monument. The center presents more than twenty-five concerts each year; it offers classical and contemporary subscription series during its main season, which runs from June through September, as well as a variety of off-season events.

Special Programs and Events: □ Classical music series. □ Contemporary music series. □ Ethnic Heritage Festivals of arts, food, sports, theater, and music demonstrations; held in spring and fall. □ Free daytime programs for senior citizens, the disabled, and schoolchildren. □ Talent Expo for New Jersey teenagers.

Grant Avenue Community Center $|♣
Kean-Brown Centre Stage
403 West Seventh Street, Plainfield 07060   201-561-0123
Performance site: Kean-Brown Centre Theater (350 seats).

The Grant Avenue Community Center, a combination cultural center and human services agency, has been producing and presenting a mix

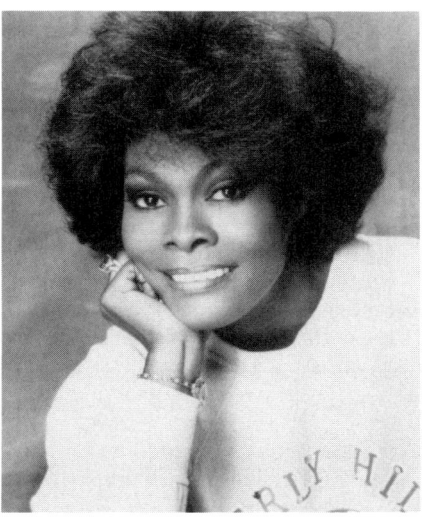

Star performers such as Dionne Warwick appear as part of the contemporary music series every summer at the state-operated Garden State Arts Center.

of music, dance, original plays, and children's theater for a cross-cultural audience since 1983. Kean-Brown was founded in 1987 as the theater division of the center. It produces one or two plays each season, sixteen performances apiece. Usually four or five actors appear in each production.

The theater arm of the center produces and presents works that feature black and minority issues and personalities. It opened its 1988 season with a play called *Forever My Darling*, set in Roxbury, a racially troubled section of Boston. In honor of Black History Month in 1989, it produced *The Black West*, a multimedia show on the history of black cowboys and pioneers that included slide presentations and dramatic depictions of Western characters.

Educational Programs and Events: □ Theater apprenticeships for young people. □ Summer performing arts program.

Jewish Community Center of Metropolitan New Jersey
$ & ♀
Cultural Arts Department
Salzman Building, 760 Northfield Avenue, West Orange
07052   201-736-3200
Performance site: at the center's Maurice Levin Theatre (500 seats).

CENTERS

ARTS CENTERS OF THE FUTURE?

A study commissioned by former Governor Thomas Kean found the following locations suitable for state arts centers:

Newark: A new, $200-million performing arts center similar to Lincoln Center, New York, is expected to house the New Jersey Symphony's home concert hall and include a theater.

Morristown, Englewood, New Brunswick, Trenton, Red Bank, Cherry Hill, and Somers Point: Recommended sites for year-round cultural centers.

Camden, Liberty State Park, Jersey City, and Waterloo Village, Stanhope: Recommended sites for outdoor performing arts centers.

More than one hundred years old, the Jewish Community Center (formerly the YM-YWHA of Metropolitan New Jersey), has a long tradition of presenting arts programs to audiences in the northern New Jersey area, at first from a building in Newark. Some events have long histories; the JCC's chamber music program, which presents performers from all over the world, began in the 1940s.

The JCC's Cultural Department presents nearly one hundred fine arts and performing arts events annually, including theater, jazz, Judaica, children's theater, and dance and jazz series. The center recently offered *Call Me Ethel . . . Merman, of Course!* and a concert by the Tokyo String Quartet, and displayed "Prints of Old Newark" in its art gallery. Three orchestras—the New Philharmonic (see Music), the Metropolitan Y Orchestra, and the Hoboken Chamber Orchestra (see Music) perform regularly at the JCC. The Y recently installed in its theater an infra-red sound system for use with headphones by the hearing impaired.

Special Programs and Events: ☐ Black History Month, including dance and jazz concerts and crafts and photography displays; annual. ☐ JCC Artists Showcase, an exhibition and sale of works by adult and gifted teen students enrolled in JCC classes. ☐ Metropolitan Y Community Orchestra. ☐ Young Artists Competition; annual. ☐ "From Our Children's Hands," an exhibit of works by students in children's classes; annual.

Educational Programs and Events: ☐ Classes in visual and performing arts for children, young people, and adults. ☐ Classes for mothers and children in music and movement.

CENTERS

John Harms Center for the Arts (RCAE) $ 👤
30 North Van Brunt Street, Englewood 07631   201-567-5797
Gallery hours: By appointment only, 9 AM—5 PM, Monday through Friday and during center events.
Performance site: at the center, a former vaudeville house (1,200 seats).

The John Harms Center for the Arts, one of the most active arts centers in the northern part of the state, was named for a well-known local promoter, who spent a lifetime bringing classical musicians to New Jersey. Prominent visiting guest artists are still part of the center's programming, and performers such as the Vienna Boys Choir and Ray Charles appear there regularly. However, the John Harms Center presents a wide range of events (more than fifty annually) in all disciplines, including art exhibits, popular singers, jazz groups, children's theater, and classical music. Its main season runs from September through June, and its subscription series include "Family Favorites," "Classics Revisited," "For Kids Only," "Stand Up and Cheer," and "Dance Magic." The New Jersey Symphony also presents a series at the center. In addition, the Creative Theater troupe, in residence since 1977, performs for children and adults and offers children's classes. The Intermission Gallery displays works by metropolitan area artists, and its shows rotate monthly.

Special Events and Programs: □ *The Nutcracker,* performed annually by the New Jersey Ballet (see Dance). □ The *Messiah;* performed annually.

Educational Programs and Events: □ Dance classes. □ Dramatics and ballet lessons. □ Gifted children's master classes taught by well-known performers.

Long Beach Island Foundation of the Arts and Sciences $ 👤
120 Long Beach Boulevard, Loveladies 08008   609-494-1241
Gallery hours: June through September, 9 AM—5 PM, Monday through Saturday; noon—4 PM, Sunday.
Performance site: at the center (400 seats).

Founded in 1947 as a summer arts center by the sculptor Boris Blai and other area artists and vacationers, the foundation now offers art classes and several concerts by popular music performers during its ten-week summer season. In 1988, jazz pianist Billy Taylor, The Inkspots, and the Marian and Jimmy McPartland Quintette appeared here. The center also presents group art shows by state and local artists and displays fine crafts.

Educational Programs and Events: ☐ Children's classes in art and puppetry. ☐ Adult classes in sculpture, watercolor, and photography.

McCarter Theatre (RCAE, AFG/DAO 1987, 1990)
Center for the Performing Arts

91 University Place, Princeton 08540   609-683-9100 (administration), 609-683-8000 (box office)
Performance site: McCarter Theatre (1,000 seats).

One of the state's busiest and most diverse cultural centers, the newly renovated McCarter Theatre Center for the Performing Arts offers theater, dance, music, children's, and young people's subscription series, in addition to special shows by performers such as George Winston, Eddie Murphy, the Kodo Drummers, and Mummenshanz.

"This will be a theater for everyone: young, old, rich, poor, black, white. . . . I want to celebrate the diverse voice of our people, to provide a home for the best writers regardless of their gender, race, political, or sexual orientation. No matter how disheartening the climate for support of the arts in this country becomes, this theater will not budge from its commitment to presenting work of quality and excellence."—Emily Mann, Artistic Director, McCarter Theatre

---

McCarter, located on the Princeton University Campus, has been entertaining and educating audiences for more than sixty years with performances by fledgling stars, famous actors, and irreverent undergraduates. It has long provided the performance space for the Triangle Club, the nation's oldest university musical theater group. During the 1930s and 1940s McCarter attracted stars and productions headed for Broadway: Princeton audiences saw performances by Lucille Ball, Gloria Swanson, and other well-known actors and actresses. *Bus Stop, Our Town,* and *Miss Lonelyhearts* had their world premieres here. In 1988, with glasnost underway, McCarter's then artistic director Nagle Jackson became one of the first Americans to direct in the Soviet Union. His production of Tennessee Williams's *The Glass Menagerie* opened at Leningrad's Gorky Theater on 19 April 1988. Although still

A Star-Studded Ivy League Stage

Perhaps no New Jersey theater group has been associated with more enduring stars than Princeton University's Triangle Club, this country's oldest university musical theater organization, which dates back to 1893.

When the Princeton Dramatic Association decided to abandon serious drama for musical comedy, Booth Tarkington, class of 1893, came up with a new name: Triangle Club, after a well-known walk on the corner of the campus at Stockton and Mercer streets.

Since Tarkington's day, present and future stage, screen, and literary stars have worked on the annual Triangle Club production, among them F. Scott Fitzgerald, Jimmy Stewart, Joshua Logan, Jose Ferrer, and, more recently, Brooke Shields.

For years the highlight of the annual Triangle Show was its preening, prancing, all-male kickline. But when Princeton went coed, the Triangle Club—and its kickline—did too. The sell-out Triangle Show can still be seen at Princeton's McCarter Theatre each spring.

---

the home of the Triangle Club, the theater is no longer owned and operated by the university. Today, it is part of one of the best-attended performing arts centers in the state. McCarter Theatre's drama season runs from October through May and includes roughly seventeen performances of each of five plays. The season also includes six free play readings, with audience/company discussions, three in the fall and three in the spring. One recent, typical theater season included a world premiere, a classic, a comedy, and an experimental play. Recent seasons have included plays such as *A Funny Thing Happened on the Way to the Forum, Dividing the Estate* by Horton Foote, and Molière's *Tartuffe*. Many McCarter productions also feature free pre-opening lectures. McCarter's annual Christmas show, *A Christmas Carol,* adapted for the stage by Jackson, has created controversy by casting Asian, black, and other ethnic actors and actresses as British Victorians. In 1989, playwright Emily Mann succeeded Jackson as artistic director.

The center offers more than one hundred events annually, plus regular seasonal events such as *The Nutcracker* by the Princeton Ballet. A recent dance series presented performances by four companies: the Feld Ballet, Dance Theatre of Harlem, Pilobolus, and the Mark Morris Dance Group. During the summer season, the theater presents special series;

in recent years a film series (with screenings of more than thirty films) and a jazz series have been offered.

Special Programs and Events: □ *A Christmas Carol:* an adaptation by Nagle Jackson of Dickens' classic; presented annually. □ Headphones available for the hearing impaired. □ McCarter Open House, a backstage tour with demonstrations by costume, lighting, and scene experts; annual. □ New Year's Eve performance of Bach's *Brandenburg Concertos,* with the New York Chamber Symphony; annual. □ *Nutcracker* by the Princeton Ballet; annual. □ Pre-St. Patrick's Day Concert; annual.

Educational Programs and Events: □ Classes in acting, scene study, and playwriting for children and adults. □ Intern program: ten to twelve interns in training each year. □ New play readings. □ Post-production seminars with discussions among directors, actors, and members of the audience. □ Pre-opening lectures for drama productions. □ School workshops and assembly programs. □ Shakespeare Summer, a four-week training program for teenagers in acting and design with McCarter professionals. □ Student matinees with post-performance seminars. □ Young Audiences subscriptions, including discounts on McCarter Training Wing classes and day-long tour/demonstration retreat.

Mid-Atlantic Center for the Arts $|例|$

P.O. Box 340, 1048 Washington Street, Cape May
08204   609-884-5404
Performance sites: Emlen Physick Estate (The center's restored
Victorian headquarters, which features an outdoor stage); Cape May
Point Lighthouse; Cape May Point State Park; Convention Hall,
Cape May.

Based in a restored Victorian house called the Emlen Physick Estate, the Mid-Atlantic Center for the Arts is a multidisciplinary organization. It emphasizes Victoriana and brings year-round performing arts events to the Cape May area. It sponsors an annual (November through March), four-performance community concert series. The center's summer theater program presents Victorian and contemporary shows by Equity companies, and the center often sponsors duet and trio performances of Victorian music or small-cast plays at various locations on holidays.

Special Programs and Events: □ Children's theater performed by guest artists. □ Shakespeare in Cape May, comprised of lectures, performances, and discussion groups, held in April. □ Victorian Week, providing

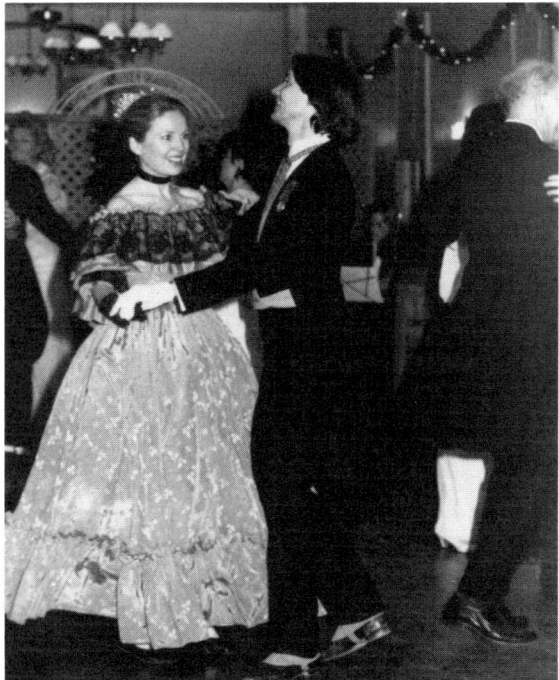

Victorian Week, which celebrates Victoriana with everything from historic house tours to a gala ball, is an annual special event at the Mid-Atlantic Center for the Arts, in the Victorian national historic landmark town of Cape May.

self-guided tours of Victorian homes; live Victorian entertainment; and lectures on Victorian architecture and the decorative arts; held in October (see Festivals).

Educational Programs and Events: ☐ Elementary school programs of workshops and lectures by theater professionals on numerous subjects from clown make-up to electronic music.

Newark Public Library ♿︎ 👤

5 Washington Street, P.O. Box 630, Newark 07101   201-733-7800
Hours: 9 AM–9 PM, Monday, Wednesday, Thursday; 9 AM–5 PM, Tuesday and Friday; 9 AM–5:30 PM, Saturday; 1–5 PM, Sunday. Performance sites: the library's Centennial Hall, auditorium, and two galleries.

CENTERS

This library has a long history as a pioneer in the movement that encouraged libraries to become cultural centers; in 1905, under the leadership of John Cotton Dana (see the Newark Museum—Visual Arts), the Newark Public Library presented one of the first exhibits of works by American artists. Since that time, the library galleries have shown thousands of works by artists of all kinds. The library also presents numerous dance, music, and theatrical events, many geared toward the different ethnic and minority groups living in Newark.

Educational Programs and Events: □ Centennial Hall Arts series. □ Music, drama, and dance performances. □ Special Populations Programs of exhibits and performances by minority and other underserved groups; the library maintains African-American and Hispanic-American rooms, devoted to cultural arts, particularly literature.

Newark Symphony Hall $ 🎭 ♿

1020 Broad Street, Newark 07102   201-643-4550 (administration), 201-643-8009 (box office)
Performance site: Symphony Hall (2,800 seats).

After completing a more than $9 million renovation, Newark's downtown Symphony Hall (built in 1925 as a mosque by the Shriners) has reopened and provides performance space for New Jersey performing arts organizations, including the New Jersey Symphony and the New Jersey State Opera. It also acts as a performing arts center in its own right, presenting annually a major concert series and fall dance and winter theater series, featuring black performing artists and ensembles such as Gallman's Newark Dance Theatre and the Crossroads Theatre Company. Every year Symphony Hall offers a free, six-week summer series for children in the adjacent Brownstone Park area, with performances by a variety of performing artists from dance troupes to storytellers and Afro-Caribbean musicians. Symphony Hall is a National Historic Landmark.

New Brunswick Cultural Center, Inc. (RCAE) $ ✎ ♿

19 Livingston Avenue, New Brunswick 08903   201-247-7200
Performance site: State Theater (1,800 seats), New Brunswick.

The New Brunswick Cultural Center was founded in 1982 with support from Johnson & Johnson, which has its headquarters in New Brunswick; Rutgers, The State University; the City of New Brunswick; and the Middlesex County Board of Chosen Freeholders as part of a plan to re-

CENTERS

New Jersey's Poet Laureate

In an era when many men of prodigious literary gifts moved to Paris, William Carlos Williams (1883–1963) stayed home in Rutherford, New Jersey, close to his childhood home, his family, and his patients. Williams has been called one of the most American of poets, a writer whose words defined the spirit of a nation. But, his work also captured the solid, quotidian soul of the northern New Jersey cities where he lived and worked: Rutherford and nearby Paterson. The head pediatrician at Passaic General Hospital, Williams tended to thousands of patients and delivered thousands of babies in his lifetime. He was just as prolific a writer, publishing volumes of poetry, some plays, short stories, and an autobiography.

The depth of his devotion to both medicine and poetry seemed impossible, and yet both defined his life. Williams was absorbed by his writing, his practice, and his roles as father, husband, and neighbor. Writing home from on board the SS *Pennland* on his way to Europe in 1927, he interrupted a prosaic letter about running into a neighbor with a burst of poetry: "I have also picked up a fellow from New Jersey who is traveling with his wife," he wrote. "They know many people in Rutherford and are related in some way to the Grays on Home Avenue. (Last night there were five separate rain storms, blue hanging curtains, off on the horizon around us while we were in sunlight as the sun went down.) Do you remember that baby that Ogden was taking care of? That's the one. They had heard of me in that way." William Carlos Williams was born and died in Rutherford. In fact, he died in the same house where he lived most of his life: No. 9 Ridge Road.

---

vitalize the city of New Brunswick. Located downtown, the center provides performance, office, studio, and gallery space for its resident cultural organizations, including the Crossroads Theatre Company, George Street Playhouse, New Jersey Designer Craftsmen, and the Princeton Ballet. Affiliate companies such as the Shoestring Players, the New Jersey Jazz Society, the Middlesex County Arts High School, and Brunswick Symphony Orchestra also have access to its services and performance spaces. The center's newly renovated State Theatre opened in 1988 with a performance by the Jerusalem Symphony. The New Brunswick Cultural Center presents annual series (more than thirty-five events) there from September through May. Programs from recent seasons have included an international symphony orchestra series, dance series, family series, and a young people's symphony series.

CENTERS

Educational Programs and Events: □ Free matinees for students in schools in Middlesex County and parts of Somerset County, including study guides and pre-performance lectures for teachers. □ Pre-performance lectures for the international symphony series.

Oakside-Bloomfield Cultural Center 💲👤
240 Belleville Avenue, Bloomfield 07003   201-429-0960
Performance site: at the center.
Gallery hours: By appointment.

The Oakside-Bloomfield Cultural Center is located in a state and national historic site: "Oakside," a Victorian mansion owned by the town of Bloomfield and administered by the Bloomfield Cultural Commission. The house was built and occupied by members of the Oakes family, which owned a nearby woolen mill (The Oakes Mills). The center opened in 1982. The house and gardens are open to visitors; house tours and a self-guided tour of the kitchen, water, and rose gardens are available. The center takes a special interest in new music; its World Music series presents contemporary music based on traditional forms, by musicians from countries such as Ireland, France, India, and Italy. It also regularly presents lecture/performances of new music by New Jersey composers, sponsored in cooperation with the Composers Guild of New Jersey (see Music). The center's gallery also sponsors an annual "Local Artists" series that highlights the work of both visual and performing artists. Oakside presents some twenty events annually during its main season, which runs from March through May.

Special Program: □ Annual Black Maria Film Festival sponsor (see Festivals).

Educational Programs and Events: □ School tours. □ Student participation in the World Music and Visual Artist series/lectures.

Ocean County Center for the Arts/The Strand Theatre 💲👤
Fourth Street and Clifton Avenue, Lakewood 08701   201-367-6688
Performance site: Strand Theatre (950 seats).

The Ocean County Center for the Arts presents more than twenty guest artists and performing arts events during its main subscription season, which runs from October through May. The 1988–1989 season included music, dance, and theater productions by performers such as Arlo Guthrie, Dizzy Gillespie, the Shanghai Acrobats and Magicians, the Princeton Ballet, and New Jersey Pops Orchestra. Red Oak Music Theater, a community theater group, presents four musicals performed five times each during the regular season. The Strand Theatre was built in 1922 as a movie/vaudeville house and is on the National Register of Historic Places. It is undergoing restoration.

Special Event: ☐ Annual *Nutcracker* performance.

Educational Program: ☐ Children's theater series for school groups.

Palisades Interstate Park Commission, New Jersey Section $|⛨

P.O. Box 155, Alpine 07620   201-768-1360
Performance sites: Fort Lee Historic Park Visitors' Center auditorium (204 seats) and outdoor locations overlooking the Hudson River—the Fort Lee Historic Park, Fort Lee; Ross Dock Picnic Area, Fort Lee; Alpine Picnic Area and State Line Lookout, Alpine; Englewood Boat Basin Area.

The Park Commission provides sites at this riverside arts and entertainment center for chamber music concerts, student piano and string recitals, vocal and piano concerts, outdoor concerts, and theater productions. The center also presents historic reenactments at lookout sites along the Palisades Interstate Parkway, within hiking distance of the Long Path and Shore Trail, two National Recreation Trails. About thirty events take place at these sites annually, many of them musical. A fee is generally charged for indoor events; outdoor events are free.

Paper Mill Playhouse (see Theater)

Park Theatre Performing Arts Center and Art Gallery
♿|$|🎭|⛨

560 32d Street, Union City 07087   201-865-6980
Performance sites: Park Theatre (1,400 seats) and Park Playhouse (140 seats), Union City.

The Park Theatre was built in 1931 as part of a Roman Catholic high school and as a showcase for the Passion Play. In 1983, it became a performing arts center, presenting dance and music and producing and presenting plays. Every Easter the Park Theatre presents the country's longest continuously running Passion Play. The play, which opened in a local auditorium in 1914, and moved to the theater in 1931, is performed ten times in English and twice in Spanish; the Spanish version

CENTERS

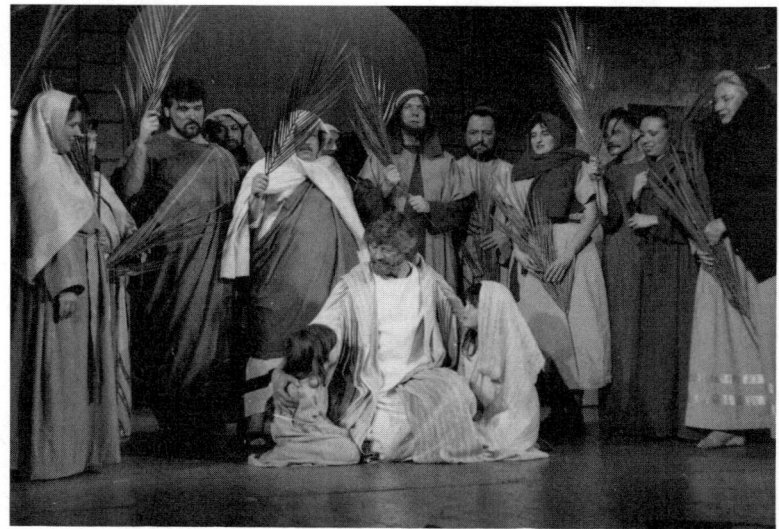

The country's longest continuously running Passion Play is performed annually at the Park Theatre Performing Arts Center.

has been featured on National Public Radio. The Garden State Concert Band, Hudson Repertory Dance Theater, and the Park Players, a community musical theater troupe, are in residence at the theater. In addition, the center presents twelve to fifteen performing arts events during its season, which runs from September through June. During the 1989–1990 season, the center produced two Equity broadway revivals, *Tintypes* and *The Sunshine Boys.* The Park Theatre Performing Arts Center offers six series, including a big-band music series, a jazz series, and a theater series featuring performances by such visiting groups as Repertory Español. The center also rents studio space to Hudson County artists.

Special Events: ◻ *The Promised Land,* an original Equity musical based on the story of Moses; annually at Passover. ◻ Passion Play, annually at Easter.

Educational Program: ◻ Visiting artists outreach program.

CENTERS

Perkins Center for the Arts $|$|🏛|🚻|

Kings Highway and Camden Avenue, Moorestown, 08057
609-235-6488
Gallery hours: During exhibitions, 12 noon–4 PM, Tuesday through Sunday.
Performance sites: at the center and at the affiliated Perkins Gallery in the Commerce Bank, Moorestown, during bank hours.

The Perkins Center, located in a Tudor home (circa 1910) in Moorestown, began offering cultural programs in 1978. It sponsors some twenty events and numerous classes during its main season, which runs from September through June. Perkins maintains a resident dance company, the Ballet des Jeunes, which performs Hans Christian Andersen's *Snow Queen* every year and has toured England, Scotland, and Wales. A resident chamber music group, the Perkins Chamber Players, composed of violinists, a cellist, and harpsichordist, offers a series. In addition, the Center presents visiting artists and groups such as the Crossroads Theatre Company (see Theater). Perkins also collaborates on performing arts programs with other southern New Jersey cultural institutions, including Appel Farm and the Walt Whitman Center. One of its major events is an annual juried photography show with nearly eight hundred entries from four states. Works from that exhibit have been included in the permanent collections of the New Jersey State Museum, the Noyes Museum, Philadelphia Museum of Art, and Smithsonian Institution. The Perkins Arboretum is also open to visitors.

Special Programs and Events: □ Ceramic exhibition; annual. □ Concert series. □ Outreach performances at homes for senior citizens and disabled persons. □ Photography exhibit; annual. □ Student art show.

Educational Programs and Events: □ Classes in ceramics, art, dance, folklore, music. □ Perkins Conservatory of Music, which offers classes for children and adults. □ Perkins Creativity Camp, a collaboration with the Walt Whitman Center, offering art and literature workshops to suburban and urban youngsters ages seven to eleven.

Princeton University $|$|

Princeton 08544   609-258-3000 (for cultural-calendar information: Richardson Auditorium Box Office, from 4 PM to 6 PM or until the start of a concert, 609-258-5000, or see the *Princeton Weekly Bulletin,* available through the Orange Key Guide Service, 609-258-3603).
Performance sites: Richardson Auditorium (800 seats), Taplin

CENTERS

Auditorium, Theatre Intime, Woolworth Center of Musical Studies, McCarter Theatre Center for the Performing Arts (see separate listing, Centers), and 185 Nassau Street.

Most active during the fall, winter, and spring months, Princeton presents cultural events that are open to the public almost every day or evening. The university provides students, faculty, and the public with arts events and programs at numerous sites on campus. Its concert series is one of the oldest college-affiliated concert series in the country. Richardson Auditorium, its primary concert hall, recently underwent extensive renovations.

The Princeton Friends of Music, a community membership organization, gives regular free concerts at Richardson that feature guest artists and advanced student performers in concerts of contemporary and classical music from all cultures. Two university concert series run from September through June. A wide variety of student and professional groups perform for the public on campus, including the The Princeton Chamber Ensemble (a group that performs many works written by graduate music students), Princeton University Orchestra, Princeton Opera Theatre, Princeton Pro Musica, the Princeton Chamber Symphony, the Triangle Club, Princeton Glee Club, Princeton Chapel Choir, and Princeton Jazz Ensemble. High-spirited a cappella groups, from the all-male Tigertones, Nassoons, and Footnotes to the all-female Tigerlilies, also give shows at Richardson Auditorium. The Art Museum (see Visual Arts) shows works from its permanent collections and hosts traveling exhibits; the John B. Putnam, Jr. Memorial Sculpture Collection (see Visual Arts) is one of the largest university outdoor sculpture collections in the country. Student plays and productions can be seen in the Theatre Intime (609-258-4950). At least two dance concerts are given annually at Richardson or 185 Nassau Street; others are presented in various campus locations by the university's Program in Theater and Dance (609-258-3676/5457). Visual arts exhibits are also held at Firestone Library (609-258-5737) and the Gest Oriental Library in Jones Hall (609-258-3182/5336). The Princeton University Film Society schedules regular screenings during the school year.

Special Programs: □ Free one-hour walking tour of campus, including selected outdoor sculptures, every day by the Orange Key Guide Service.

Educational Programs and Events: □ Many lectures and symposia are open to the public, including lectures on music theory and history

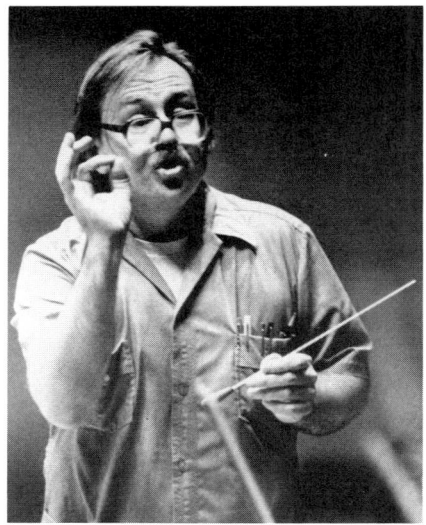

Jens Nygaard directs the Rutgers University Orchestra, one of the many university and guest ensembles that perform regularly at the state university's New Brunswick campus.

sponsored by the Department of Music; check *Princeton Weekly Bulletin*.

Rutgers, The State University of New Jersey [$]

New Brunswick 08903   201-932-7591 (University Arts Services), 201-932-7511 (box office)
Performance sites: Rutgers Art Center, New Brunswick (Nicholas Music Center and Philip J. Levin Theater), Downtown Arts Building, Loree Gym, Walters Hall Gallery, Kirkpatrick Chapel, and at other Rutgers campuses.

The state university is one of New Jersey's most active cultural centers, presenting dozens of events and programs in music, dance, opera, theater, and the visual arts. While other Rutgers campuses present performing and visual arts events and programs, New Brunswick, home of the university's Mason Gross School of the Arts, is the hub of performing arts activity.

Though busiest during the academic year, Rutgers arts programs run year-round. In fact, Rutgers's Summerfest (see Festivals) is one of the largest and most successful summer arts festivals in the state. There is an arts event on campus almost every day of the week; the University Arts Services office (201-932-7591) publishes a calendar listing events and programs in all disciplines. Rutgers organizations and institutions reach outside the campus; many events of interest to the public originate with the Mason Gross School of the Arts and take place at the Rutgers Arts Center, which includes Nicholas Music Center, the Philip J. Levin Theater, and Walters Hall Gallery. Classical and contemporary music; star, faculty, and student soloists; and ensembles and orchestras all find an audience in Rutgers concert and recital halls. Regular series include Music at McKinney; a dance series with visiting artists; opera at Rutgers; the seventy-four-year-old university concert series; Theatre-at-Rutgers Series with performances by graduate students, Equity actors, and faculty members; and the Philip J. Levin Theater Company, a summer Equity theater group.

The Rutgers Concert Bureau (201-932-9067/9288) sponsors a program that encourages advanced faculty and students by booking engagements for them throughout New Jersey, New York, Pennsylvania, Connecticut, and Delaware. This arrangement gives Rutgers students a chance to perform and audiences an opportunity to hear and see emerging young artists and faculty from the Rutgers Doctor of Music Arts/Artist Diploma Program. The bureau also arranges for on-site lecture/recitals.

Special Programs and Events: □ Princeton Ballet repertory season (see Dance). □ Summerfest (see Festivals).

Educational Program: □ Lectures in connection with some performances.

Stockton Performing Arts Center $ 👤
Stockton State College, Jim Leeds Road, Pomona 08240
609-652-4607 (administration) and 609-652-9000 (box office)
Performance site: at the center (550 seats).

Located on the campus of Stockton State College in the Pinelands west of Atlantic City, the Stockton Performing Arts Center presents pop, classical, and stage performers throughout the year. The main season runs from October through May and consists of forty to fifty events. It includes theater, dance, jazz, and classical music series and a children's summer theater. The programs feature guest artists, ensembles, and orchestras such as the Batsheva Dance Company of Israel, the Negro Ensemble Company, the Atlanta Symphony Orchestra, and the Prague

Symphony Orchestra. The center also offers a New Jersey Chamber Music Society series. Special events have included performances by Harry Connick, Jr., and by the New York City Opera's national company. The Stockton Chamber Players, a community music group, is in residence.

Special Event: ☐ Jersey Shore Summer Music Festival at Stockton, presenting jazz, classical, and popular performers.

Educational Programs and Events: ☐ Matinees for elementary and high school student groups. ☐ Occasional dance master classes in connection with Stockton State College.

Union County Arts Center $

Rahway Theatre, 1601 Irving Street, Rahway 07065   201-499-0441
Performance site: Rahway Theatre (1,350 seats).

A non-profit corporation called Rahway Landmarks is renovating and operating the Rahway Theatre as the headquarters for the Union County Arts Center, to provide performance space for community performing arts groups as well as a subscription season of professional dance, theater, and music. Like the New Brunswick Cultural Center, the Union County Arts Center is part of a downtown revitalization effort. The theater, a former film and vaudeville house opened in 1928, is on the New Jersey Register of Historic Places.

Special Events: ☐ Annual Black History Month program. ☐ *Nutcracker* by the New Jersey Dance Theater Guild; annual.

Walt Whitman Center for the Arts and Humanities (see also Poetry listings) $ ♿

2nd and Cooper Streets, Camden 08102   609-757-7276
Hours: 10 AM–4 PM, Monday through Friday; evening and weekend hours vary.
Performance site: at the center (190 seats).

The center was founded in 1971 and named in honor of Walt Whitman, who spent his final years in Camden. In addition to poetry and writers series (James Baldwin read here in 1986 and seven Pulitzer Prize winners appear here annually), the Walt Whitman Center for the Arts and Humanities also presents theater, music, and visual arts events. It offers nearly one hundred events during its September-through-May season, including a Saturday children's theater series. A

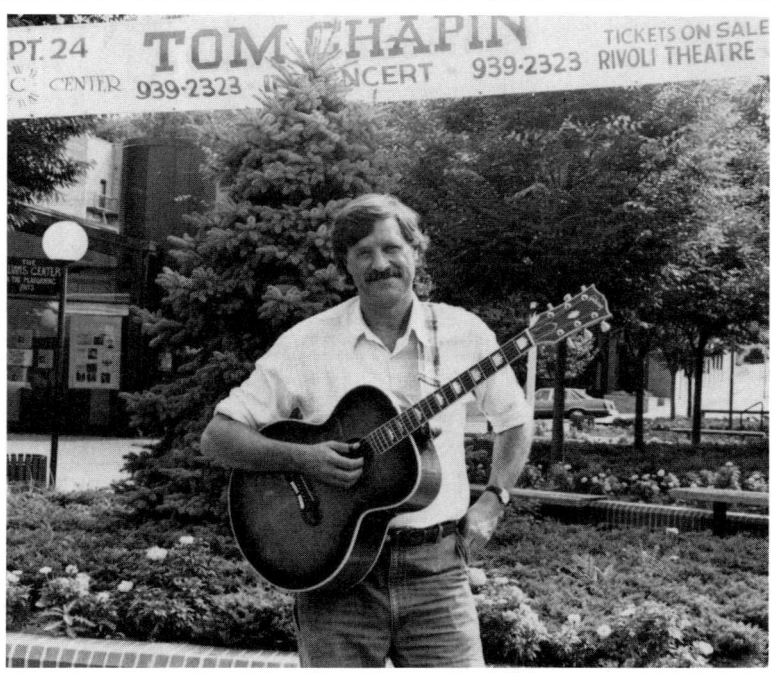
Performing artists such as folk singer Tom Chapin appear regularly during the main season at the William Carlos Williams Center for the Arts.

fine arts gallery (admission is free) displays changing exhibits by New Jersey and other artists. The center collaborates with the Appel Farm Arts and Music Center and the Perkins Center for the Arts in presenting "Sharing the Arts," a program of dance, theater, music, and other events.

Special Event: □ Camden Poetry Award Competition.

Educational Programs and Events: □ Creativity Camp (see Perkins Center for the Arts). □ Arts, music, and theater programs for children, including "Music of Brazil," "Introduction to Opera," "Shakespeare," "Music Project," "Jazz Synthesizers," and "Computers and Composers." □ Summer Children's Theatrical Series: "Ten Fridays of Fun." □ Walt Whitman Month art exhibits and symposia.

CENTERS

POETRY

Both northern and southern New Jersey can claim great poets; Walt Whitman lived in Camden and William Carlos Williams practiced medicine and wrote in Rutherford. Today, poetry in the state is kept alive at two major poetry centers, a major poetry festival, and at performing arts centers, universities, colleges, local libraries, community centers, and cafés (such as Maxwell's in Hoboken) that present poetry readings, classes, and/or workshops. The state's most active poetry centers and programs are listed below. Two of the best sources of information on poetry centers, readings, organizations, magazines, and festivals are the *New Jersey Poetry Resource Book* and the *Poetry Calendar,* published by The Poetry Center at Passaic County Community College (see below).

The Geraldine R. Dodge Poetry Project
  95 Madison Avenue, P.O. Box 1239, Morristown 07960
  201-540-8442
  The highlight of the Geraldine R. Dodge Foundation Poetry Project is its annual international Dodge Poetry Festival (see Festivals). But, the project is a comprehensive poetry program designed to reach the public through not only the festival, but also through schools and radio and television broadcasts. The program was featured on a Bill Moyers series on PBS. Poets have made more than one-hundred-eighty visits to New Jersey schools under the program since its inception. In addition, "The Poet's Voice" (recordings of poetry read at the Dodge Poetry Festival) has been broadcast over the public radio station WBGO, Newark, and the film *Poets in Person* (also based on the Poetry Festival) has been presented on national public television. Program-sponsored school workshops help teachers learn about and teach poetry.

The Poetry Center at Passaic County Community College
  College Boulevard, Paterson 07509   201-684-6555
  Established in William Carlos Williams's territory, this center presents a full schedule of poetry readings, including its Distinguished Poets Series. It sponsors the annual Paterson Poetry Prize, which has attracted entries from poets from across the country. The center's *Poetry Resource Book* lists poetry organizations throughout the state. The center also publishes the *New Jersey Poetry Calendar; Horizontes,* a Spanish-language poetry journal; and *Footwork,* an annual poetry collection.

CENTERS

The Walt Whitman Center for the Arts and Humanities
  Second and Cooper Streets, Camden 08102   609-757-7276
  Established in 1971 as a poetry center, but now also a performing arts center (see Centers), the Walt Whitman Center for the Arts and Humanities presents a poetry and writers series, which features distinguished poets and seven Pulitzer Prize winners annually. It also sponsors the annual Camden Poetry Award competition, open to poets not only from this country but from all over the world, and a Walt Whitman Poetry Series which encourages readings by senior citizens, high school students, and other local poets.

William Carlos Williams Center for the Arts
  Park Avenue at Williams Plaza, Rutherford 07070   201-939-6969
  Named for New Jersey's most famous poet, the Center sponsors occasional poetry series and readings.

Poetry readings also are offered by the following organizations:

The Arts Council of Princeton
  102 Witherspoon Street, Princeton 08442   609-924-8777

Barron Arts Center
  582 Rahway Avenue, Woodbridge 07095   201-381-7691

County College of Morris
Great Swamp Poetry Series
  Route 10, Randolph 07869   201-361-5000, extension 383

The Newark Public Library
  Five Washington Street, Newark 07101   201-733-7800

Princeton University
Creative Writing Program Reading Series
  Princeton University, Princeton 08544   609-452-3000

Rutgers, The State University
Rutgers Poetry Series
  New Brunswick 08901   201-757-6117

Seton Hall University
Poetry in the Round
  South Orange 07070   201-761-9388

CENTERS

Stockton State College
Visiting Writers Series
   Jim Leeds Road, Pomona 08240   609-652-1776

Trenton State College
Annual Writers Conference
   Hillwood Lakes, CN 4700, Trenton 08650   609-771-3254

YM-YWHA of Metropolitan New Jersey
The Poets Forum
   760 Northfield Avenue, West Orange 07052   201-762-5403

YM-YWHA of Northern New Jersey
Poets' Café
   One Pike Drive, Wayne 07476   201-595-0100

The War Memorial Theatre [$][♿]
Performing Arts and Conference Center

West Lafayette Street and Memorial Drive, Trenton 08608
609-984-8484
Performance site: at the center (1,900 seats).

Created under the provisions of the New Jersey War Memorial Act, which allocated public funds for war memorials, the Trenton War Memorial opened in 1932. Since then, every governor of the state, except one, has been inaugurated in its elaborate, gold-domed auditorium. The War Memorial, owned by the state, is on the National and New Jersey Registers of Historic Places and is expected to undergo a nearly $10 million renovation.

The War Memorial annually presents a major concert series by the New Jersey Symphony. In addition, it is the home of the Greater Trenton Symphony and frequent performance site for the Garden State Theater Organ Society (the War Memorial houses the Moller pipe organ, once located in a Trenton movie theater) and the Trenton Civic Opera Company. The center offers more than one hundred theater, music, dance, and other events annually, primarily music.

Special Programs and Events: □ Annual performances of *The Nutcracker* by the Princeton Ballet.

CENTERS

Educational Programs and Events: ☐ Student shows by the New Jersey Symphony, Greater Trenton Symphony, and others.

William Carlos Williams Center for the Arts $ ⚕

Park Avenue at Williams Plaza, Rutherford 07070   201-939-6969
Gallery hours: 10 AM–10 PM, Monday through Friday; noon–10 PM, Sunday.
Performance sites: performances at Marcus Hall (160 seats); films in two affiliated theaters: the Sammartino and Wentworth cinemas. (The center is restoring the 1922 Rivoli Theatre, which seats 400, to provide additional performance space.)

When the old Rivoli Theatre was ravaged by fire in 1977, a group of area residents raised funds to restore it and establish an arts center. The William Carlos Williams Center for the Arts was incorporated in 1978. Today, the center hosts about fifty events annually during its main season, which runs from September through May. The center offers a children's theater series. Recent programs have included a performance by the Amsterdam Guitar Trio and a Cole Porter revue by the 13th Street Repertory Company. The Williams Center gallery presents monthly art exhibits.

Special Events: ☐ Free outdoor concerts in July. ☐ Occasional poetry readings.

YM-YWHA of North Jersey $ ♿ ⚕

One Pike Drive, Wayne 07470   201-595-0100
Performance site: Rosen Auditorium (440 seats).

The YM-YWHA of North Jersey presents between eighty and one hundred cultural events and programs annually. It sponsors several arts series, including a children's theater series, a star performers series, and music and lecture series. The Poets' Café offers occasional poetry readings. The art gallery presents one show/sale each month featuring items from paintings and sculpture to rugs and jewelry.

Special Programs and Events: ☐ Signing for the hearing impaired at all children's theater productions.

Educational Programs: ☐ Dance, drama, music, and art classes for children and adults. ☐ Dance classes for disabled persons.

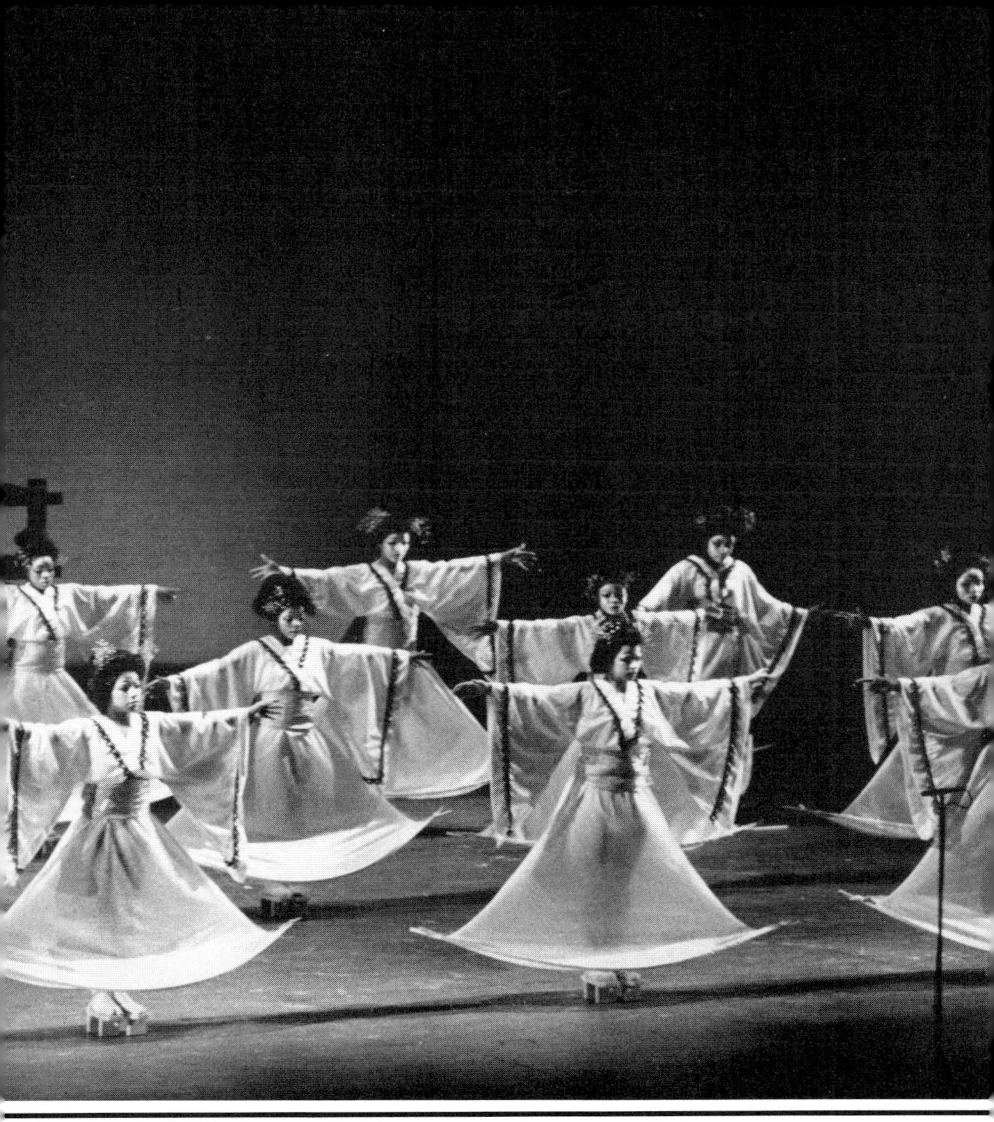

DANCE

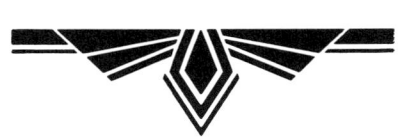

Overleaf: A scene from the Newark Community School of the Art's original ballet production to commemorate its twentieth anniversary, *And Still the Snowflakes Fall.* The ballet was composed by Randall Svane and choreographed by Roberto Arteaga.

DANCE

American Ballroom Theater Company, Inc. 💲

39 Harding Avenue, Clifton 07011   201-779-4466
Performance sites: at performing arts centers, concert halls, and festivals statewide and nationwide and on tours of Canada and Europe.

The American Ballroom Theater Company, based in the Clifton studio of artistic director Pierre Dulaine, has made a specialty of elevating ballroom dancing to the level of art without taking the fun out of it. The pieces in the company repertory are choreographed and based on social dance steps: waltzes, tangos, jitterbugs, and rhumbas. But instead of whirling away on a dance floor, company dancers perform on professional stages, to music by artists as different as Gershwin and Elvis Presley. Founded by two accomplished competition ballroom dancers, Dulaine and Yvonne Marceau, the American Ballroom Theater Company's first performance was a workshop production called *Sheer Romance,* a choreographed social history of ballroom dancing.

The American Ballroom Theater performs at venues that include the Kennedy Center in Washington, D.C., and the Brooklyn Academy of Music. It also appears regularly at the annual summer dance festival at Jacob's Pillow. The troupe consists of a corps of seven couples, six of whom perform in each production. Generally, the American Ballroom Theater Company introduces at least one new work each year into its repertory. The company performs during a year-round season, with a hiatus in August.

Educational Programs: ☐ Classes and workshops in social dancing for adults and children in connection with tour performances; occasional.

Beyond the NJ Turnpike Dance Company 💲

28 Rose Trail, Andover 07821   201-691-1856 or 201-361-5000 x450
Performance sites: throughout the northeast; in residence at the County College of Morris.

The Beyond the NJ Turnpike Dance Company, founded in 1983, chose its name to make the point, facetiously, that there is more to New Jersey than one infamous highway and that artistic activity goes on west as well as east of the turnpike. This modern dance troupe, composed of eight regular dancers, performs works by its artistic directors and cofounders, Joann Staugaard Jones and Argenis Belle, as well as by guest choreographers. Among the works recently added to its repertoire are *Katsura,* based on movements of strollers in parks in Tokyo and New

DANCE

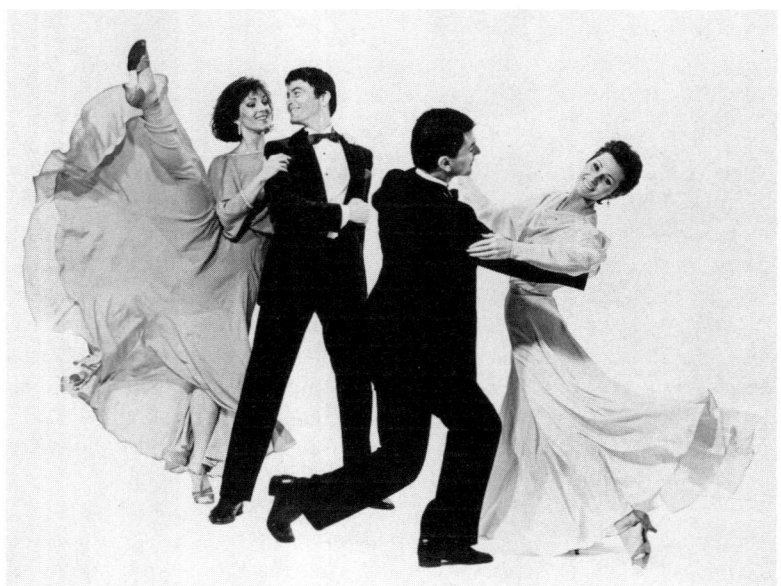

The American Ballroom Theatre has turned ballroom dancing into a performing art, in which choreographed dances such as fox trots, rumbas, and waltzes are set to music by artists from Gershwin to Elvis Presley. Photo: Tom Caravaglia.

York City and *Arena*, a "play/dance" inspired by a 1944 science fiction story about a fight for survival between a human and an alien. The company makes a point of using dancers from many different racial and cultural backgrounds. It helped train the second black dancer ever to perform with the Radio City Rockettes. Jennifer Jones, a BTNJT alumna, joined the kickline for a Super Bowl halftime show in January 1988.

Carolyn Dorfman Dance Company 💲🚻
2780 Morris Avenue, Suite 2-C, Union 07083   201-687-8855
Performance sites: in schools and theaters throughout New Jersey and in New York City and on state and out-of-state tours.

The Carolyn Dorfman Dance Company was founded in 1982 by dancer and choreographer Carolyn Dorfman. This modern dance company performs works that tackle a wide range of subjects, many concerning human relationships and communication. *Lifeline*, for in-

DANCE

stance, uses movement and rope to illuminate the connections among family members and generations. Another work, *Conversations*, includes a piece called *Duet for Two*, in which two women communicate through movement, while their shadows carry on an entirely different "conversation." Dorfman recently commissioned a new work, *Dancing in the Dark*, set to music of the forties and fifties and choreographed by Garden State Ballet artistic director Peter Anastos. The company also emphasizes education; it gives many performances and workshops for school audiences. It maintains a repertory of some ten pieces, and regularly commissions new works from guest choreographers. The company introduces two to three new works annually. Programs consist of four to five pieces. The Carolyn Dorfman company gives some thirty performances annually, most from September through June.

Educational Programs and Events: □ Audience discussion sessions after performances. □ Educational touring program: lecture/demonstrations on modern dance. □ Master dance and choreography classes for students from kindergarten through college.

Center Dance Collective $|\text{\textdollar}|\text{\textsterling}|$

18 Davenport Street, Somerville 08876   201-526-8876
Performance sites: Mill Hill Playhouse, Trenton, and Somerset County Vo-Technical School, Bridgewater, with appearances throughout metropolitan New York, New Jersey, and New England, and in Europe.

Located in Somerville, where Ruth St. Denis, a pioneer of modern dance, was born, the Center Dance Collective has one of the largest repertoires of Denishawn works in the country. The term Denishawn derives from the names of St. Denis and her husband and collaborator, Ted Shawn. Together they developed a new, fluid dance technique, inspired in part by Oriental and Indian dance traditions. Founded in 1979, the company emphasizes but is not limited to Denishawn works. Center Dance Collective produces two Denishawn and two new works annually. It performs to the music of classic and contemporary composers, and it often uses New Jersey dancers, set designers, choreographers, and musicians.

Denishawn works are reconstructed with the help of dance historian Jane Sherman, who was the youngest member of the Denishawn company in 1926 and who maintains notes on original productions. Most

DANCE

Ruth St. Denis: Pioneer of Modern Dance

Young Ruthie Dennis (1877–1968) of Somerville became one of America's most exotic early modern dancers. In the years after she left New Jersey, Dennis changed her name, adding "St." and subtracing an "n" for dramatic effect; took Europe by storm; and introduced Americans to a fluid, expressive technique that drew on dance traditions of the Far East and India. She sometimes costumed herself in elaborate headresses and flowing gowns in her performances, and in other ways

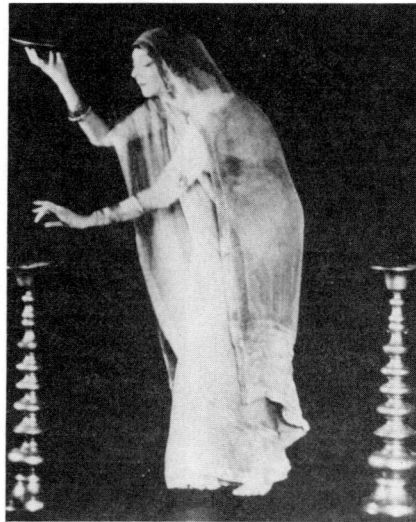

turned her back on the constrictions of classical ballet. She choreographed dances set in Indian temples and villages, with names like *Incense* (see photo), *Cobra,* and *The Yogi.*

But it was as a collaborator rather than a star that Ruth St. Denis made her mark. She and her husband Ted Shawn founded the Denishawn School of Dance in Los Angeles. There they nurtured the outstanding talents of, among others, Martha Graham and Doris Humphrey. Though the marriage foundered, the couple's influence on dance did not. Shawn went on to found the country's foremost dance center and festival, Jacob's Pillow. St. Denis continued to choreograph and dance until she was eighty-nine.

Ultimately, modern dance moved away from the Denishawn style and toward a simpler, more "American" choreography, pioneered in part by St. Denis's student Martha Graham. But today, the Denishawn legacy lives at the Center Dance Collective in Somerville, which maintains one of the largest repertoires of Denishawn works in the country. A documentary film titled *Denishawn,* produced by the collective in 1988, presents Denishawn works performed by Center Dance Collective dancers. In keeping with St. Denis's passion for stunning sets, many of the works were filmed in front of imposing Greek columns at the Masonic Temple in Trenton.

DANCE

of the company's contemporary works are created by the collective's two main choreographers: founder Michelle Mathesius and artistic director Janet Rowthorn. Recent additions to the repertory include *Criterium,* based on the Somerville bicycle race of the same name, and *Roots and Wings,* a look at the vicissitudes of impending motherhood, performed by one choreographer while she was expecting her first child. The Center Dance Collective maintains a corps of eight full-time dancers and two free-lance, using an average of ten performers in each production. The company follows a fall and winter/spring schedule, usually presenting one or two summer workshops.

A documentary film produced by the Center Dance Collective and titled *Denishawn* examines the life and work of St. Denis and traces the development of the Denishawn style. It contains clips of original performances by St. Denis and Shawn as well as contemporary performances of Denishawn works by Collective dancers. The company has also developed a live dance-history program called *Dance Heritage,* which illustrates the history of the modern dance movement and features Collective dancers performing Denishawn and other landmark works.

Educational Programs and Events: ☐ Dance workshops. ☐ Documentary film *Denishawn* available on loan. ☐ "Living Dance History" program for elementary and high school students. ☐ Master classes for disabled persons. ☐ Spring tour of New Jersey vocational schools.

Dance Alliance (see New Jersey Center for the Performing Arts—Dance)

DanceCompass (See Nicholas Rodriguez and DanceCompass)

Danmari, Ltd. (DAO 1987) $☧
Yass Hakoshima Mime Theatre
New Jersey Center for Mime, 239 Midland Avenue, Montclair 07042   201-783-9845
Performance sites: Memorial Auditorium, Montclair State College (1,000 seats), and on state, national, and international tours.

Danmari's name is taken from the Japanese word for silence or mime. Drawing on French pantomime and Japanese Noh dance traditions, Yass Hakoshima, the company's founder and principal performer, has created his own style of mime, which he shares with audiences not

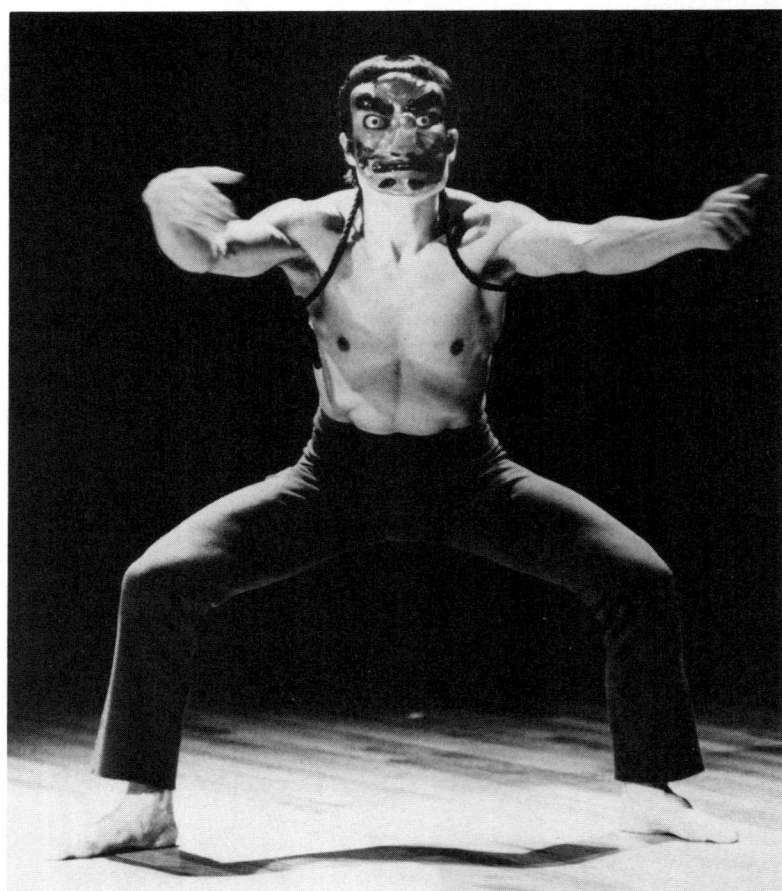

Yass Hakoshima of Danmari Ltd. combines dance and theater in his mime performances, which show the influence of Japanese Kabuki and French pantomime traditions.

only in New Jersey but throughout the world. His goal is to tell stories with movement, combining dance moves with dramatic, symbolic gestures. The Japanese-born Hakoshima has developed a thirty-five-piece repertoire containing works that explore various objects and beings in motion, such as *Balloon* and *Eagle*. His short programs consist of five or six pieces; his long ones of nine or ten. Hakoshima generally introduces two to three new works each year, and he appears between forty and sixty times annually, usually on tour. He occasionally collaborates with other New Jersey performing arts organizations. For example, in 1988 he performed to Charles Ives's Second String Quartet with the New Jersey Chamber Music Society. Hakoshima also performs with his wife, dancer Renate Boue. He created New Jersey's first professional mime institute at Montclair State College in 1982 as an educational offshoot of his performing company. There students learn all aspects of the art of mime, from philosophy to choreography.

Special Programs and Events: ☐ Appearances with the New Jersey Chamber Music Society and other performing and visual arts organizations.

Educational Programs and Events: ☐ Mime workshops consisting of summer and winter programs designed to introduce students to techniques of mime, T'ai Chi, commedia dell'arte, and Kabuki.

Garden State Ballet $ ♿

45 Academy Street, Newark 07102   201-623-0267
Performance sites: in residence at the Count Basie Theatre, Red Bank (1,400 seats); also Park Theatre, Union City; Essex County College, Montclair State College, and at sites throughout the state.

The Garden State Ballet, founded in 1961, emphasizes classical ballet during its fall/late-winter/spring season. It maintains seventeen corps dancers. Its artistic director and choreographer, the well-known Peter Anastos, has a sense of humor; in addition to presenting serious classic ballets, the company occasionally performs comic works, including parodies of ballet legends and history. A recent spoof, *Yes, Virginia, Another Piano Ballet,* starred male dancers in ballet slippers tip-toeing with mock delicacy. December is always *Nutcracker* month. In 1989, the company premiered four new ballets. The company recently performed Anastos's *Gloria,* based on Vivaldi's choral work, accompanied by the Ars Musica Chorale.

Special Programs and Events: ☐ *Nutcracker* Youth Concerts in December. ☐ Annual Newark dance festival.

Educational Programs and Events: ☐ Scholarship program for talented ballet students. ☐ School of the Garden State Ballet. ☐ Workshops and apprenticeships for dancers and choreographers.

DANCE

Geulah Abrahams Danceworks (Danceworks, Inc.) $
108 Clover Lane, Princeton 08540   609-924-7483
Performance sites: in New Jersey, New York, and on European and United States tours.

Danceworks was founded in 1985 by Geulah Abrahams, a former member of the Princeton University dance program's faculty and the Paul Taylor Dance Company who studied with Merce Cunningham and Doris Humphrey. As Danceworks' artistic director Abrahams often collaborates with professionals from other disciplines. For her 1982 production of *A Soldier's Tale,* Princeton-based, post-modern architect Michael Graves designed the sets and Michael Pratt, associate director of the New Jersey Symphony, conducted the Stravinsky music. In 1986, Abrahams presented *Photoformance,* a collage in which slides were projected on and around dancers, at the American Dance Festival in North Carolina and at several European photography festivals. Three years later, Danceworks presented *Physics Art* at the Museum of Science and Industry in Los Angeles, a work choreographed by Abrahams with the help of her physicist-husband. While some pieces are experimental, others draw on long-standing dance traditions; for instance, the company recently performed Stravinsky's *Les Noces,* based on a traditional primitive Russian wedding. *The Word Hopi Means Peace* was inspired by American Indian dance forms. The Geulah Abrahams company performs between four and eight times annually with four to twelve free-lance dancers appearing in each piece. The repertory consists of some six pieces (usually movement-oriented rather than theatrical) and two or more are added each year.

Hudson Repertory Dance Theatre $ 🛉
300 Whiton Street, Jersey City 07304   201-432-5534
Performance sites: Park Theatre Performing Arts Center, Union City (1,400 seats) and on tours of colleges throughout the metropolitan area.

The Hudson Repertory Dance Theatre is a "multiethnic" company. Conceived as a New Jersey version of the Dance Theater of Harlem, it is dedicated to providing performance opportunities for young black, Hispanic, and other minority artists. The company was founded in 1983 by dancer/choreographer Joel Harrison. It performs mainly contemporary works that emphasize character and historic settings. For instance, one work created by Harrison called *Ain't No Thing* is set

When Industry and Art Meet

In New Jersey, where there are more scientists per square mile than in any other state, the line between science and art sometimes blurs. Scientists become artists and vice versa. Clyde Lynds, a sculptor from Wood-Ridge, has inscribed concrete columns with fiber optics, creating primitive symbols with high-tech lights. Shown is his *Stele LX— Night Swallowing the Sun*. Lillian Schwartz, a consultant for AT&T Bell Laboratories, has invented computer sculptures, which move according to electronic demands.

Artists use science as a subject—and a medium. At Appel Farm Arts and Music Center, dancers attached by electrodes to a biofeedback monitor have created their own peculiar "music." With help from her scientist-husband, Geulah Abrahams, artistic director of Danceworks, has developed a dance inspired by the laws of physics.

Surrounded by industries that excel at scientific research (New Jersey laboratories account for one-fifth of the nation's private research and development dollars), a number of New Jersey museums and arts organizations take an interest in the relationship between technology and art. The Bergen Museum of the Arts and Sciences, founded by a group of artists and scientists, at first devoted itself almost exclusively to that subject. In 1987, the Morris Museum presented an exhibit featuring high-tech art employing robots, holography, and computer graphics. The following year, students enrolled in a computer-art program at William Paterson College and the college's Ben Shahn Galleries showed their electronically executed landscape and abstract "paintings."

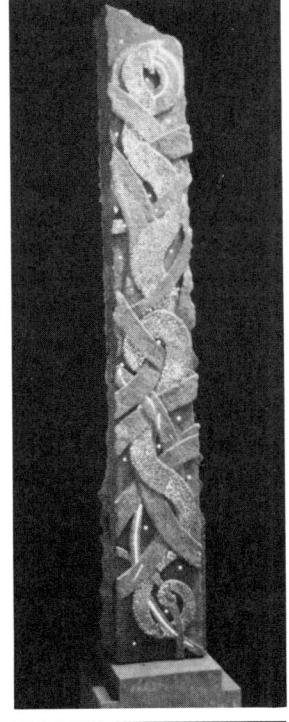

"Almost everything done in painting and sculpture today is somewhat redundant," explains sculptor Clyde Lynds. "There are new ways to do it, but not vitally new ways. Movement is so much a part of life. The only real way you can achieve new experience in art is with new materials."

DANCE

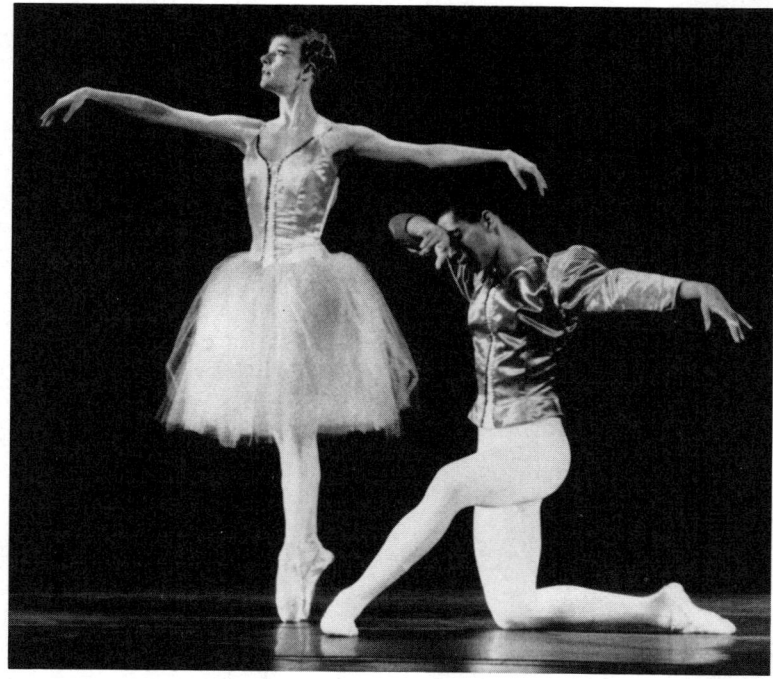

The Hudson Repertory Theater casts dancers of many ethnic backgrounds in its classical and contemporary productions, such as the ballet "Legacy."

in turn-of-the-century France. Danced to the music of Scott Joplin, it concerns a flimflam man who tries to sell love. An annual Christmas production of *Ebenezer's Dream* sets *Nutcracker*-like scenes in the antebellum South.

Special Event: ☐ Annual Christmas production.

Educational Programs and Events: ☐ Lecture/demonstrations in association with the Hudson Repertory Dance Theatre School.

Mount Laurel Regional Ballet Company

216 Church Road, Mount Laurel 08054   609-235-5342
Performance sites: Thomas E. Harrington Middle School Theatre (750 seats) and on tours of New Jersey, New York, Pennsylvania, and Delaware.

DANCE

Founded by dancer and choreographer Lorraine McAdams, this company performs mainly in southern New Jersey communities. The Mount Laurel Regional Ballet presents at least one world premiere annually in addition to standard classics such as *The Nutcracker* and *Firebird*. Between two and forty dancers may appear in any one production; the regular corps consists of thirty-three dancers. McAdams recently choreographed the production of the opera *Susannah* for the Hollybush Festival (see Music).

> "Most children in the Nutcracker party scene aspire to someday be the Sugar Plum Fairy or Clara. This year, a little eight-year-old dancer said she 'wanted to be the giant, Mrs. McAdams.' No doubt she wants to be a director!"—Lorraine McAdams, Artistic Director, Mt. Laurel Regional Ballet

Special Event: ◻ Annual New Jersey Invitational Festival of Dance, showcasing between five and thirteen dance companies.

Educational Programs and Events: ◻ Apprenticeship program, during which students from the company's school dance with the company. ◻ School of the Mount Laurel Regional Ballet. ◻ "The Making of a Dancer," a lecture/demonstration presented annually at public schools and schools for disabled persons. ◻ Young audiences tour.

New Jersey Ballet Company (DAO 1987, 1990) $ 🛉

270 Pleasant Valley Way, West Orange 07052   201-736-5940
Performance sites: in residence at the Paper Mill Playhouse, Millburn (1,200 seats), and the Wilkins Theatre, Kean College, Union (209 seats); affiliated with Newark Symphony Hall, the John Harms Center, Englewood, and the New Jersey State Opera; also on statewide tours.

Founded in 1958, the New Jersey Ballet has used dance to illuminate history and social history. In 1987, E. G. Marshall narrated a new ballet about the United States Constitution, and in 1976, in honor of the American Bicentennial, the company presented *Off to the Sea* by Edward Villella, based on New Jersey's maritime history. The company staged an all-American program at the Hollybush Festival in 1986, appearing on the same bill as the Kirov Ballet of Leningrad. In 1989, the company visited Taiwan.

DANCE

Villella, formerly a principal dancer with the New York City Ballet, has worked with the company since 1966 and is now its artistic advisor. The New Jersey Ballet performs more than eighty concerts and one hundred lecture/demonstrations annually. It maintains a corps of sixteen dancers, with occasional appearances by guest artists and apprentices. The company has more than one hundred works in its repertory, which includes standard ballet classics, such as *Sleeping Beauty,* as well as contemporary pieces, including numerous George Balanchine works. It usually introduces three or four newly choreographed works during its fall/winter/spring season.

Special Program: □ *Nutcracker* Month in December.

Educational Programs and Events: □ "On School Time," a program of ballet demonstrations, and "Introduction to Dance," which illustrates dance-training techniques and encourages student participation. □ New Jersey School of Ballet.

New Jersey Center for Mime (See Danmari, Ltd.—Dance)

New Jersey Center for the Performing Arts $ & //
17 Division Street, Somerville 08876   201-526-6074

The New Jersey Center for the Performing Arts is the state's largest dance service organization. It concentrates on dance classes, workshops, and programs and provides performance spaces, technical assistance, advice, and, through the Dance Alliance, an allied organization, information to dancers and dance companies throughout the state. At the same time, it has also offered classical and jazz concerts, writing competitions, and children's theater programs. Founded in 1978, the center recently has moved to concentrate even more heavily on dance. Jointly with the New Jersey State Council on the Arts, it also sponsors dance workshops and showcases throughout the state.

Special Programs and Events: □ Beaux Arts Festival of dance, music, and vocal performances. □ Center Space Dance Series (see Festivals). □ Jazz series. □ Somerset County Teen Arts Festival.

Educational Programs: □ Workshops for choreographers.

New Jersey Dance Alliance (See New Jersey Center for the Performing Arts)

DANCE

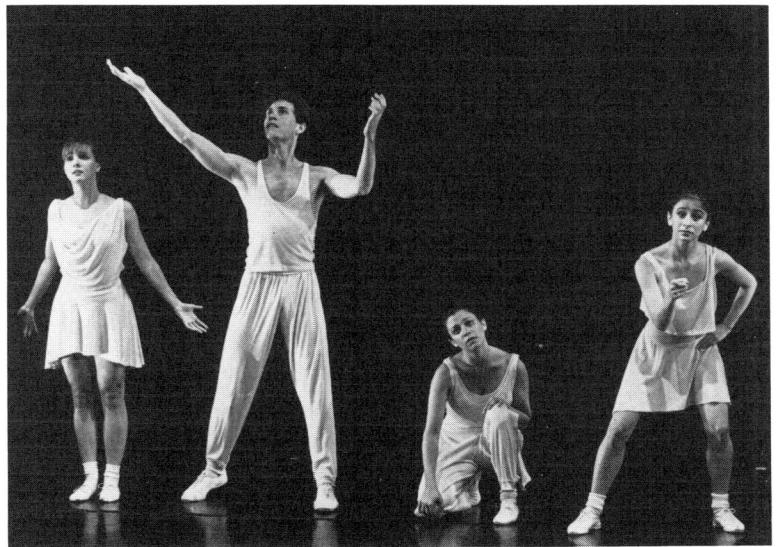

Choreographer Carolyn Dorfman's dance company often examines social relationships, as in this piece, called "Conversations." Photo: Johan Elbers.

Nicholas Rodriguez and DanceCompass (DAO 1989)
$ ⚥

P.O. Box 43115, Montclair 07043   201-746-6427
Performance sites: Montclair State College's National Memorial Auditorium (1,000 seats), with appearances in schools and theaters throughout the metropolitan area.

The work of this troupe largely reflects the philosophy and style of one man: Nicholas Rodriguez, a Paterson native who cofounded the company in 1984 with executive director Sharon Stephens and holds the positions of artistic director and choreographer.

Nicholas Rodriguez and DanceCompass is a modern dance troupe with a flair for politics and romance. One piece, called *Terms of Reference*, was danced while a tape of excerpts from the congressional Iran-Contra hearings played in the background. At the other end of the spectrum, the troupe performs *By Candlelight* to songs by Tony Bennett. In addition to performing works from its repertory, the company introduces two or three new productions annually: two company works and one solo or small group work. During the 1989–1990 season, the troupe acquired a Paul Taylor work. It maintains a corps of six dancers, and with some free-lancers, about eight dancers usually appear in each production. Recently, Nicholas Rodriguez and Dance-Compass commissioned music for *Triple Talk* from Raphael Rudd, a New Jersey composer and harpist who has collaborated on works with British rock star Pete Townshend.

Educational Events: ☐ Dance education programs for New Jersey schools and dance troupes.

Princeton Ballet (DAO 1988, 1990, MIO) [$][♦]

17 Livingston Avenue, New Brunswick 08901   201-249-1254
Performance sites: State Theatre, New Brunswick, (1,800 seats), and McCarter Theatre, Princeton (1,000 seats) and on tours of New Jersey, New York, and other northeastern states.

Dancer Audree Estey, the wife of a Lawrenceville English instructor, founded the Princeton Ballet Society in 1954. Today, it is a regional company performing repertory and new works (about four new ballets are introduced annually) during its fall and spring seasons, between September and June. The twenty-four-piece repertory includes works by Princeton Ballet artistic director Dermot Burke (such as *Evening Dances,* choreographed for five couples and set in a Victorian parlor) and by Antony Tudor, Paul Taylor, and José Limon. Each program consists of three to four pieces, often a mix of neo-classics such as *Reflections* by Gerald Arpino and contemporary works by choreographers such as Limon. Between two and twelve dancers may appear in each production. The company annually presents the fifth-longest-running, full-length production of *The Nutcracker* in the country, falling into line after the San Francisco Ballet (1949), the New York City Ballet (1954), Ballet West (1955), and the Washington Ballet (1961). The Princeton Ballet is the resident dance company of the New Brunswick Cultural Center and dance company-in-residence at McCarter Theatre in Princeton.

Special Programs and Events: ☐ Annual *Nutcracker* performances at McCarter Theatre, the Trenton War Memorial Theatre, Middlesex County College, and the State Theatre in Easton, Pennsylvania. ☐ Ballet School biennial production. ☐ Dance Power company performance with a guest artist; annual. ☐ June Repertory Season, including performances of the entire repertory.

DANCE

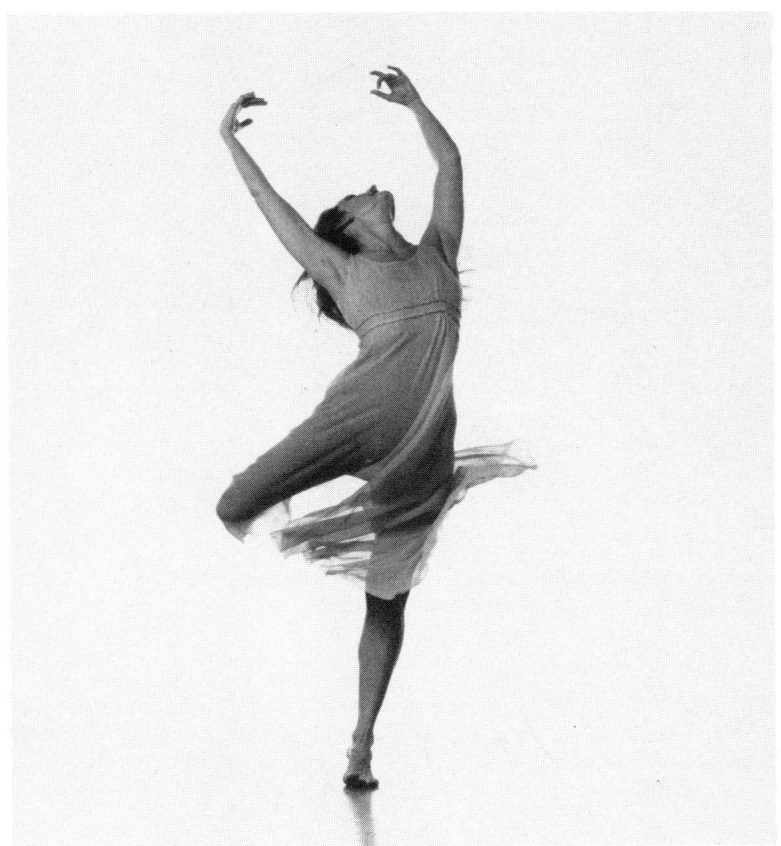

The Center Dance Collective revives works choreographed by the New Jersey–born pioneer of modern dance, Ruth St. Denis. Here a dancer performs her "Schubert Waltzes." Photo: Lois Greenfield.

Educational Programs and Events: ☐ Dance Power, an after-school enrichment and training program for New Brunswick third graders, offered in conjunction with the New Brunswick Board of Education. ☐ Residential workshops consisting of five-week summer programs at Princeton University that are open to advanced students nationwide. ☐ School of Princeton Ballet with studios in Princeton, New Brunswick, West Windsor, and Cranbury. ☐ Workshop Sampler, four-week program open to dancers age eleven and up.

DANCE

Teamwork Dance $
1209 Canal Road, R.D. 1, Princeton 08540   201-359-6752
Performance sites: college and school auditoriums throughout New Jersey, Pennsylvania, and New York.

Teamwork Dance was founded on the campus of Princeton University in 1981 by choreographers Mary Pat Robertson (who came to Princeton after training with Merce Cunningham and Twyla Tharp) and an athlete with no formal dance training, John Watson Stewart. The company frequently weaves drama and athletics into its dances. One work in the company repertoire, *Mixed Doubles,* incorporates allusions to tennis movements; another, *Wanting Contact,* makes reference to football movements and is set to rock music. Teamwork's early style owed much to the influence of Stewart, a soccer player who still appears with the company. Recently, artistic director Robertson has concentrated on multidisciplinary collaborations; Teamwork has appeared with the vocal ensemble Voices (see Music) and the New Jersey Percussion Ensemble. She is administrative director of the School of the Princeton Ballet.

Special Program: □ Annual concert at Mercer County College, Mercerville.

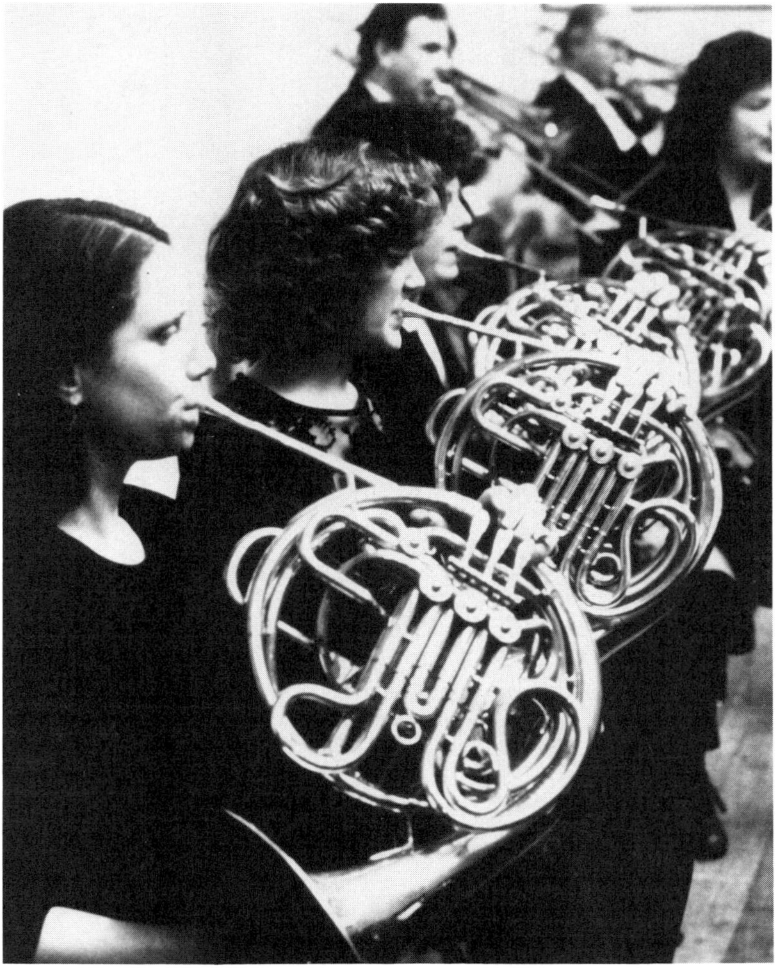

MUSIC

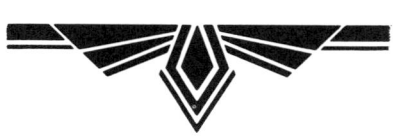

Overleaf: During the 1989–1990 season, the New Jersey Symphony Orchestra's French horn section was an all-female enterprise.

MUSIC

All Seasons Chamber Players $\boxed{\$}\boxed{\&}$
115 Orchard Road, Demarest 07627   201-768-1331
Performance sites: in arts centers, churches, libraries, and public spaces throughout the metropolitan New York–New Jersey area.

Founded in 1981, the All Seasons Chamber Players performs music for flute, violin, cello, and piano and piano duets in every program. Each includes four or five pieces from its repertoire; perhaps a Beethoven serenade for violin and flute or Ravel piano trio. The All Seasons Chamber Players occasionally presents period works in historic locations. The group has performed at a number of National Trust properties, including Lyndhurst, a castle-like mansion on the Hudson, and the Mohonk Mountain House. In 1987, an All Seasons concert sponsored by the New Jersey Historical Society featured American works from the time of George Washington that had not been played for a live audience since the late 1700s. Another program titled "Music for Queen Victoria" presented music of the late nineteenth century. The group has also performed contemporary music, some by New Jersey composers. It gives about sixteen concerts each year, during a fall and spring season. Several of its regular corps of five players are union musicians.

Special Events: □ Annual performance at the Arts Festival of Bergen County. □ Special performances for the disabled.

Educational Programs and Events: □ Lecture-style introductions to chamber music concerts; occasional. □ Lecture/demonstrations. □ Meet the Composer sessions; occasional.

The Bridgeton Symphony $\boxed{\$}$
P.O. Box 872, Bridgeton 08302   609-451-1169
Performance site: Bridgeton High School Auditorium (1,000 seats).

Bridgeton Symphony's director Russell Meyer combines familiar classic works with unusual or contemporary music during the orchestra's four-concert, July-through-May season. The orchestra, comprised of a core of about fifty regular, union, free-lance musicians, often performs major works by Beethoven and German romantic composers. Occasionally, humor is injected into the proceedings; the Bridgeton Symphony recently presented Jacques Ibert's *Suite Symphonique Paris,* which includes a part for police whistles. The Bridgeton Symphony frequently performs with young guest artists and a volunteer, fifty-to-seventy-member chorus. It accompanies the Vineland Regional Ballet for an annual *Nutcracker* and presents a yearly outdoor pops series.

"This orchestra survived on a shoestring for eight years because its founders believed that Central New Jersey's population needed access to live music. The Board was made up of musicians who handled all the responsibilities—marketing, bookkeeping, and administration—and dipped into their own pockets when funds were low. Their dedication to Central New Jersey was rewarded in 1988 when the New Brunswick Cultural Center chose their orchestra as an affiliate member."—Carol Roan, Executive Director, The Brunswick Symphony Orchestra (formerly the Garden State Symphonic Orchestra/Pops)

Educational Programs: ☐ Pre-concert "conversations" with the conductor. ☐ School outreach performances.

The Brunswick Symphony Orchestra $ ⚥
(formerly Garden State Symphonic Orchestra/Pops)
New Brunswick Cultural Center, 19 Livingston Avenue,
New Brunswick 08901   201-247-7200
Performance sites: throughout central New Jersey, primarily at the State Theatre, New Brunswick (1,800 seats).

The Brunswick Symphony Orchestra, with a corps of about sixty-five free-lance, union players, was founded in 1980. It offered its first subscription series in the 1989–1990 season and is the only orchestra member of New Brunswick Cultural Center. The orchestra gives five concerts during its regular subscription season, which runs from October through April, plus at least one additional free summer concert. The program at each concert usually includes a familiar work, a contemporary work, and a work that falls somewhere in between. Musical director and conductor Raymond Wojcik regularly presents an "informance," prefacing one selected concert piece with a mini-lecture during which soloists play—and he explains—themes from each composition.

Special Programs and Events: ☐ Free summer concerts in connection with Rutgers Summerfest. ☐ New Year's Eve concert with guest artist.

Educational Programs and Events: ☐ Musical enrichment program. ☐ Orchestra ensembles perform in Central Jersey schools. ☐ Lecture and demonstration study sessions to prepare children for concerts. ☐ Pilot project teaching "International Musical Geography." ☐ Teacher workshops.

MUSIC

Cathedral Symphony 💲
Cathedral of the Sacred Heart, 89 Ridge Street, Newark 07104
201-484-4600
Performance site: Cathedral of the Sacred Heart (2,200 seats).

The Cathedral Symphony was founded in 1983 by conductor Thomas Michalak and the Archdiocese of Newark, which donated performance space at the Cathedral of the Sacred Heart. The French gothic cathedral, begun in 1899 and finished in 1953, is a New Jersey and national historic site. A setting that includes stained glass windows, marble, a soaring atrium, and dramatic acoustics gives an otherworldly quality to performances of Mozart's *Requiem,* Bach masses, and similarly majestic music by the Cathedral Symphony. The symphony's annual concert series includes seven major performances, often with vocalists, from September through May. Programs vary with the season; however, a number draw on the German tradition. During the 1988–1989 season, the symphony presented "An Afternoon of German Romanticism," with soloist Jerome Hines. Another program included works by Bernstein, Stravinsky, and Wagner. In addition to major concerts, there are three or four chamber music performances and four organ recitals annually, both by visiting organists and by the cathedral's organist and director of music, David Fedor. The Cathedral Symphony, directed by Michalak's successor, Keith Clark, is an all-union, free-lance orchestra, composed of a corps of forty to fifty players.

Special Programs and Events: ▫ Annual Christmas concert. ▫ Annual Viennese New Year's Eve concert.

Educational Programs and Events: ▫ Orchestra workshops in conjunction with Montclair State College. ▫ Pre-concert lectures on music and architecture. ▫ Tours of the cathedral by the New Jersey Society of Architects, Newark/Suburban Chapter, before each concert.

Colonial Symphony 💲♿
205 Madison Avenue, Madison 07940   201-377-1310
Performance sites: Madison Junior School auditorium (850 seats), other school auditoriums in Morris and Essex counties, and occasional out-of-state locations.

The Colonial Symphony was founded in 1950 by Dr. John Karlin, a Bell Laboratories research scientist, and named for the colonial heritage of the northwestern New Jersey area it serves. In 1988, the symphony

MUSIC

United in Song

New Jersey maintains a rich choral music tradition, and its choral groups perform in churches and concert halls across the state. Often composed of volunteers (most of whom audition for membership and parts), these groups may appear alone or with opera companies, professional soloists, symphonies, and other ensembles. One of the state's leading choral groups, the Pro Arte Chorale (368-C Paramus Road, Paramus 07652, 201-445-9052) was designated a Distinguished Arts Organization by the New Jersey State Council on the Arts. Founded more than twenty-five years ago, Pro Arte has developed a tradition of performing unusual or rarely performed works, such as Berlioz's *The Trojans;* during a three-year American music project the group has concentrated on new American works. The chorale regularly appears with the New Jersey Symphony Orchestra and presents an annual concert series at the John Harms Performing Arts Center.

A number of choruses regularly commission works and perform world premieres; the Summit Chorale/Music, of Summit, for example, has been commissioning works and performing New Jersey and world premieres since 1949. In 1989, the Masterwork Music and Art Foundation of Morristown presented the world premiere of Giannini's Mass Number 2. Other choral groups, such as the North Jersey Philharmonic Glee Club and the Ric-Charles Choral Ensemble, draw on black vocal traditions, showcasing gospel, blues, and spiritual music. The Monmouth Civic Chorus of Red Bank concentrates on large, formal masterworks for chorus such as Bach's *St. Matthew Passion* and Berlioz's *Requiem*. It also presents Gilbert and Sullivan comic operas.

appointed a new maestro: Yehuda Gilad, formerly conductor of the Santa Monica (California) Symphony Orchestra. The all-union, forty-eight-member orchestra is composed of free-lancers (including a loyal corps of about thirty musicians), and presents four different concert programs each season, which runs from October through April. The Colonial Symphony performs each six times, repeating two of its programs. It strives for a mix of classical and contemporary music and usually presents a program of all-Baroque music, using a smaller orchestra, at Christmas.

Educational Programs and Events: ☐ Chamber music assemblies and workshops for young people and professionals. ☐ Pre-concert lectures by prominent musicologists.

MUSIC

Composers Guild of New Jersey $|🎵|

202 Central Avenue, Ship Bottom 08008   609-494-8513
Performance sites: various indoor, outdoor, and historic sites statewide.

One of the most active and innovative musical organizations in the state, the Composers Guild of New Jersey presents the work of New Jersey composers to the public, often performed by New Jersey ensembles. It is also a membership organization that serves the state's composers, both student and professional. Since the organization's founding in 1980, the guild has presented hundreds of performances of new music by dozens of composers, some nationally prominent. It often sponsors performances of new music in settings that suit particular musical themes. For instance, a 1988 "Seascapes" benefit concert for the Marine Mammal Stranding Center in Brigantine was offered at two oceanfront locations: the Chalfonte Hotel in Cape May and The Ketch in Beach Haven. An electronic music concert series, "Music of the Spheres," has been presented at several museum planetariums. The Composers Guild solicits new scores and matches music with musicians. It frequently presents multidisciplinary programs; one musical/visual arts event at the Noyes Museum combined works by Mozart and Roger Sessions with a show of paintings by a contemporary artist. The Composers Guild also publishes a catalogue offering scores, tapes, and compact discs.

> "Only two or three men read music. Thus we believe it is amazing that we learn music by sight reading, perform a new concert annually and sing all our concerts from memory."—David E. Peniston, Business Manager, North Jersey Philharmonic Glee Club

Special Programs and Events: ☐ The Capital Music Festival (see Festivals). ☐ Chamber orchestra competitions. ☐ Choral contests. ☐ New Jersey Composers Forum for young composers. ☐ Regional and international exchange programs.

Educational Programs and Events: ☐ "Hands-on" in-school workshops on music composition featuring New Jersey composers and performers. ☐ Workshops and symposia with composers.

MUSIC

Garden State Concert Band [$][♿]
15 Bellevue Terrace, Bloomfield 07003   201-338-8140
Performance sites: Park Theatre Performing Arts Center, Union City (1,400 seats) and at outdoor sites during statewide tours of New Jersey and New York.

The Garden State Concert Band, founded in 1979 by bandmaster Dominick J. Ferrara, performs band music throughout the year. Its three-concert series at the Park Theatre includes a late-fall performance of holiday music; a winter opera program, featuring a soloist; and a spring presentation called "Masterworks for Band." The band consists of thirty-five to forty regular, free-lance, union musicians. Summer performances are free of charge and feature lighter music: sing-alongs, Sinatra tunes, Broadway musical hits, big band numbers, and classical overtures. The band takes an interest in new music; it tries to perform at least one new work each year, and in 1989 it presented a world premiere by New Jersey composer Ellen Spokane.

Special Event: ◻ Holiday concert in December.

Educational Program: ◻ Band instrument on-site demonstrations for children.

Garden State Symphonic Orchestra/Pops (see Brunswick Symphony Orchestra)

Garden State Theatre Organ Society [$][♿][♿]
907 Best Court, Ridgewood 07450   201-233-5121
Performance sites: in old-time music halls and theaters where restored pipe organs stand. Most regular performances are at the War Memorial Theatre, Trenton (1,900 seats). Other performances sites include: Convention Hall, Asbury Park; Union County Arts Center (former Rahway Theatre), Rahway; Immaculate Heart of Mary Chapel (former Astor Theatre), North Bergen; Pascack Theatre, Westwood.

Founded in 1973, the society, a branch of a national organization devoted to preserving theater organs and promoting their music, presents concerts that feature professional concert organists, playing both contemporary and traditional tunes. One well-known performer, Father James Miller, an Eastern Orthodox priest, recently played jazz- and blues-influenced numbers during a society-sponsored performance. The year-round season includes an annual holiday show at the Trenton War Memorial consisting of carols and selections from the *Messiah*. Most

MUSIC

ARTS BROADCASTS AND ARTS-ORIENTED BROADCASTERS

"The Arts"
c/o Middlesex County Cultural and Heritage Commission, 841 Georges Road, New Brunswick 08902   201-745-4489
Monthly cable show on the arts

Newark Public Radio, Inc.—WBGO FM (DAO 1990)
54 Park Place, Newark 07102   201-624-8888
Public radio station presenting jazz, poetry readings, and other New Jersey arts programming

New Jersey Network
New Jersey Public Broadcasting Authority, 1573 Parkside Avenue, CN777, Trenton 08625   609-530-5252
Public television station presenting New Jersey arts programming, including "State of the Arts," a program focusing on the New Jersey arts world

"State of the Arts"
c/o New Jersey Network, New Jersey Public Broadcasting Authority, 1573 Parkside Avenue, Trenton 08625   609-530-5252
Twice-weekly show on the arts

Thirteen-WNET/Educational Broadcasting Corporation
Gateway One Center, Newark 07201   201-643-3315
Public television station presenting New Jersey arts programming

---

other programs stress music from the 1920s and 1930s; occasionally musicians play contemporary hits that work well on an organ (such as music from Andrew Lloyd Weber's *Phantom of the Opera*). Silent film classics come alive when they are accompanied by the tones of a theater organ. The Garden State Theatre Organ Society sponsors showings of silent movie classics accompanied—as they originally were—by a theater organist. A recent showing of *Dr. Jekyll and Mr. Hyde* at the old Rahway Theatre featured music from the Mighty Wurlitzer. The society is developing a program for the visually impaired, which would acquaint participants with individual sounds of the horseshoe-shaped theater organ (such as drum, cymbals, xylophone) and explain how they are produced and combined.

Special Programs and Events: ☐ Free early evening performances at the Pascack Theatre.

MUSIC

Educational Programs and Events: ☐ Organ instruction program for students in participating public schools. ☐ Organ tours, during which audience members are encouraged to try playing the organ. ☐ Roundtable discussions with musicians following concerts.

Greater Trenton Symphony Orchestra $

28 West State Street, Room 507, Trenton 08608   609-394-1338
Performance sites: The War Memorial Auditorium, Trenton (1,900 seats), and various auditoriums on statewide tours.

Originally known as the Trenton Symphony, the Greater Trenton Symphony Orchestra's first concert took place on March 13, 1922. In its more than sixty years, the symphony has grown from a group of forty amateur musicians to a regular corps of seventy-five to eighty musicians, most from the Trenton-Philadelphia area. Fundamentally a classical orchestra, the group occasionally performs contemporary works but does not present or commission world premieres. Its October-through-May subscription season is built around six performances of six different concert programs, including an annual Christmas concert. In the 1988–1989 season, one program included oil heir/composer Gordon Getty's *Plump Jack,* Mendelssohn's Overture to *A Midsummer Night's Dream,* and Beethoven's Ninth Symphony. The Greater Trenton Symphony, an all-union free-lance orchestra, has performed with classical and popular celebrities such as tenor Plácido Domingo and comedienne Phyllis Diller.

Educational Program: ☐ "Mini-orchestra" school performances.

Hoboken Chamber Orchestra (DAO 1987, 1988, 1989) $ ♪ ♩

22 Hudson Place, Hoboken 07030   201-653-1999
Performance sites: Demarest Auditorium, Hoboken (900 seats), in schools throughout Hudson County, and at other sites during occasional statewide tours.

The Hoboken Chamber Orchestra performs a mix of contemporary and classical music, taking a special interest in American works and pieces by New Jersey composers. It presents about five local premieres annually and recently performed the premiere of "Antifonys" by Montclair resident George Walker. The orchestra also performs frequently with New Jersey theatrical, dance, choral, and musical groups. For instance, each movement of its performance of *Peer Gynt* was accompanied by a dramatic reading by actors of the East Lynne Company (see

MUSIC

"Bad Boy of Music"—George Antheil

He wore an Oscar Wilde-style cape, custom made, with an armpit pocket for a pistol. Trenton-born George Antheil (1900–1959) was perpetually ready for battle, not only with possible assailants on the streets of Paris, where he lived as an expatriate, but also with the musical establishment. A classically trained concert pianist, Antheil composed outrageously "modern" music that enraged audiences and critics alike. The Paris premiere of his *Ballet méchanique,* which featured nine pianos, electric bells, a xylophone, assorted drums, and an airplane propeller, so offended audience members in the Théâtre des Champs Élysées that they stood in the aisles in protest. Antheil fans in attendance—among them, fellow expatriate Ezra Pound—shouted out words of support. Antheil seemed to relish the attention; he titled his autobiography *Bad Boy of Music.*

Born in 1900, Antheil moved to Europe in 1922, first living in Berlin, then moving to Paris, where he became the center of attention in a group that included Pound, James Joyce, Pablo Picasso, and W. B. Yeats. (Pound wrote a book of music criticism on Antheil, and commissioned two violin sonatas from him.) The composer's irreverent music was known for its jazz references, dissonance, and wit. *Ballet méchanique,* his most famous piece, was followed by such works as *Jazz Symphonietta* and the operas *Transatlantic* and *Helen Retires.* Antheil also began, but never finished, an opera based on Joyce's *Ulysses.* In his later years, the composer mixed music and bathos; he worked scoring films in Hollywood and writing a syndicated advice-to-the-lovelorn column. He appeared with the Greater Trenton Symphony during its 1931–1932 season. Recently the New Jersey Percussion Ensemble performed *Ballet méchanique,* accompanied by Teamwork Dance, which choreographed a piece for the event.

Theater). Beethoven's *Coriolanus Overture* and Ninth Symphony were performed in conjunction with the Pro Arte Choral and Chamber Symphony of Princeton. The orchestra was founded in 1981 when now musical director Gary M. Schneider assembled a group of musicians to play for the arts and cultural festival called Hoboken Celebration '82. The next year the orchestra became fully professional. It now has a six-concert season, which runs from September through May. With its seventy-member community chorus, it presents the *Messiah* every December. The Hoboken Chamber Orchestra performs about twenty-four times annually with thirty-seven union free-lance musicians, who are under contract for the season.

MUSIC

Special Programs and Events: ☐ *Messiah* concert presented annually in December. ☐ New American Works for Chamber Orchestra Competition, which is open to contestants of any age from across the country; biennial. ☐ Young Artists Competition, in which New Jersey high school musicians compete and after which the winner performs a concerto with the orchestra; biennial.

Educational Programs and Events: ☐ Children's concerts in Hudson County schools, featuring lectures and encouraging audience participation.

The Hollybush Festival [$][&][♿]
P.O. Box 707, Glassboro 08028   609-863-6043
Performance sites: The Hollybush Opera Theater, Wilson Concert Hall, Glassboro State College (1,000 seats) and other auditoriums during statewide tours.

The Hollybush Festival suggests that music is a diplomatic language; it was inspired by a landmark in American-Soviet relations: the 1967 "Hollybush" summit meeting of President Lyndon Johnson and Soviet Prime Minister Alexei Kosygin, which took place on the Glassboro campus. The interest in Soviet-American affairs is ongoing; in 1987, in honor of the summit's twentieth anniversary, the festival presented its own "Artistic Summit" featuring an American opera, *Susannah*, and a Russian opera, *Love for Three Oranges*, with a Soviet-American cast.

The Hollybush Festival takes place each May, when the festival offers eight to ten performances of four productions. While Hollybush presents traditional repertory works and less frequently performed standards, its artistic director prefers an experimental approach. For instance, a 1989 production of *Carmina Burana*, usually produced as a ballet or concert piece, was staged as an opera. And Hollybush set Puccini's *Tosca* in Central America instead of Italy.

Special Programs and Events: ☐ Holiday Family Opera in December. ☐ Holiday productions for handicapped persons and the learning disabled; free.

Educational Program: ☐ "Hollybush Too!" an educational program that provides music literacy progams in schools throughout southern New Jersey during multi-week residencies.

MUSIC

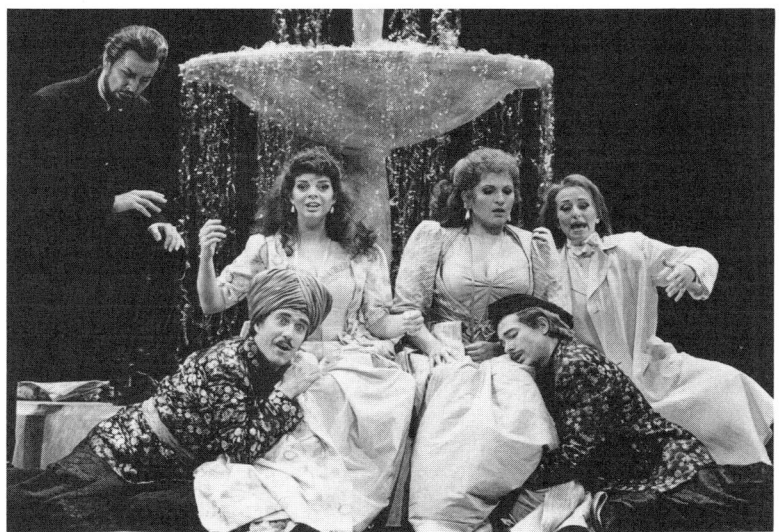

Noted for its ensemble casts, the June Opera Festival frequently presents works by Mozart, such as *Così Fan Tutte*. Photo: Robert Faulkner.

June Opera Festival of New Jersey (DAO 1987, 1988)
$ 🎭 🎟

65 South Main Street, Building B, Pennington 08534   609-737-7711
Performance sites: Kirby Arts Center, the Lawrenceville School, Lawrenceville (800 seats).

From June through early July, picnics and opera go hand in hand at the June Opera Festival; audiences dine on the lawn outside the Lawrenceville School's Kirby Arts Center before a musical performance. Spectators can order a picnic to be picked up with their tickets at the box office.

Founded in 1983, the June Opera Festival offers all its operas in English and works with an ensemble cast. Every summer thirty-one young American singers (many returning as festival alumni) spend three weeks in rehearsals and performances. The June Opera Festival includes five performances of two operas, plus one concert. The festival attempts fresh interpretations of classics and has presented such popular works as Mozart's *Così fan tutte,* Britten's *A Midsummer Night's Dream,* and Gilbert and Sullivan's *The Mikado.* Mozart works are frequently performed, and the festival recently repeated for the first time its production of *The Marriage of Figaro* with an orchestra of period and reproduction instruments. Opera casts vary, but average fifteen to twenty singers, in addition to the chorus.

Educational Programs and Events: ◻ Spring tours of "Opera For Kids, Too," a children's opera program featuring classics such as *Hansel and Gretel* and spoofs on serious opera, for instance, such tongue-in-cheek "classics" as *Ring of the Fettuccines.*

New Jersey Chamber Music Society (MIO/AFG; DAO 1988, 1989, 1990) $ 🚹 ♿

73 South Fullerton Avenue, Montclair 07042   201-746-6068
Performance sites: Union Congregational Church, Upper Montclair (500 seats), in addition to other sites during statewide and out-of-state appearances.

The New Jersey Chamber Music Society (originally the Montclair Chamber Music Society) has achieved a reputation that has spread beyond the borders of the Garden State, through appearances at Spoleto, the international arts festival in South Carolina; in Washington, D.C.; New York City; and on PBS and National Public Radio. The group regularly performs commissioned, contemporary music, presenting at least one world premiere annually. In 1984, it introduced a piece commissioned from New Jersey composer Loretta Jankowski, *Paterson Songs: A Work in Seven Parts,* inspired by poems of William Carlos Williams. And in 1988, it presented the world premiere of a commissioned work, Katherine Hoover's piano quintet *Da Pacem.* In addition to new works, the New Jersey Chamber Music Society often performs chamber works by Brahms, Beethoven, Mozart, and twentieth-century composers. Guest artists have included the Guarneri String Quartet and harpist Susan Jolles. In 1988, the society appeared with Yass Hakoshima (see Danmari, Ltd.—Dance), performing Charles Ives's Second String Quartet.

The New Jersey Chamber Music Society was founded in 1974 by pianist Bernice Silk and flutist Peggy Schecter. Within four years the group attracted a star; in 1978, the mezzo-soprano Marilyn Horne performed with the company. The New Jersey Chamber Music Society consists of

MUSIC

Corporate Culture

A Union singing group, The Celebration Singers, traces its origins back to 1938, when it acted as the official New Jersey Exxon (then Esso) men's chorus and went by the name The Esso Choristers. After the men left for the Second World War, Esso's female employees took over the enterprise. Ultimately, the choristers went coed. The chorus continued to be funded by Exxon until 1978, when the company determined that most chorus members were no longer employees.

Today, the Celebration Singers, an all-volunteer organization, still sings popular classics (Jerome Kern, Cole Porter, and Rodgers and Hammerstein) in five- to eight-part harmony at benefits and other gatherings. In 1988, the thirty-five-member ex-Exxon chorus celebrated its fiftieth anniversary.

---

thirteen to fifteen union, free-lance musicians, usually averaging appearances by seven to eight per concert. There is a loyal core of ten or twelve performers, including artistic directors Silk and Schecter. The group presents about thirty performances annually, including a seven-concert series from October to May and two three-concert series at the Stockton Performing Arts Center (see Centers) and the Morris Museum (see Visual Arts).

Educational Program: ☐ Thirty-concert workshop program for urban young people, including the disabled and mentally retarded.

New Jersey Pops $

95 Vere Terrace, Livingston 07039   201-992-7191
Performance sites: at various auditoriums during statewide tours and occasional out-of-state performances.

True to its name, this orchestra, founded in 1977, brings audiences popular music from all genres and eras: Hollywood film scores, Broadway show tunes, familiar classics, marches, and big-band music. It presents about forty concerts annually, during a year-round touring season. Summer concerts, often in outdoor locations, are almost always free. A corps of forty union musicians (the orchestra size ranges from fifty-five to seventy-five depending on the event and works performed) presents a variety of audience favorites, from Tchaikovsky's *1812 Overture* to "76 Trombones," from Meredith Wilson's Broadway show *The Music Man*. The orchestra also plays patriotic songs, and its signa-

MUSIC

ture sign-off is Sousa's "Stars and Stripes Forever." At Christmas time, the New Jersey Pops concerts center on seasonal works such as "March of the Toys," "Winter Wonderland," and the *Nutcracker Suite*.

America the Beautiful

The music for "America the Beautiful," the rousing hymn that is considered this country's second national anthem, was written by a New Jerseyean: Newark resident Samuel A. Ward (1847–1903).

New Jersey State Opera $[$][⚑]

Symphony Hall, 1020 Broad Street, Newark 17102   201-623-5757
Performance sites: in residence at Symphony Hall (2,800 seats) and at other auditoriums during statewide tours.

Founded by a group of suburban opera lovers in 1965, the New Jersey State Opera presents opera in the grand European tradition. Alfredo Silipigni, who has served as musical director since the company's inception, favors Italian themes and composers; during the 1987–1988 season the company performed *Iris* by Pietro Mascagni, Mozart's *Don Giovanni,* and Verdi's *Il Trovatore.* The New Jersey State Opera often casts internationally known singers in leading roles, accompanied by young singers (sometimes competition winners) and two choruses, one volunteer, one professional. It has a reputation for reviving rarely performed Italian operas, such as *Iris,* with traditional stagings and performances. Another Mascagni work, *Lodoletta,* which was recently performed by the company, had not been heard in the United States since 1919. In honor of its twenty-fifth anniversary, the company plans to stage a world premiere of *Frederick Douglass* by New Jersey resident Ulysses Kay during its 1990–1991 season. During its 1987–1988 season, the New Jersey State Opera added supertitles, English translations projected on a screen, to its performances. While controversial among opera purists, supertitles are designed to help audiences follow an opera's plot. The New Jersey State Opera's season generally runs from January through the spring and includes three to four productions annually, with two performances of each work. One of those productions usually tours, presenting about five performances at various locations.

Educational Programs and Events: ▫ "Let's Make an Opera," in-school programs featuring performers. ▫ Operalogues prior to each performance. ▫ Young Artists Competition in June for young opera singers (under thirty-four) from across the country.

MUSIC

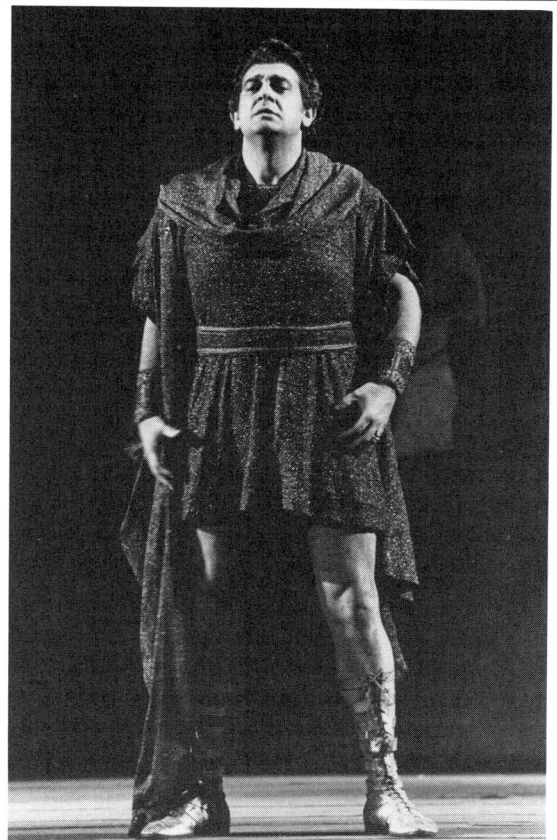

The New Jersey State Opera concentrates on Italian works, casting internationally known singers in starring roles. Here Plácido Domingo appears in its 1980 production of *Aida*. Photo: Robert Heffernan.

New Jersey Symphony Orchestra (AFG, DAO 1987, 1988, 1990) $ 👶

Robert Treat Center, 11th Floor, 50 Park Place, Newark 07102
201-624-3713 (administration); 201-624-8203 or 1-800-ALLEGRO (box office)
Performance sites: in residence at Symphony Hall, Newark (2,800 seats), with major concert series also presented at the John Harms Center for the Arts, Englewood (1,200 seats); Count Basie Theatre, Red Bank (1,400 seats); War Memorial Theatre, Trenton (1,900 seats);

MUSIC

the orchestra also makes statewide tours and annual appearances at Carnegie Hall, New York City.

Under the musical direction of the Paris-born, Harvard-educated conductor Hugh Wolff, the New Jersey Symphony Orchestra has become one of the most prominent arts organizations in the state. The orchestra has received favorable reviews from New Jersey and New York critics alike and national publicity through an article in *People* magazine and a segment on the CBS Sunday Morning show. Known for his bold conducting style, Wolff has helped secure the symphony a reputation as an orchestra capable of achieving national stature.

Founded in Montclair in 1928 as an outgrowth of the Eintracht Orchestra and Singing Society of Newark, the symphony first served largely Essex County audiences. It became fully professional in 1968. For years, without a hall to call its own, it traveled the state, appearing in various community and school auditoriums. Hard financial times and union troubles hit in 1980, and the New Jersey Symphony fell silent for sixteen months before returning in better health in October 1981. Four years later, Hugh Wolff was chosen as music director, and since then the organization has generated new glamour, funds, and enthusiasm. The Wolff repertoire includes the works of classic and modern composers: Beethoven (for whom the conductor is said to have a particular affinity and talent), Brahms, Mahler, Stravinsky, Debussy, and Ravel. Having spent a number of years in Paris, Wolff also favors the works of French composers. One recent program examined turn-of-the-century composers: titled "Music Turns the Century," it included Debussy's *Prelude to the Afternoon of a Faun;* Strauss's *Don Quixote,* and Ives's Symphony No. 2. In 1989, the orchestra commissioned its first new American work in nearly twenty years: Concerto for Chamber Orchestra by the Teaneck composer Ezra Laderman.

The symphony's main season of nearly 170 performances includes a major concert series (with the full orchestra averaging eighty-five musicians), chamber orchestra (thirty-five musicians) series; winter pops series; and annual December performances of the *Messiah* and *Nutcracker* (with the New Jersey Ballet). The symphony's chamber orchestra series is offered at Richardson Auditorium in Princeton (800 seats), the State Theatre in New Brunswick (1,800 seats), the John Harms Center for the Arts in Englewood (1,200 seats), and the Pingry School in Martinsville (800 seats). A recent winter pops series featured "Lake Wobegon Revisited" with the author Garrison Keillor, and an ap-

MUSIC

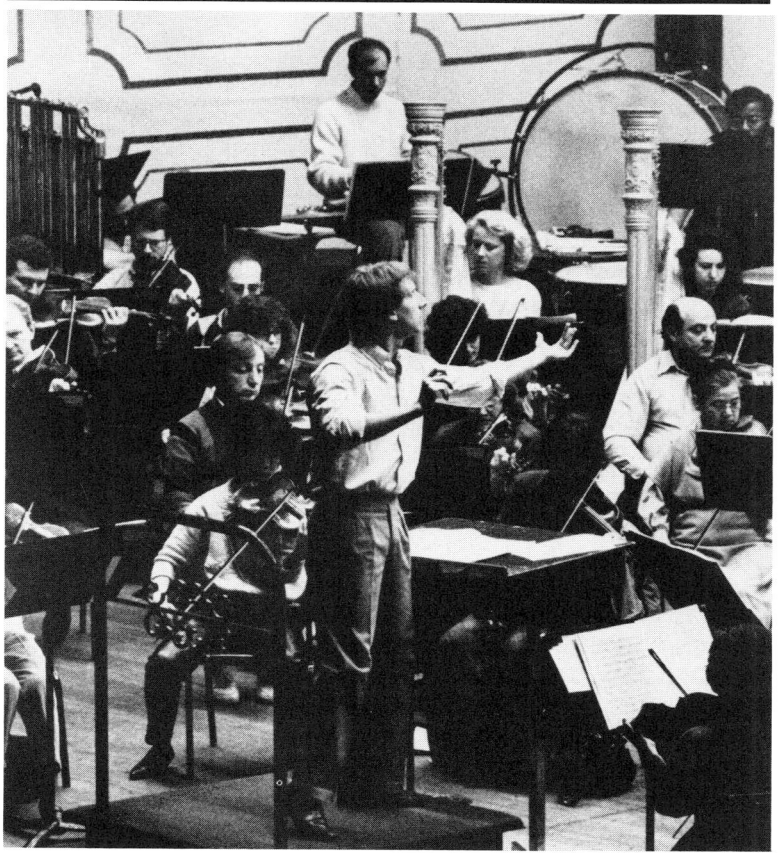

Artistic Director Hugh Wolff conducts the state's largest orchestra, the New Jersey Symphony Orchestra. Photo: Arthur Paxton.

pearance by Johnny Carson's band leader, Doc Severinsen. The symphony has frequently appeared with other New Jersey performing arts organizations, including the New Jersey Ballet, Westminster Symphonic Choir, and the American Boychoir. Its summer season concentrates on outdoor concerts at the Garden State Arts Center, Giralda Farms, and in various parks. In addition, throughout the year popular guest artists and virtuosos such as pianist Marvin Hamlisch and violinist Itzhak Perlman appear with the symphony. The orchestra has a regular contract corps of seventy-five union musicians.

MUSIC

Special Programs and Events: ☐ Always changing. One concert featured actor Dudley Moore on the piano, Itzhak Perlman on the violin, and Yo-Yo Ma on the cello. ☐ Young Artists Concerts of free performances by winners of the Young Artists Auditions; New Jersey musicians (under twenty) annually compete for a chance to perform with the orchestra at a free concert each spring. ☐ Young People's Concert: annual free concert at holiday time.

Educational Programs and Events: ☐ Schooltime concerts at locations around the state. The 1988 program, titled "Pan American Passages," included works by Herb Alpert, Aaron Copland, Mexican composer Carlos Chavez, and Brazilian Heitor Villa-Lobos. ☐ "Spotlight" concerts for schoolchildren, at which are played young people's favorites such as *Peter and the Wolf* and *Carnival of the Animals* (with puppets portraying the animals) in the symphony's regular locations.

New Philharmonic $ 🎭
19 Beach Place, Maplewood 07040   201-762-8499
Performance sites: The Morris Museum, Morristown (300 seats) and Maurice Levin Theatre, JCC of Metropolitan New Jersey, West Orange (500 seats), and chamber music concerts at private homes, clubs, and restaurants in Morris, Essex, and nearby counties.

"I was ready to change into black tie after the dinner break between dress rehearsal and the performance of a 'Wholly Mozart' concert. A search of all likely and unlikely places failed to turn up my tuxedo, so my concert dress consisted of my second-best blue jeans and a jacket borrowed from a sympathetic clarinet player. My opening remarks that night began in the appropriately classic manner: 'A funny thing happened to me on the way to the concert hall.'"—Leon Hyman, conductor, The New Philharmonic of New Jersey

---

The New Philharmonic orchestra was founded in 1977 by Leon Hyman, musical director and conductor, and Karen Pinoci, associate director and conductor. On the theory that socializing and classical music can go hand in hand, the New Philharmonic added to its regular full orchestra series a "Music for Singles" series in 1988 with a chamber music performance at the Unitarian Fellowship in Morristown. These "mixers," in "singles" concert series, are also presented in hotels, such as the Short Hills Hilton. Many of the musicians have been playing with the orchestra since its founding. About thirty-five freelance performers (nearly all union) appear at any one concert. The

MUSIC

main season runs from October through May and includes nine orchestra performances, ten chamber music concerts, and six "Music for Singles" events. The New Philharmonic generally presents one or two world premieres a year (in the 1988–1989 season it introduced *Sinfonia* by New Jersey composer Ting Ho), and most concert programs include some contemporary works. Hyman tends to contrast works of different styles, periods, and composers: a 1988 performance included pieces by Haydn, contemporary composer John Sichel, and Beethoven.

Special Programs and Events: □ Chamber musicales in private homes. □ "Family Goes to a Concert": Sunday afternoon concerts to which children accompanied by parents are admitted free of charge; family reception and music demonstration and discussion follow. □ "Wholly Mozart" concert; annual.

Educational Programs and Events: □ Composer/audience discussion sessions before world premieres. □ "Concerts in the School": symphony concerts that one or several schools attend. □ Post-concert conversations with artists. □ Pre-concert lectures on period and composer by the musical director. □ "Quartet of Music Making," in-school lecture demonstrations exploring the composer/conductor/music/audience components of a performance. □ "Sounds Like Fun!" presents performances and instrument demonstrations by small ensembles for elementary and secondary school audiences.

Opera at Florham $ ♿

Fairleigh Dickinson University, 285 Madison Avenue, Madison 07940
201-593-8620
Performance sites: Fairleigh Dickinson University, in the Dreyfuss Theatre (400 seats) and Lenfell Hall (200 seats).

Founded in 1982, Opera at Florham attempts to make opera both entertaining and educational. The Opera at Florham season, which runs from October to May, includes two full productions (two performances of each) and four cabaret-style evenings of arias and ensemble recitals. The productions include an average of thirty professional singers and thirty musicians. Artistic director and conductor Charles Del Rosso tries each year to present one well-known opera and one rarely performed; in 1988, Opera at Florham presented Dvořák's little-known work *Rusalka*. Opera at Florham considers itself the only company in the country and perhaps the world that helps audiences understand the opera by offering a "Living Libretto." Prior to each opera, actors and actresses perform a play in English that dramatizes the plot line. After a

MUSIC

Harriet Ware, A Musical Poet

To neighbors in Plainfield she might have been Mrs. Hugh Khrumbhaar of Terrill Road, the wife of an architect/engineer. But in the world of classical music, she was simply Harriet Ware. Born in Wisconsin in 1877, this child prodigy was said to have composed her first musical piece at the age of three. She later studied in New York, Paris, and Berlin. But it was in her Plainfield studio that she wrote many of the works that earned her a reputation in a field long dominated by men.

In 1927, Ware's "Women's Triumphal March" became the national processional song for the General Federation of Women's Clubs. Delegates to the club's national conventions march to it to this day. (The music to the club's national song, "America the Beautiful," was written by another New Jerseyean: nineteenth-century Newark native Samuel Ward.)

Ware also wrote several operettas, including *Waltz for Three* and *The Love Wagon*, which were produced at the Paper Mill Playhouse in Millburn, where she served on the music committee. The author of cantatas and a choral cycle, she set literature to music, composing a score for the Book of First Corinthians and the poem "The Rose is Red." Ware's symphonic poem *The Artisan* was performed by the New York Symphony Orchestra in 1929.

She died in 1962, having moved to the west side of Manhattan, but never having abandoned her Plainfield home, Lambkins Farm.

---

brief intermission, with the libretto still fresh in the audience's memory, the opera itself is performed. Informal cabaret evenings feature young artists singing arias before audience members who are seated at small tables with refreshments. Performers discuss the music and composer after the show. Recent cabaret programs have included: "The I's Have It: The Music of Rossini, Bellini and Donizetti" and "Mozart and Friend: The Music of Mozart Compared with That of His Rival Antonio Salieri." Opera recitals are held in Lenfell Hall in The Mansion; full productions in the Dreyfuss Theatre.

Special Programs and Events: ☐ Dress rehearsals free of charge to high school students. ☐ Vocal competition for aspiring young opera singers ages eighteen through thirty-five; annual.

Educational Event: ☐ "Operalogues" consisting of evening seminars open to the public, held a few days prior to the opening of each production, and conducted by the Opera at Florham's artistic director.

MUSIC

Opera/Music Theatre International Inc. (see Education and the Arts)

Philharmonic Orchestra of New Jersey [$]
67 Mountain Boulevard, P.O. Box 4064, Warren 07060
201-356-6165
Performance site: Pingry School, Martinsville (800 seats).

Founded in 1987, the Philharmonic Orchestra of New Jersey serves audiences in the burgeoning suburbs in the Somerset, Hunterdon, and Morris area with an annual subscription series and young people's concert. Directed by George Marriner Maull, the Philharmonic is composed of free-lance, union musicians, many of them recent conservatory graduates. Roughly half of the musicians are regular Philharmonic performers. Maull, who also conducts the New Jersey Youth Symphony (see Education and the Arts), favors late romantic and twentieth-century works. Programs during a winter/spring season of three concerts usually include a major symphony or concerto, overture, and incidental or ballet music. One recent performance combined dance music by several different composers into one dance "suite." The Philharmonic Orchestra usually consists of seventy-five to one hundred musicians, depending on the works performed.

Educational Program: ☐ Music-listening class for adults.

Solid Brass [$][🎵][♪]
Five Sunset Drive, Chatham 07928   201-522-1221 or 201-635-1854
Performance sites: throughout the New Jersey–New York metropolitan area and tours of the northeast.

Solid Brass's repertoire includes four programs: "Christmas with Solid Brass" (French, German, and Spanish carols as well as selections from the *Messiah*), "Solid Brass at the Opera" (music from *Don Giovanni, Carmen,* and *The Magic Flute*), "Made in America" (Sousa marches, Civil War songs, and works by George Gershwin), and "Solid Brass Goes Pops" (light popular music) as well as a varied program featuring Renaissance to baroque, romantic, and contemporary music. The ensemble performs between fifty and one-hundred-and-fifty times annually, with a corps of fifteen to twenty regular musicians. Solid Brass incorporates sixteenth-century festive music in many of its concerts. Founded in 1982, the group includes musicians on percussion, trombone, horn, trumpet, and tuba, who frequently change the works in each program, adding to their repertoire and drawing from a wide

MUSIC

range of music from medieval to jazz. Solid Brass also performs contemporary works, some composed by ensemble members. The group presents at least one world premiere each year; in the 1988–1989 season it presented works by two New Jersey composers: Carl della Peruti and David Sampson. It has performed choral works with the Summit Chorale Music Inc. and the Westminster Choir. Members of Solid Brass have performed widely not only in New Jersey but also with the Metropolitan Opera, New York City Ballet, and New York City Opera.

Special Program: □ Christmas concert in Morris County.

Educational Programs and Events: □ In-school performances. □ Master classes for high school and college students. □ Workshops in rehearsal techniques, performance attitudes, repertoire, and arranging for other ensembles.

South Jersey Symphony Orchestra [$]

27 Columbia Avenue, Pitman 08071   609-582-2374
Performance sites: high school and college auditoriums in Princeton, Millville, Mount Laurel, Cape May, Ocean City, Atlantic City, Tuckerton, Glassboro, and Cherry Hill.

On an annual tour of southern and central New Jersey concert halls, this orchestra presents more than twenty performances of five programs, offering series at numerous regular locations. Artistic director Samuel Muni presents mainly orchestral standards by Mozart, Handel, and other classical composers, along with occasional twentieth-century works. During the 1989–1990 season, the symphony, in association with the Composers Guild of New Jersey, introduced its first world premiere. The orchestra consists of union and nonunion free-lancers who are under contract for the series. There is a regular corps of between forty and fifty performers.

Special Event: □ Annual outdoor, free summer concert.

State Repertory Opera [$]

363 West South Orange Avenue, South Orange 07079
201-763-7969
Performance sites: Montclair High School (1,500 seats); William Carlos Williams Center, Rutherford (200 seats); and Brookdale Community College, Lincroft (370 seats) and in area churches and recital halls.

MUSIC

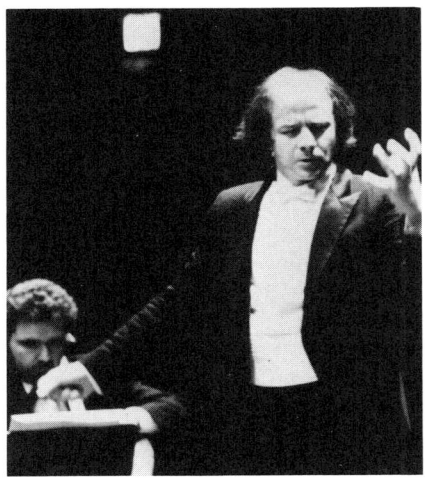

Samuel Muni conducts the South Jersey Symphony Orchestra, which offers series in eleven central and southern locations.

Originally a children's opera company, the State Repertory Opera was founded in 1975. It gives priority to New Jersey singers and occasionally performs works by New Jersey composers. All of its operas are performed in English. A small company, it does not present operas that call for large casts, but concentrates on manageable classics such as *The Barber of Seville, The Marriage of Figaro,* and *The Magic Flute.* Casts usually number about thirty (including the chorus), accompanied by an orchestra of thirty union, free-lance musicians. In addition, the company also stages revivals of rarely performed operas, such as the parody of Handel's work, *The Dragon of Wantley.* The State Repertory Opera generally presents one major production and occasional musical revues during its season, which runs from October to May. Its director sometimes experiments with programming; a recent performance of *The Dragon of Wantley* was preceded by *The Brickdust Man,* a twelve-minute, eighteenth-century curtain raiser.

Special Programs: ☐ "In Celebration of Christmas" concert series; annual.

Trenton Symphony Orchestra (see Greater Trenton Symphony Orchestra)

MUSIC

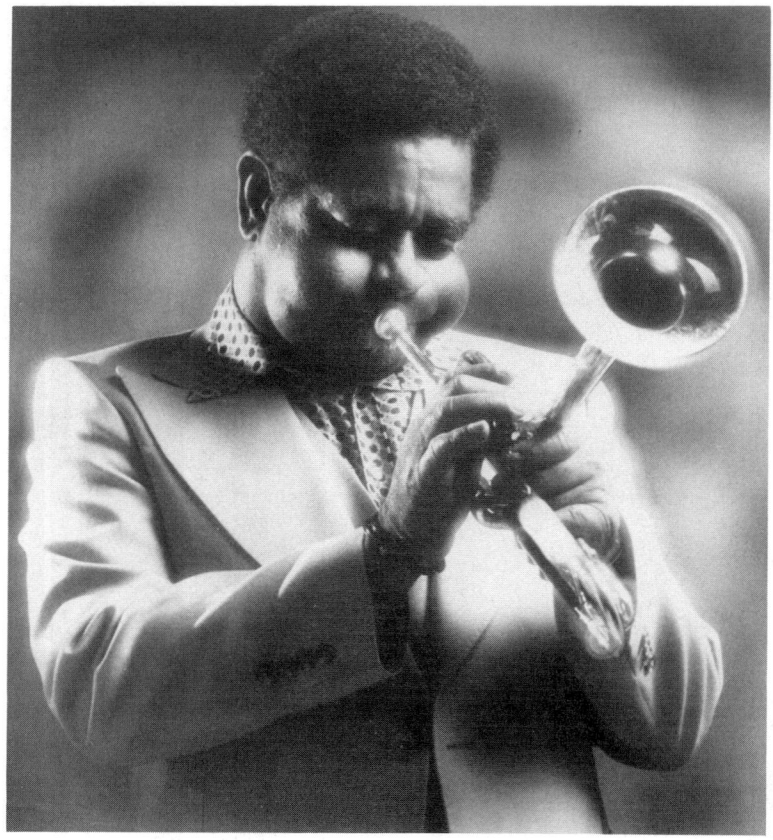

Unity Concerts, the state's longest continuously running non-university concert series, presents both classical and popular artists, including jazz performers such as Dizzy Gillespie.

Unity Concerts (DAO 1987) 💲🚻

22 Valley Road, Montclair 07042   201-744-6770
Performance sites: Montclair High School's Community Auditorium (1,500 seats) and the Glenfield Auditorium, Montclair (580 seats).

Founded in 1920 under the auspices of the Unitarian Church, Unity Concerts considers itself the longest-running, non-university classical concert series in New Jersey. Two of the state's most prominent music

MUSIC

organizations—The New Jersey Symphony Orchestra (formerly the Montclair Symphony) and the New Jersey Chamber Music Society (formerly the Montclair Chamber Music Society)—were presented by Unity Concerts early in their career. The season includes a major series of seven regular concerts and one bonus concert, an Orpheus Chamber Orchestra series of three concerts, and occasional appearances by guest artists. The main season, emphasizing classical works, runs from October through May. In addition to presenting well-known artists, Unity Concerts showcases promising young artists. Its series feature a roughly equal number of soloists and ensembles; one to one hundred-and-ten performers may be on stage at any given performance.

The Unity Concerts autograph book reflects a tradition of bringing internationally known performers to New Jersey: it begins with the 1923 signature of Polish composer and pianist Jan Paderewski. Over the years the concert series has featured many of the world's musical stars, among them cellist Pablo Casals, pianist Sergei Rachmaninoff, and flutist James Galway.

Educational Programs and Events: □ In-school assemblies.

Voices $ ♿

P.O. Box 404, Pennington 08534   609-883-6598
Performance sites: All Saints Church, Princeton, and Richardson Auditorium, Princeton University (800 seats), and elsewhere throughout the metropolitan area.

Voices concerts are performed by twelve professional singers, culled from nearly forty members, and a pianist. The group's forte is the performance of new works, especially pieces by New Jersey composers, but it also presents classical works as well as occasional popular pieces by Cole Porter and George Gershwin. A recent program included "Four Bizarre Songs" by Moseh Budmor and madrigals by Monteverdi. Often concerts follow a theme; for instance in 1988 Voices presented "Impressions of the Orient," works influenced by oriental music but written by Western composers. The group's composing contest for children attracts dozens of scores by children over the age of five; a contest kit complete with staff sheets and composing suggestions is designed to make the task easier for children under twelve.

Special Programs and Events: □ Capital Music Festival (see Festivals). □ Children's Composition Contest; annual. □ Family concert; annual.

MUSIC

Educational Programs and Events: ☐ Assembly programs. ☐ Children's opera in schools. ☐ Master classes. ☐ Music parties for pre-schoolers. ☐ Music workshops.

Walden Trio $\boxed{\$}\boxed{\ast}$

95 Palisades Avenue, Leonia 07605   201-836-4683
Performance sites: at colleges and community centers throughout the state and on nationwide tours.

Founded in 1973, the Walden Trio consists of cellist Maxine Neuman, a Bennington College professor; flutist Gwendolyn Mansfield Holtham; and pianist Joan Stein. The Walden Trio concentrates on creating a fresh approach to music; it researches scholarly literature for new information on frequently performed works. Dedicated to developing and performing new music, the group regularly commissions and performs works by contemporary composers, occasionally from New Jersey. Stein, Mansfield, and Holtham frequently discuss works with audience members before or after a performance. The trio adds one new work each year to its repertoire, which includes baroque, classical, and romantic works, from trios by Jean Loeillet and Bach to pieces by Ned Rorem.

Educational Programs and Events: ☐ Community chamber music workshops. ☐ Master classes for young people and adults.

Wayne Chamber Orchestra $\boxed{\$}$

The William Paterson College of New Jersey, Wayne 07470
201-595-2694 (administration), 201-595-2371 (box office)
Performance sites: in residence at Shea Center for Performing Arts, William Paterson College, Wayne (960 seats).

Founded in 1986, the Wayne Chamber Orchestra was cosponsored by the Wayne Area Chamber of Commerce and William Paterson College. Concentrating on traditional American music rather than new music, the group includes at least one American work and one European classic in every program. It has celebrated such occasions as the ninetieth birthday of Virgil Thomson and the fiftieth anniversary of the death of George Gershwin with performances of the composers' works. The orchestra also has presented theme concerts, performing music by immigrant composers in honor of the American Bicentennial and music by women composers, sung by women soloists, during Women's History Month. The company also revives rare classics; during its first season, it performed works by Barber, Copland, Cowell, and Joplin. The

MUSIC

"To provide an instrument for the great sacred choral works of the renaissance, baroque, and classic eras, Maestro Garyth Nair constructed a small positif organ several years ago. Four of the ranks operating the organ were salvaged and restored from pipes of American organs built in the third quarter of the nineteenth century—a period generally regarded as the last era of classic organ builders in this country. The organ design allows it to be dismantled into three units so it can be moved more easily. But that sounds easier than it actually is. Our stage crew of Chorale members attempts to follow Mr. Nair's detailed instructions for transport, assembly, and dissembly. With much gnashing of teeth, a few expletives, occasional strained muscles or bruised fingers, the job gets done, of course; but it's usually a struggle."—C. Y. Haas, Summit Chorale/Music

---

orchestra presents four performances each season, which runs from September through June. It consists of about forty professional, union free-lancers and ten student performers.

Educational Programs and Events: ☐ "Musical Notes," a pre-concert lecture series. ☐ Outreach lectures at Wayne Public Library and other sites.

Westfield Symphony Orchestra $ & ♿

P.O. Box 491, Westfield 07090   201-232-9400
Performance sites: The Presbyterian Church, Westfield (950 seats) and Westfield High School Auditorium (1,100).

The Westfield Symphony Orchestra was founded as a community group and presented its first performance on 4 June 1983. Since then it has become a professional orchestra with sixty-five contract, free-lance musicians. The season, which runs from October through April, includes five concerts, with one performance of each. The Westfield Symphony presents one concert opera every season. It performed Beethoven's *Fidelio* in Carnegie Hall in 1986, and in 1988 presented *Tosca* in a production featuring more than 160 singers and musicians. In addition to concert opera, the music director has a particular interest in Mahler, though works by Mahler are not included every year.

Special Programs and Events: ☐ Programs for the handicapped in conjunction with Children's Specialized Hospital. ☐ "Sounds of the Season," an annual holiday family concert.

MUSIC

Educational Programs and Events: ☐ "Assistant to the Conductor" program for high school students. ☐ Master classes for high school and junior high school students. ☐ Pre-concert previews. ☐ "Upbeat Live" series for elementary schools during which young people sit among musicians as they play. ☐ Workshops for elementary schools.

An Artistic Patriot

Francis Hopkinson (1737–1791) was a Renaissance man. A native of Bordentown, he is considered the United States' first "native" composer; his 1788 *Seven Songs for Harpsichord or Forte Piano* (dedicated to George Washington) was the nation's first published book of music. A signer of the Declaration of Independence and a New Jersey Constitutional Convention delegate, Hopkinson also had an eye for design; he helped develop motifs for the American flag and the Great Seal of New Jersey.

West Jersey Chamber Music Society $ ♿ ♀

P.O. Box 211, Moorestown 08057   609-778-1899
Performance sites: Moorestown area churches and middle school auditoriums.

The West Jersey Chamber Music Society combines a professional chamber orchestra and professional chorus under a single director. Founded in 1980 under the name Musica Sacra, the West Jersey Chamber Music Society evolved from the music program at the First Presbyterian Church. The emphasis is on works written for chorus and orchestra: masses and cantatas by major classical composers. For instance, the group has performed a chamber version of the *Messiah*. The season, which runs from October through July, usually includes one contemporary work. The society divides its four-concert series between programs for orchestra only, for chorus only, and for both. A loyal core of twelve musicians and singers respectively appear regularly in the fifteen-to-thirty member orchestra and twenty-member chorus.

Special Programs and Events: ☐ Moorestown Bach festival; annual. ☐ Summer concert, free of charge; annual.

Educational Programs and Events: ☐ Workshops at the Perkins Center for the Arts for children, including the developmentally disabled.

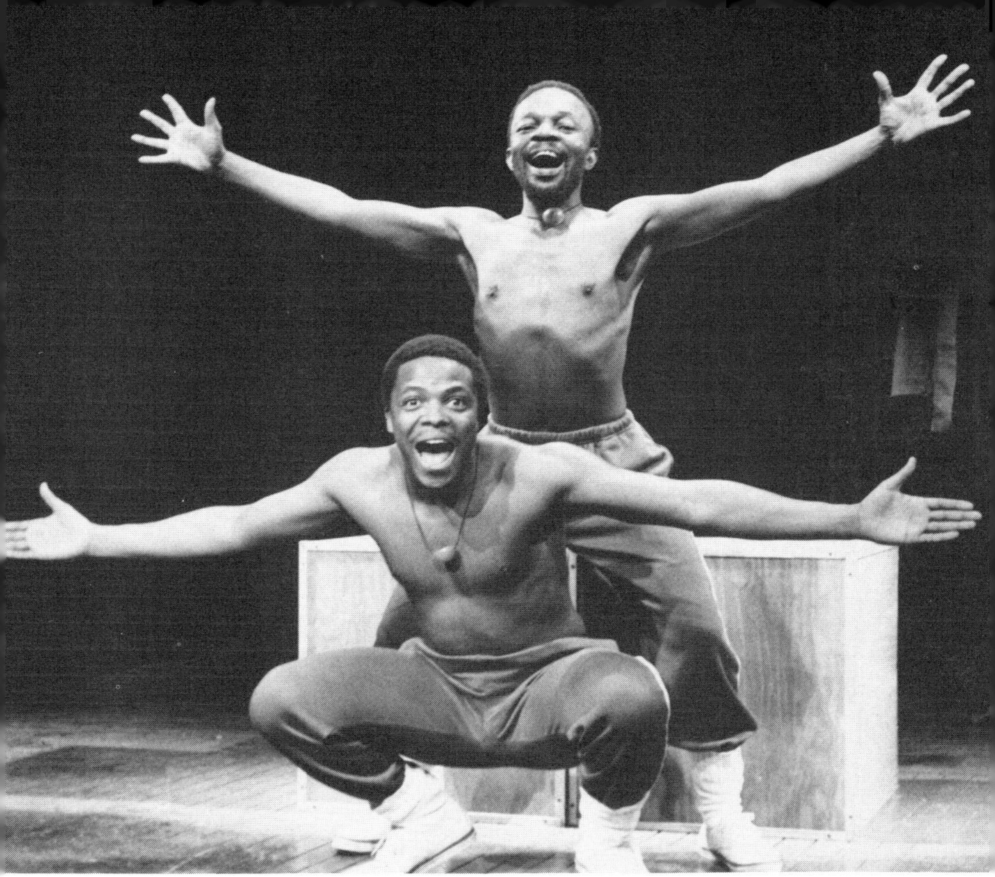

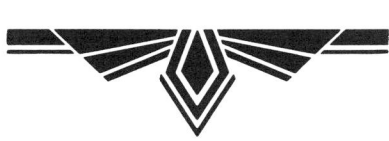

THEATER

Overleaf: Tsepo Makone (standing) and Fan Kekana (crouching) in the Crossroads Theatre production of *Woza Albert!* Photo: Eddie Birch.

THEATER

The American Stage Company (DAO 1990)
P.O. Box 336, Fairleigh Dickinson University Campus, Teaneck 07666   201-692-7720 (administration), 201-692-7744 (box office)
Performance sites: Becton Theatre, Fairleigh Dickinson University's Teaneck campus (300 seats) and other auditoriums during occasional out-of-state tours.

The American Stage Company, so named because it performs new and classic American plays, was founded in 1985 by Jim Singer and Ted Rawlins, two New York actors. Convinced they needed a "name" to give the new company credibility, they asked Paul Sorvino, a popular movie and television actor who lives in Englewood, to act as artistic director. Funding from a local businessman and the promise of space at Fairleigh Dickinson helped them open with a production of *All the King's Men*. A comedy that premiered at the American Stage, *Other People's Money* by Jerry Sterner, opened Off Broadway in 1989. It is one of five productions that has moved to New York. The American Stage presents four or five mainstage productions annually (usually twenty performances of each). World premieres dominate the season, which runs from October through May, and the company usually takes a traditional, naturalistic approach to the works it undertakes. An average of four performers appear in each production.

Educational Programs and Events: □ American Stage Conservatory provides year-round classes in acting, scene study, and improvisation. □ Master classes. □ "Moving to Music" programs for children. □ Pre-teen and teen workshops.

Centenary Stage Company
Centenary College, Hackettstown 07840   201-852-1400
Performance site: Centenary Stage Company Little Theater (170 seats).

Founded in 1987 by Carl Wallnau, a New York actor and Centenary College drama teacher, the Centenary Stage Company is the only Equity company in this corner of northwest New Jersey. The company performs a wide range of plays, from revivals to contemporary works on the Centenary College campus during its October-through-May season. Wallnau has a particular liking for modern British dramas by playwrights such as Tom Stoppard, and generally the company offers at least one American premiere each year. Centenary Stage produces four mainstage productions annually, with twelve performances of each. Between two and nine actors and actresses appear in each production.

THEATER

Under the auspices of its Women Playwrights Project, the company annually presents four staged readings and one full mainstage production of new plays by women that are selected from nationwide submissions.

Educational Programs and Events: □ Area elementary school drama festival, during which children stage original or revival plays during a one-day contest. □ Outreach program in which high school students discuss productions with actors, directors, and set designers after a show.

Crossroads Theatre Company (AFG, DAO 1988, 1990)

320 Memorial Parkway, New Brunswick 08901   201-249-5581 (administration), 201-249-5560 (box office)
Performance sites: Crossroads Theatre (135 seats) and other auditoriums during state and nationwide tours.

The brainchild of two Rutgers University drama students, Rick Khan and L. Kenneth Richardson, the Crossroads Theatre Company was founded in 1978 to provide theater opportunities for black actors, actresses, and audiences. It concentrates on developing new works and new artists, and its productions use black and multiracial experiences as touchstones. In addition to offering revivals of such hits as *Bubblin' Brown Sugar, Eubie,* and *Ain't Misbehavin',* the Crossroads Theatre Company presents new plays each year, some written by New Jersey playwrights. In fact, the 1989–1990 season was devoted to world premieres. In the ten years since its founding, Crossroads has become a leading black theater company. In 1986, its production of an original play, *The Colored Museum,* moved to Joseph Papp's Public Theatre in New York and later to London. Crossroads presents five productions, a mix of dramas, musicals, and comedies, during its regular season, and it usually offers a Christmas musical. Generally there are more than thirty performances of each production, in which between one and eight actors and actresses appear. Crossroads has staged a number of plays by Trenton resident Don Evans, and in 1987, it produced *Spell #7* by Trenton native Ntozake Shange, author of *For Colored Girls.* . . . Crossroads staged readings and discussions of new works are open to the public. The company, whose season runs from September through May, is a resident member of the New Brunswick Cultural Center. In the 1989–1990 season Crossroads introduced Genesis, a two-week-long new-play festival, featuring several world premieres, followed by discussion sessions with the playwrights. A new 260-seat theater in the New

THEATER

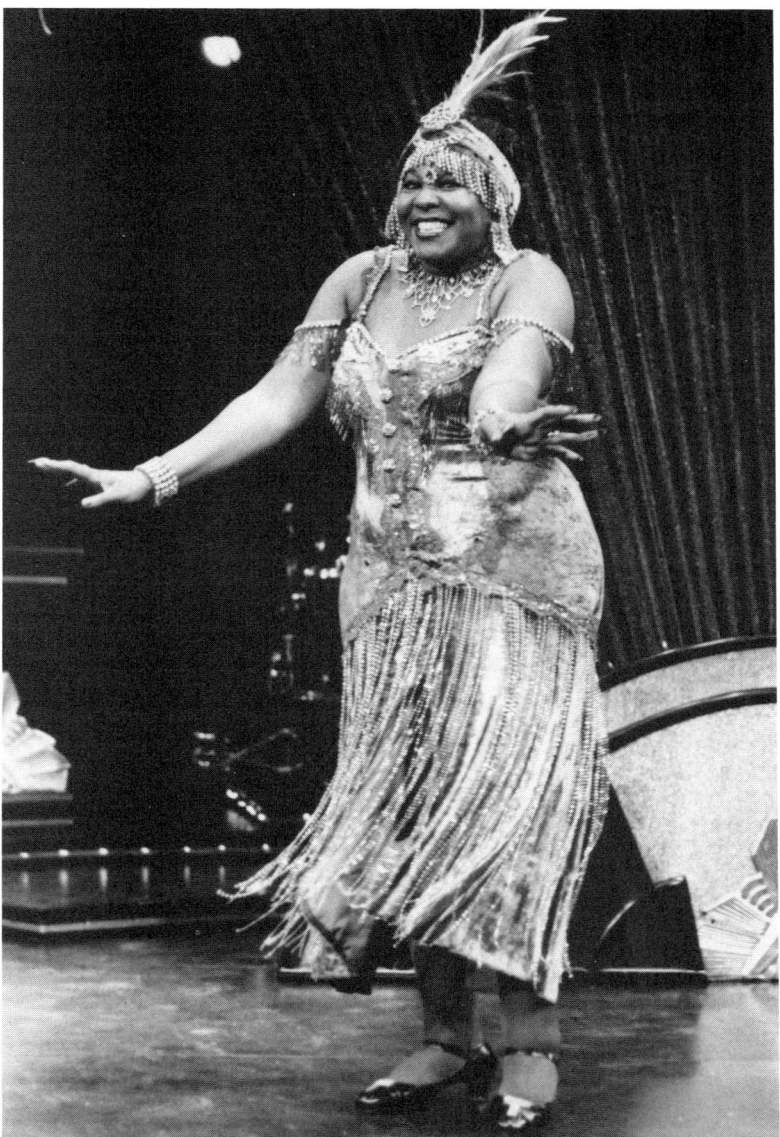

The Crossroads Theatre Company produces plays with black actors and audiences in mind. Here Sandra Reaves-Phillips appears in *The Late, Great Ladies of Blues & Jazz*. Photo: Eddie Birch.

THEATER

One Artist's Struggle

An international star, Princeton-born Paul Robeson (1898–1975) inspired awe and controversy. Audiences admired his magnificent baritone voice and stage presence. But many—including the United States Government—criticized him for his strong stand on behalf of independence for African countries and his close relationship with the Soviet Union and its citizens.

Certainly, Robeson was outstanding in many areas. A Phi Beta Kappa graduate of Rutgers and an all-American football player, he entered law school at Columbia University before launching a career as a singer and actor. At first, stardom eluded him in the United States, but he was acclaimed in London and a favorite among European audiences.

His moving interpretation of "Old Man River" in the 1932 revival of the musical *Show Boat* captivated American audiences. But it was the title role in *Othello* (1943), Broadway's longest-running Shakespearean production, that finally brought him great acclaim in his na-

---

Brunswick Cultural Center Complex is expected to open in the 1990–1991 season.

Special Programs and Events: □ For Black History Month, a production that opens at Crossroads, then tours the state. □ "New Play Rites," a development program for new and established playwrights, with staged readings.

Educational Program: □ Crossroads Internship for young people interested in professional theater careers. □ Post-performance discussions with playwrights and cast during previews of new works. □ Newroads touring company performs at schools, corporations, and festivals nationwide.

East Lynne Company Inc. 🎭 $

281 Lincoln Avenue, Secaucus 07094   201-863-6436
Performance sites: summer residency at the Mid-Atlantic Center for the Arts, Cape May, and appearances at other auditoriums during nationwide tours of colleges, museums, and other institutions.

The East Lynne Company was founded by Warren Kliewer, a professor who turned to acting. It is the country's only theater company that regularly revives nineteenth- and twentieth-century theater works. East

THEATER

tive land. The success was bittersweet for Robeson, who wanted more opportunities in American theater not only for himself but for all black actors and singers.

"I came to understand that the Negro artist could not view the matter simply in terms of his individual interest, and that he had a responsibility to his people, who rightfully resented the traditional stereotyped portrayals of Negroes on stage and screen," the actor explained in his 1958 autobiography, *Here I Stand.* "So I made a decision: if the Hollywood and Broadway producers did not choose to offer me worthy roles to play, then I would choose not to accept any other kind of offer."

Inspired by Robeson's vision, The Robeson Gallery at Rutgers University, Newark, was founded to show the work of contemporary minority artists. Edward Pierson, a baritone from Elizabeth, also keeps alive the star's memory by performing works from his repertoire throughout the state under the auspices of the Carter G. Woodson Foundation.

Lynne takes its name from a popular nineteenth-century novel and play by Mrs. Henry Wood, which was widely performed in both England and America. The company stages long-forgotten plays, such as *The Politician Outwitted,* written in 1788 by Samuel Low, and the long-running stage adaptation of *Rip Van Winkle.* East Lynne has toured widely with its adaptation of the 1892 Charlotte Perkins Gilman story *The Yellow Wallpaper,* about a woman tormented by patterns on the wall. Another production, *Demon Rum,* was a recreation of a nineteenth-century temperance meeting.

The East Lynne Company gave its first performance at the Jersey City Public Library in 1981. Today, in addition to producing plays, the company sponsors symposia on various aspects of theater and theater history; it recently held a conference on the Barrymore family, which traces its dramatic roots back to Elizabethan England. East Lynne has staged more than twenty-five productions, introducing several new plays each year. The cast size of each production varies from one to about eleven.

Educational Programs and Events: □ Classes and symposia on productions and theater history.

THEATER

Ensemble Theatre Company 🐚$
89 Lincoln Park, Newark 07102   201-648-0569
Performance site: Newark Symphony Hall Studio Theatre (80 seats).

Founded in 1981 by Rutgers graduates, the Ensemble Theatre Company takes an experimental approach to theater. It presents four or five productions each year, usually at least one classical work (such as *Antigone* or *Macbeth*), a new work, and a rarely performed play or adaptation of a novel. It also stages plays based on Afro-American stories and issues. Up to seven actors and actresses appear in each production, including the theater's three founding members, and these make up a regular corps.

The Ensemble Theatre Company recently presented a modern-dress *Macbeth* in which the title character was a police officer to whom the Witches appeared while he was drinking a beer. In the 1989–1990 season, the company presented the world premiere of *Ice House*, by Judyie Al-Bilali, a work that was developed as part of the Crossroads Theatre Company's New Play Rites program.

Special Event: □ Annual production at the Crossroads Theatre Company.

Forum Theatre Group 🐚$🕴
314 Main Street, Metuchen 08840   201-548-4670 (administration), 201-548-0582 (box office)
Performance site: Forum Theatre, Metuchen (400 seats).

Founded in 1983 by long-time Metuchen resident Peter Loewy, this Equity theater company is based in the Forum Theatre, a former vaudeville theater (circa 1926). It specializes in revivals and works that had short Broadway or Off Broadway runs: mostly musicals, but some comedies and dramas. The theater recently presented the American premiere of *Mr. Cinders*, a London musical, and the Broadway hits *Dream Girls* and *Sunday in the Park with George*. The main season, which runs from October through June, offers five productions, presenting between sixteen and twenty-two performances of each. Anywhere between six and thirty actors and actresses appear in a given production. A seven-production children's series presents visiting companies such as the Pushcart Players (see Education and the Arts) performing works for young audiences.

THEATER

Special Programs and Events: ☐ Film showings of classic and second-run films, occasionally focusing on one director such as John Huston or Frank Capra. ☐ Theatre for Young Audiences, a series of spring and winter productions for children.

Educational Programs and Events: ☐ "Kindermusik," an introduction to notes, instruments, and music basics for pre-school children, ages two to six. ☐ Theater workshops for all ages.

Foundation Theatre 👤$♿

Burlington County College, Route 530, Pemberton 08068
609-894-9311, x423 (administration), 609-894-2138 (box office)
Performance site: Foundation Theatre, Burlington County College Campus (240 seats).

Formerly a summer theater, the Foundation Theatre recently added spring and fall productions to its season. Founded in 1974, the company offers three mainstage productions of musicals, mysteries, comedies, or dramas and one children's theater production during the summer. Generally the fall production is a world or New Jersey premiere and the spring production is a classic, such as a Shakespeare play. Recent summer offerings have included *Berlin to Broadway with Kurt Weill* and *Cliffhanger,* a murder mystery. Producing director Julie Ellen Prusinowski takes theatrical risks: in April 1989, she honored Shakespeare's birthday by presenting *Much Ado About Nothing* set in the post–World War I era.

Special Programs and Events: ☐ Dance performances; occasional. ☐ Student matinees.

Educational Programs and Events: ☐ Discussion sessions with producer, director, and actors following the Fall Event and Spring Classic, performances of new and classic plays respectively. ☐ Explorer Post for the Boy Scouts of America where scouts work at the theater.

George Street Playhouse (DAO 1988) 👤$♿

9 Livingston Avenue, New Brunswick 08901   201-846-2895 (administration), 201-246-7469 (box office)
Performance sites: at the Playhouse (370 seats).

The George Street Playhouse stages both revivals and new plays. Founded in 1974, it presents seven productions annually, between October and June. George Street tends to reinterpret well-known works, often with nontraditional casting and settings. It presented a cross-cultural cast in *The Subject Was Roses* and set *Man of La Mancha* in Nicaragua. During the 1989–1990 season, George Street presented four world premieres. In addition to new works, the season often contains a mix of musicals, comedies, and dramas. Generally there are thirty-two performances of each production, with between two and seventeen actors and actresses in each. George Street occupies a renovated YMCA building in downtown New Brunswick and is a resident theater of the New Brunswick Cultural Center.

Twice a year, the George Street Playhouse sponsors "Educators' Night," so that New Jersey teachers can preview the plays its outreach touring company is prepared to perform in schools throughout the tri-state area. Examples of such plays are: *Lives Worth Living,* which examines a young woman's relationship with her mentally retarded brother, and *Rock n Roll from William Shakespeare,* which presents *Taming of the Shrew, Macbeth,* and *A Midsummer Night's Dream* to rock music.

Educational Programs and Events: ☐ Theater classes for children and adults. ☐ Outreach touring company.

Loaves and Fish Theatre Company ♿ $

P.O. Box 4098, Jersey City 07304   201-451-8784 (administration), 201-795-5053 (box office)
Performance site: in residence at the Roy Irving Theater, St. Peters College, Jersey City (140 seats).

Notwithstanding its name—and its affiliation with St. Peters College—this regional company does not produce theological plays. Founded in 1986, Loaves and Fish agreed in the first season to serve as advisor to the St. Peters Drama Club in exchange for performance space. Producing director Douglas Farren has as his goal producing plays that combine a ring of truth with beautiful language. In 1986, the company's production of *Return to the River,* about a black man who bucks the tide in an predominantly white corporation, had a short run Off Broadway. The company produces three plays a year, presenting fifteen performances of each. Usually four or five actors and actresses appear in each production. The company recently presented the New Jersey premiere of *Triple Play,* three one-act plays by Rutgers professor Joseph Hart that reflect on three stages of adult life: young adulthood, middle age, and retirement age.

THEATER

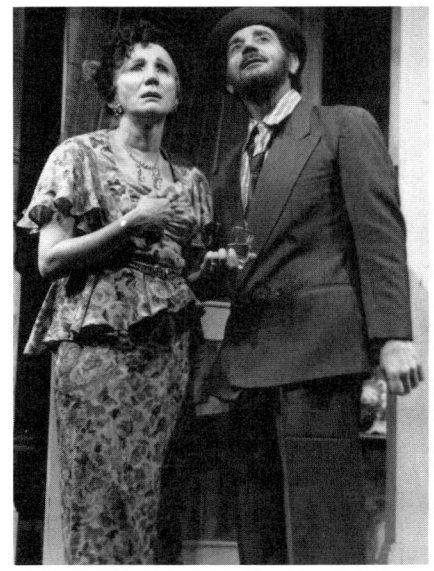

Artistic director and Academy Award–winning actress Olympia Dukakis appears with Anthony Ponzini in the 1988 production of *The Rose Tattoo* at the Whole Theatre, which closed its doors in 1990 due to financial problems. Photo: Barry Morgenstein.

Special Program: □ "The Genesis Series," staged readings of new plays in area restaurants, auditoriums, and community centers.

Educational Program: □ In-school drama workshops for Hoboken elementary and high school students.

McCarter Theatre (see Centers)

New Jersey Shakespeare Festival $ 🖉 🛉

Drew University, Route 24, Madison 07940   201-377-5330 (administration), 201-377-4487 (box office)
Performance site: The Bowne Theatre, Drew University, Madison (240 seats).

The New Jersey Shakespeare Festival does not limit itself to Shakespearean plays; it also performs revivals of American plays such as *The Crucible* and *A Streetcar Named Desire*. Founded in Cape May in 1963, the festival has had permanent guest status at Drew since moving on campus in 1972. Members of its resident company appear in three Shakespearean plays each season, giving between twenty-two and thirty-five performances of each. The classical repertory rotates daily through October. At the end of the season, two or three contemporary plays are performed, usually twenty-eight times each. The company takes an ensemble approach, the actors alternating in leading and supporting roles. While many productions are traditional, adhering to Shakespeare's descriptions of time and place, others take a more experimental tack; the festival has presented a World War II *Coriolanus* and a feminist version of *Taming of the Shrew*.

In 1990 the New Jersey Shakespeare Festival became one of a handful of theaters in the world to have staged all thirty-eight plays written by Shakespeare. All plays run full length; the Festival does not make cuts.

Special Programs and Events: ☐ Monday Night Special performances: dance, jazz, mime, comedy, and children's and visiting theater company productions; summer. ☐ Shakespeare Festival Colloquium, consisting of company performances and guest lecturers from all over the country; annual.

Educational Programs and Events: ☐ Intern classes in acting, weaponry, and other theater techniques. ☐ Intern Program in which candidates for membership in Actors Equity perform in supporting roles, as understudies, and in understudy matinees and workshops.

New Jersey Theatre Group (New Jersey Professional Theatre Foundation) (DAO 1989) $ ⏀

6 Afton Drive, Florham Park 07932   201-593-0189

The New Jersey Group represents Actors Equity, non-profit theaters. Established in 1978 by five original member theaters, it is now composed of nine full (senior) member theaters and eight associate members from all over the state. The association considers itself the only statewide organization of its kind in the country. It serves and promotes professional, Equity theater in New Jersey and provides information, technical assistance, and other resources to members of the theater community and sponsors some performances for New Jersey audiences. It also publishes an annual calendar outlining member theaters' seasons.

Special Event: ☐ New Jersey Plays: a series of three readings of new plays by New Jersey authors presented at three different member theaters each fall.

Educational Programs and Events: ☐ Developing Theatres Program that provides consultants to member theater companies at low cost. ☐ Job

THEATER

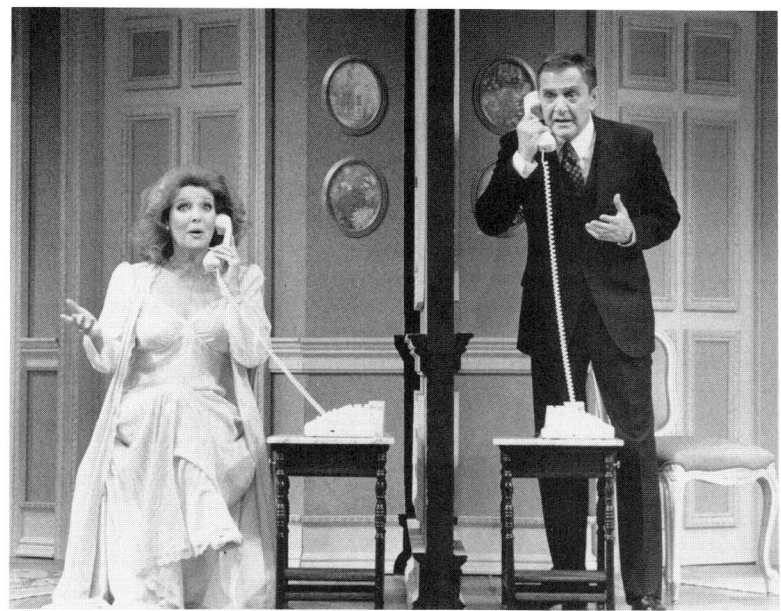

Known for its elaborate, Broadway-style productions, the Paper Mill Playhouse often presents well-known actors. Here Millicent Martin and Tony Randall appear in *Two in One*. Photo: Gerry Goodstein.

fair; annual. □ New Jersey Theatre Conference; annual. □ Theater Symposia series.

Paper Mill Playhouse (SCAE, AFG, DAO 1987, 1988, 1989, 1990) 🐾 $ ♿ 🚹

Brookside Drive, Millburn 07041   201-379-3636 (administration), 201-376-4343 (box office)
Performance site: Paper Mill Playhouse (1,200 seats).
The Renee Foosaner Gallery: Open one hour before stage performances and during intermission and also noon to 3 PM Fridays.

With the largest subscription base and earned income of any regional theater in the country and seasons full of Broadway stars and revivals, the Paper Mill Playhouse has convinced some critics and subscribers that it is more Broadway than Broadway. Since its founding in 1934, its productions have featured hundreds of stars, for example, Colleen

THEATER

Dewhurst, Tony Randall, Jason Robards, Jr., and Robert Vaughn. Broadway and Off-Broadway revivals such as *Shenandoah, The King and I,* and *Steel Magnolias* are standard Paper Mill fare. In 1989, its elaborate production of *Show Boat* appeared on PBS television's "Great Performances."

The Paper Mill is interested in new plays as well, and it sponsors as many as nine staged readings annually in the "Musical Theatre Project." Under the auspices of that project, it recently developed and produced the musical *Sayonara,* an adaptation of a James Michener novel. The theater's September-through-June season includes six mainstage productions: two musicals in the fall and two in the spring (usually forty-eight performances of each) and a drama or comedy in the winter (usually forty performances). As many as fifty or more performers may appear in any one production. The Paper Mill also acts as a performing arts center, presenting dance and musical performances, and art exhibits in its upstairs gallery. Every year the New Jersey Ballet performs *The Nutcracker* at the theater. A leader in providing handicapped access, the theater offers more services and facilities for the disabled than any other major theater in the state. Special programs and facilities include: removable seats for wheelchair access, audio-described performances for the visually impaired, sign-interpreted and infra-red system performances for the hearing impaired, and Braille playbills.

Special Programs and Events: ☐ Musical Theatre Project, which is dedicated to producing new musicals and revitalizing old ones. ☐ *Nutcracker* performances by the New Jersey Ballet; annual. ☐ Summer Festival of jazz, classical music, and dance.

Educational Program: ☐ "On-School Time," a performance/lecture program for schoolchildren.

Park Theatre Performing Arts Center and Art Gallery (see Centers)

The Passage Theatre Company ♿$

221 East State Street, Trenton 08608   609-392-0766
Performance sites: The Mill Hill Playhouse, Trenton (120 seats).

The Passage Theatre Company, founded in 1985, develops and produces new American plays. It casts minority actors in works with themes that appeal to urban and multiethnic audiences. And it explores different play structures. For example, *American Shorts,* a series of

THEATER

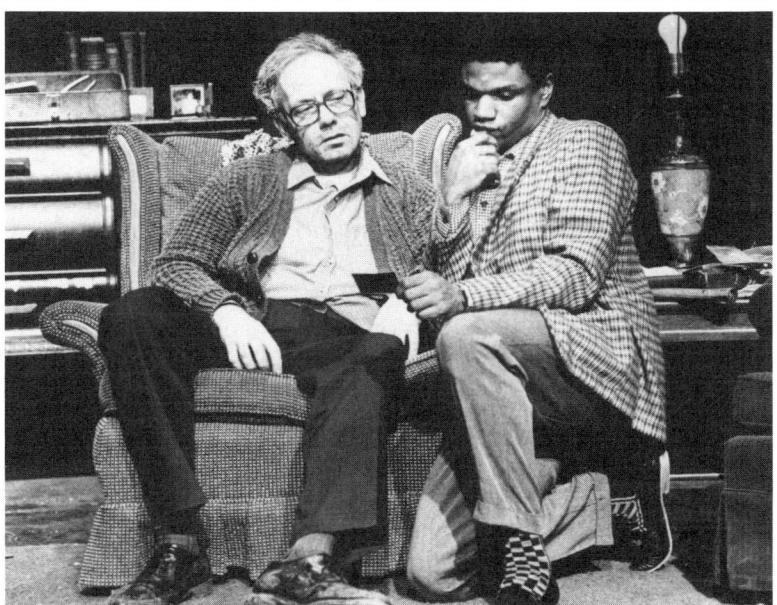

New works by Trenton or New Jersey playwrights, such as *In This Fallen City* by Bryan Williams, frequently are commissioned by Trenton's Passage Theatre Company. Photo: Andrea Kane.

three one-act plays, honored American working-class heroes. Many of this theater's works are commissioned from Trenton playwrights. The Passage Theatre Company made its debut with a production of *The Undoing*, a play by Trenton native and founding member William Mastrosimone. Perhaps Trenton's most famous dramatist, Mastrosimone wrote *Extremities*, which played on Broadway and then became a movie starring Farrah Fawcett. Though not restricted to Trenton subjects or playwrights, the company stages many works written by Trenton natives, or set in Trenton, or similar urban/multiethnic locales. *Essentials* told the story of a black woman running for political office in the Deep South. Passage presents three major projects (roughly twenty to twenty-two performances each) and several readings and workshops during its season, which runs from September through June.

Special Programs and Events: ◻ Lunchtime series of short plays performed during the weekday lunch hour; audience members are invited to bring a brown-bag lunch. ◻ Readings and workshops. ◻ *The*

THEATER

Madonna Project, an annual pageant, performed in both Italian and English as part of Trenton's Feast of Lights; it traces the history of that festival.

Educational Programs and Events: ☐ Classes at St. Joe's Reform School, Trenton, and the New Jersey School for the Arts, Trenton.

Playwrights Theatre of New Jersey 🎭 $ ♿ ⛔ ♿

33 Green Village Road, Madison 07040   201-514-1787 (administration), 201-514-1940 (box office)
Performance site: Playwrights Theatre of New Jersey (100 seats).

The Playwrights Theatre, founded in 1987 by Drew University theater arts department chairman and playwright Buzz McLaughlin, focuses on new play development and education. It brings a new play to life in three steps, giving it a reading, a staged reading, then a full production. Some plays never reach the full-production stage, others receive a final, polished premiere at Playwrights Theatre, a renovated school building in Madison. The Playwrights Theatre encourages playwriting not only among professionals but among students, the disabled, juvenile offenders, and prisoners. In 1987, it gave a staged reading of *Spine* by Bill C. Davis, an established dramatist and author of the Broadway play *Mass Appeal.* It recently presented a reading of *Come as You Are* by N. Richard Nash, author of *The Rainmaker.* The Playwrights Theatre cast recently opened in the new play Off Broadway.

The theater annually presents one fully staged production (twelve performances) and five staged readings (three performances each). An average of four or five actors and actresses appear in most productions. With the exception of the fully staged plays, productions are spare; staged readings emphasize the content of the play, not the set, which generally consists of modular boxes assembled to resemble doors, walls, and other architectural and decorative concepts. Producing artistic director McLaughlin tends to favor plays that offer insight into the human spirit, often realistic serious dramas and comedies. The Playwrights Theatre's main season runs from September through May. Staged readings and most festival productions are free of charge.

Special Programs and Events: ☐ The Madison Young Playwrights Festival (see Festivals). ☐ The New Jersey Young Playwrights Festival (see Festivals). ☐ The Playwrights Information Center, which provides information on the practical aspects of playwriting from submission procedures to production advice. ☐ Special Needs Playwriting Projects for

THEATER

The Trenton Muse

The seat of New Jersey's state government may not seem a likely spot for the dramatic muse, but a number of prominent contemporary playwrights have called that city home.

Ntozake Shange's play of poems, *For Colored Girls Who Have Considered Suicide, When the Rainbow Is Enuf* went to Broadway. So did William Mastrosimone's drama about a rape victim, *Extremities*, which later became a motion picture starring Farrah Fawcett.

Michael Cristofer's grueling Pulitzer Prize–winning drama, *The Shadow Box*, about a group of cancer patients in a hospice, also played on Broadway before becoming a television production starring Joanne Woodward. And Don Evans's play *A Lovesong for Miss Lydia*, which had its premiere at the Crossroads Theatre in New Brunswick, was produced by the Public Broadcasting System.

As a founding member of Trenton's downtown Passage Theatre Company, Mastrosimone devotes himself to keeping the city's theater world vibrant. A number of his plays, including *The Undoing*, set in nearby Chambersburg, have had their premieres here, and the theater regularly produces works by other area playwrights.

---

the handicapped (at Cheshire Home, Florham Park), substance abusers, and prisoners.

Educational Programs and Events: ☐ Gifted and talented play-writing symposia. ☐ Playwriting workshops at all levels for adults. ☐ Playwriting for Teachers. ☐ Playwriting In-The-Schools.

Renegade Theater Company (DAO 1989) ♿ $

P.O. Box M109, Hoboken 07030   201-798-6860 (administration), 201-659-1480 (box office)
Performance sites: various locations in Hoboken.

New American plays, some by New Jersey playwrights, are a specialty at the Renegade Theater Company, which employs a regular ensemble of twelve to fifteen actors and actresses. The New Jersey filmmaker John Sayles sits on the company's advisory board, and Renegade performed a one-act play by Sayles during one of its festivals. It has also staged David Mamet's children's play *Revenge of the Space Pandas*. Founded in 1985 by a group of actors and actresses (some of whom had taken the same New York City acting class), the Renegade Theater

THEATER

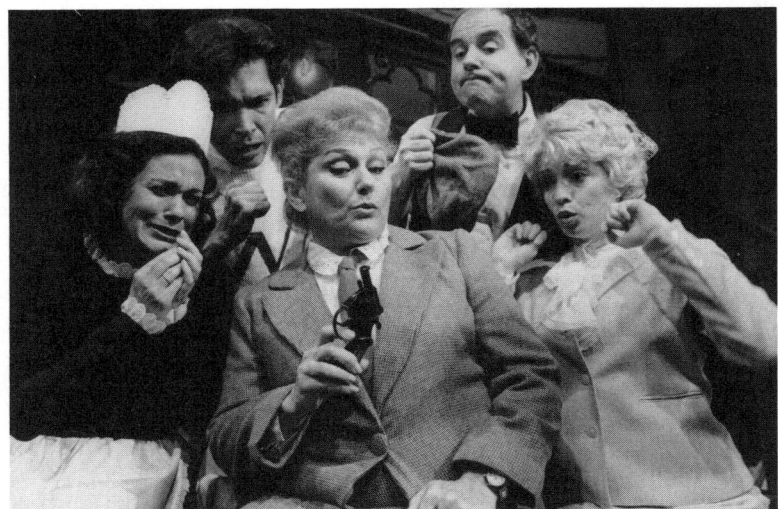

A smoking gun was at the heart of the action in the South Jersey Regional Theatre's 1988–1989 musical murder mystery *Something's Afoot*.

Company presents two to three mainstage productions annually, each usually featuring between two and five actors and actresses and being given fifteen performances. The company works with a resident composer, whose music accompanies some productions.

Special Programs and Events: □ Annual One-Act Play Festival, during which new plays are performed together for four weeks in April and May. □ New play workshops/laboratories. □ Writers series consisting of occasional public play readings.

South Jersey Regional Theatre 🐕 $ ♿ 🚻

Bay Avenue, Somers Point 08244
Performance site: The South Jersey Regional Theatre (300 seats).

The South Jersey Regional Theatre, founded in 1977, is the only professional, full-season (September through June) theater company in southern New Jersey. Each of its seasons generally includes a comedy, a classic, a musical, and, often, a mystery. While emphasizing theater productions, the South Jersey Regional Theatre's long-range plan is to become a multidisciplinary performing arts center; it offers four jazz

THEATER

"Before interviewing farm families for our show about New Jersey farm life, most of the actors held certain stereotypes about farmers. Like most people, we assumed that the farmers we would talk to wouldn't be interested or knowledgeable about the arts, would be uneducated, unfashionable, and probably unsophisticated. In short, we assumed farmers had nothing in common with actors. Much to our delight, we met farm families that boasted members who had two or more advanced degrees, were opera buffs or studying acting, were practicing professional artists and craftsmen and who exhibited the very latest fashion in clothing and interior design."—Carolyn O'Donnell, Producing Artistic Director, Stageworks Touring Company

and two classical concerts annually and hosts art exhibits. The theater produces six plays during its main season, usually presenting about thirteen performances of each. An average of four performers are cast in each production.

Special Program: ◻ Performances for groups of disabled persons brought to the theater under grants.

Educational Programs: ◻ Equity membership candidate intern program offers classes in technical theater and stage management. ◻ Outreach workshops for southern New Jersey schools.

Stageworks Touring Company $
Speech/Theatre/Dance Department, Glassboro State College,
Glassboro 08028   609-863-7150
Performance sites: in residence at Glassboro State College Campus and on tours of the tri-state area.

Founded in 1979 by actress and Glassboro State professor of theater Carolyn O'Donnell, this non-Equity, professional company first produced mime shows. In 1986, it presented its first original play, based on the history of Gloucester County. It continues to find drama in New Jersey history and personalities; it develops original plays based on oral history, regional history, and folklore. In 1988–1989, the company toured the state with a production of *For Goodness Sake,* based on oral histories of seventy-five modern-day New Jersey farm families. Stageworks emphasizes plays about New Jersey; and it produces works geared toward minority and ethnic populations.

THEATER

Stageworks reaches audiences who rarely travel to urban theater centers. A new production based on regional and oral history and folklore is mounted every two years; the company plans to present shortly a work about a family in the Pinelands. Stageworks maintains a short resident season on the Glassboro campus, staging two productions (about five performances each) in the winter and the fall. When not on campus, it tours with five productions, presenting about thirty-five performances annually. Two one-act plays, one about domestic violence and date rape, the other about drug and alcohol abuse, recently were commissioned from Glassboro professor and playwright Toni Libro. An average of three or four actors appear in each production; a corps of regular actors and actresses appear play after play.

Educational Program: ☐ Stage One Theatre School.

Whole Theatre (DAO 1987)
544 Bloomfield Avenue, Montclair 07042   201-744-2996
(administration)

Olympia Dukakis, Whole Theatre's producing artistic director, gained national prominence when she won an Oscar for her performance in the movie *Moonstruck*. Yet Dukakis had been a star in Montclair for a long time; she was one of a group of actors and actresses who left New York and founded Whole Theatre in 1973. She and the theater usually steered clear of the traditional in favor of taking theatrical risks. For instance, the 1989–1990 season included a *King Lear* with feminist overtones that examined the theme of male tyranny.

During the 1989–1990 season, citing "severe financial difficulties," Whole Theatre closed its doors. Although there is scant hope for the theater's revival, several of its educational programs, featuring Whole Theater artists, may continue to serve New Jersey teachers and students under a different name.

Whole Theatre presented its first play in a Montclair church; then moved to its own small downtown theater. It developed many new plays, but also presented American and European classics. Each play was cast individually; artistic director Dukakis often drew on a regular corps of

---

"Any cutback is a setback. We are very fragile, we cultural institutions, whether big or small."—Samuel Miller, speaking at the 1990 Congress of Artpride, the New Jersey arts advocacy organization

actors and actresses as well as directors and set designers. Whole Theatre cast many prominent actors and actresses over the years, from Linda Hunt to Jose Ferrer.

Special Programs and Events: □ Arts workshops for special populations from the gifted and talented to urban children. □ "The Gathering," a support group for women writers. □ Staged reading series.

Educational Programs and Events: □ Outreach Programs: teacher development and other programs for elementary and secondary, and college students. □ Theatre School, classes for young people and adults.

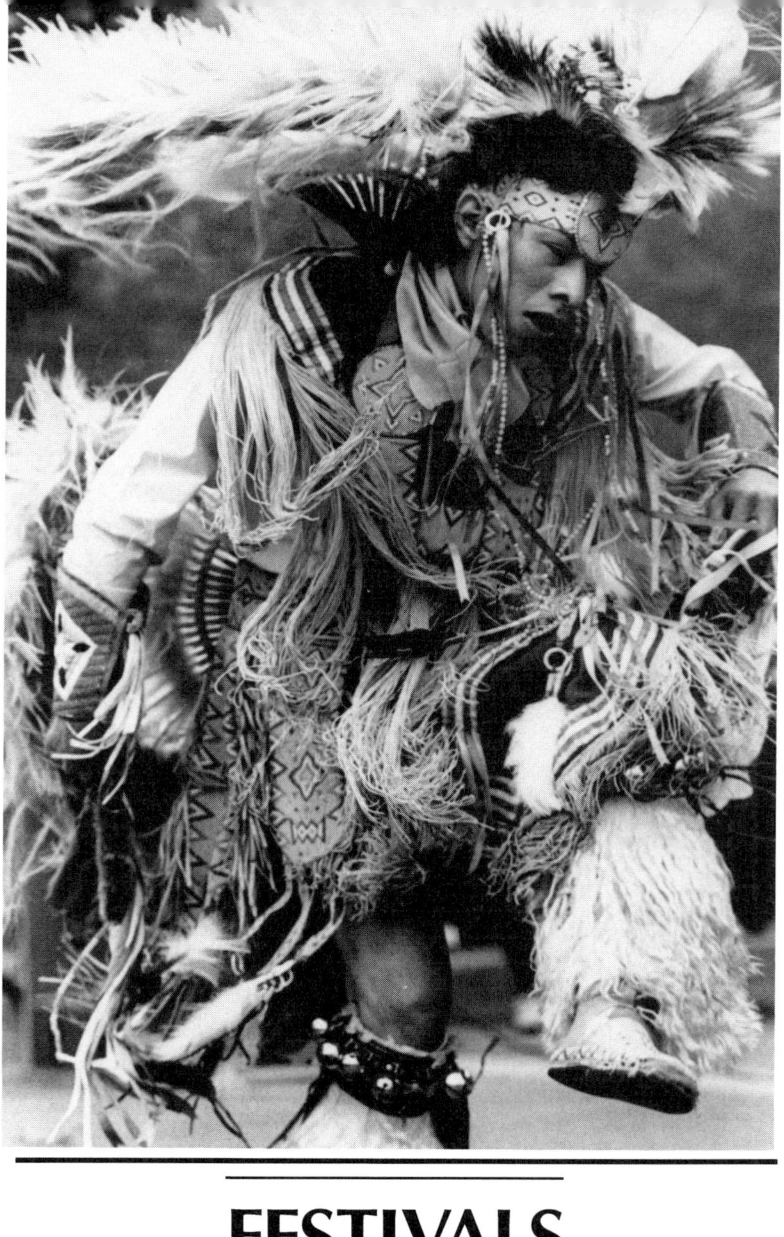

FESTIVALS

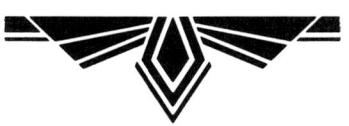

Overleaf: Native American dancers appear each year as part of the Powhatan-Renape Nation's American Indian Arts Festival.

FESTIVALS

Allaire Crafts Fair 🎭🎨
c/o Crafts Coordinator, New Jersey State Council on the Arts, 109 West State Street, CN 306, Trenton 08625   609-292-6130
Held: annually in July
Location: Allaire State Park, Wall Township.

This juried outdoor craft show, with about one hundred exhibitors, takes place in a historic setting. It features sales and demonstrations of crafts of all kinds, from fiber art, to woodcarving, stained glass work, potting, and glass blowing.

American Indian Arts Festival 💲🎭🎨
Powhatan Renape Nation, Rankokus Indian Reservation, P.O. Box 225, Rankokus 08073   609-261-4747
Held: annually in October; the first day is youth day, for schoolchildren only
Location: the Indian Reservation, Rankokus Road, near Mt. Holly.

At least one hundred artists—flutists, hoop dancers, war dancers, sand painters, jewelers, potters, weavers, and sculptors—demonstrate their talents at this juried festival, which its organizers consider the largest Indian arts exhibit east of Santa Fe. Now in its eighth year, the Indian Arts Festival is hosted by the Powhatan Renape Nation, one of the oldest Indian nations in North America.

Arts in Education Showcase 💲🎨
c/o Arts Council of the Essex Area, Montclair State College, Upper Montclair 07043   201-744-1717
Held: annually in September or October
Location: Montclair State College, Upper Montclair.

This showcase displays the work of theater, dance, and other organizations that produce fine arts and performing arts programs for school audiences. Each group presents a twenty-minute overview of its program. The showcase also includes arts-in-education exhibitions, featuring study guides, aids, and other arts-in-education materials. It is cosponsored by the Office of Cultural Programming, School of Fine and Performing Arts, Montclair State College.

Barbershop Festival of Champions 💲🎭
Great Auditorium, Ocean Grove 07756   201-775-0035
Held: annually in August
Location: Great Auditorium, Ocean Grove.

FESTIVALS

This festival features performances by barbershop singing champions from up and down the East Coast.

Black Maria Film and Video Festival (DAO 1987) $⃞ ♫⃞
c/o The Thomas A. Edison National Historic Site, Main Street and Lakeside Avenue, West Orange 07052   201-736-0796
Held: annually in the winter/spring season
Location: at colleges, libraries, performing arts centers, and other sites across the state and country.

Inspired by Thomas A. Edison's inventive spirit and his experiments with film in his studio/shed called Black Maria, this film festival exhibits winning film and video entries by independent media artists from across the country and abroad.

Capital Music Festival 🌲
Composers Guild of New Jersey (see also Music)
202 Central Avenue, Ship Bottom 08008
Held: annually, October through May
Location: New Jersey State Museum and other sites.

This festival highlights the works of contemporary New Jersey composers, performed for the most part by the New Jersey instrumental and vocal groups. Classical music by composers such as Mozart and Bach is also included.

Center Space Dance Series
c/o The New Jersey Center for the Performing Arts
18 Divison Street, Somerville 08876   201-526-6074
Held: annually during ten weekends from October to May
Location: Somerset County Vocational and Technical High School, Bridgewater.

These dance weekends feature informal showings of works by New Jersey dancers and choreographers.

Dance Sampler 🌲
c/o New Jersey Dance Alliance, 18 Davenport Street, Somerville 08876   201-526-6074
Held: annually in April
Location: indoor and outdoor Trenton locations, including the State

FESTIVALS

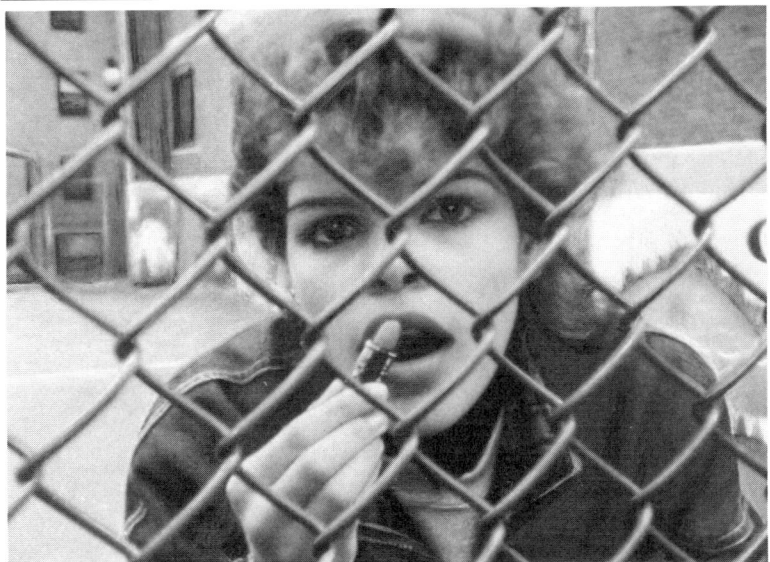

"Pinky" is a character in Kate Davis's *Girltalk*, one of the works by independent filmmakers presented during the annual Black Maria Film Festival.

House Annex Lawn, historic Mill Hill Playhouse, and New Jersey State Museum stage and sculpture garden.

Sponsored by the New Jersey Dance Alliance, the sampler presents a day of performances by New Jersey dancers and dance companies and features New Jersey choreographers.

Dodge Poetry Festival $ 🎨 👤

The Geraldine R. Dodge Foundation, 95 Madison Avenue, Morristown 07960   201-540-8442
Held: annually in October
Location: Waterloo Village, Stanhope.

This festival, sponsored by the Poetry Program of the Geraldine R. Dodge Foundation, is a three-day event featuring readings by a number of prominent poets, such as Allen Ginsberg, Joyce Carol Oates, Octavio Paz, and Robert Bly. It also includes workshops for teachers and high school students.

FESTIVALS

Hollybush Festival (see Music)

Jazz It Up
c/o William Paterson College, Jazz Studies and Performance Program, Wayne 07470   201-595-2268
Held: annually in spring
Location: Willowbrook Mall, Wayne.

This festival offers performances by internationally known jazz musicians and members of the William Paterson College jazz program, including bassist Rufus Reid and William Paterson College's Latin Jazz Ensemble and Big Band, led by keyboard player Chico Mendoza.

June Opera Festival (see Music)

Madison Young Playwrights Festival [$][🏛]
The Playwrights Theatre of New Jersey, 33 Green Village Road, Madison 07940   201-514-1940
Held: annually in March
Location: The Playwrights Theatre

This festival presents performances of plays about growing up, written by young people ages ten to seventeen. Recent productions have included *You'll Get Grandma's Biscuits,* by a ten-year-old, and *Route to The Problem,* by an eighteen-year-old.

Mediamix Media Arts Festival [$]
P.O. Box 1623, New Brunswick 08903   201-249-9623 or 201-249-1375
Held: annually from September through April
Location: hosted by the Rutgers University Film Co-op and Rutgers University Libraries Media Services at various Rutgers, New Brunswick, locations.

This festival presents visiting film and video artists and classic and avant-garde films and videos, including rarely shown works by François Truffaut, Werner Herzog, Orson Welles, and Stanley Kubrick.

New Jersey Teen Arts Festival [🏛]
New Jersey State Teen Arts Program
841 Georges Road, North Brunswick 08902   201-745-3898
Held: annually in May and June

FESTIVALS

First in Film

America's motion picture industry was born not in Hollywood but in northern New Jersey. In his workshop in West Orange, Thomas Edison and a lab assistant, W.K.L. Dickson, developed the first American moving picture in a dark shed called Black Maria. The Edison Company operated the nation's first film studio. Edison began his work with the idea that he could invent a machine that "would do for the eye what the phonograph does for the ear." How could he make photographs move? Edison and his helper devised a camera called a kinetoscope and film strips that, when run over moving wheels, played back the "moving pictures." The first motion picture actors and actresses were none other than Edison lab assistants, clowning for the camera. Eventually the studio raised its creative standards, developing and recording the first real movies: *Day in the Life of a Fireman* and *The Great Train Robbery*.

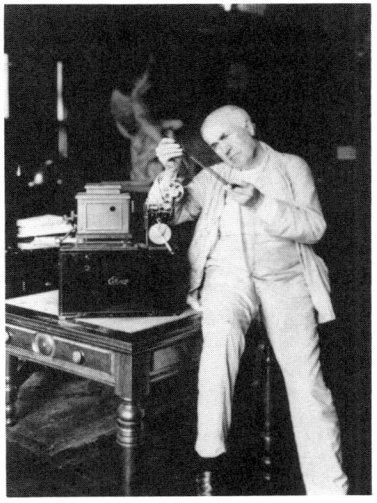

As the medium gained sophistication, the film industry moved from West Orange to Fort Lee, which became the headquarters for nearly twenty companies and seven studios in the early years of the twentieth century, including those operated by legends such as Fox, Goldwyn, and Selznick. Many silent film stars, including Mary Pickford, began their careers not in California, but on the Palisades bluffs overlooking the Big Apple. Today, the Thomas A. Edison Media Consortium, in the spirit of Edison's first experiments, sponsors the annual Black Maria Film and Video Festival.

Location: individual county festivals at sites in each of twenty-one counties, and during the State Teen Arts Festival at the Mason Gross School of the Arts, Douglass Campus, Rutgers, The State University, New Brunswick.

During this festival, New Jersey teenagers share creative impulses and insights with professionals while experimenting with various media and methods in the visual arts, writing, film and video, dance, music, and

FESTIVALS

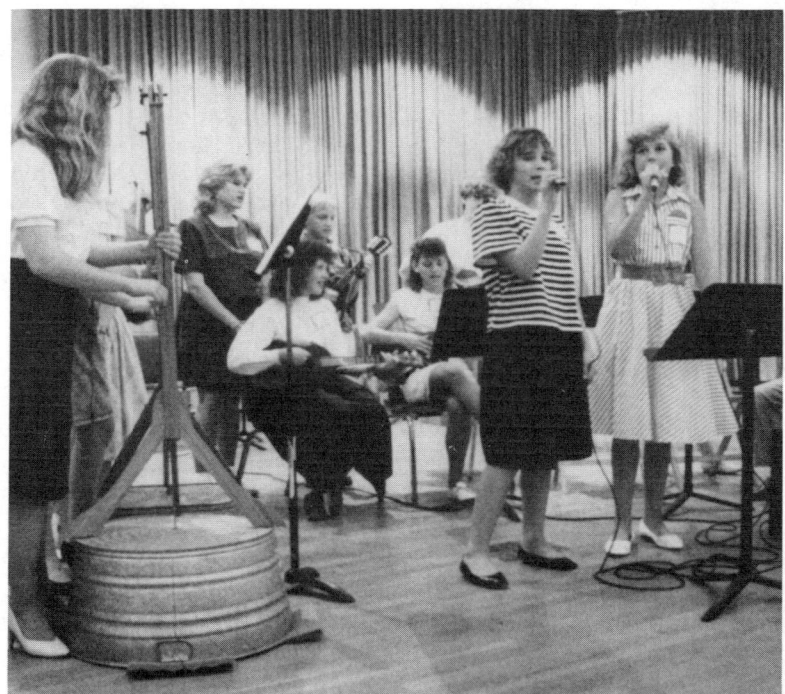

The Alloway Folk Singers from Salem County perform on country-style instruments, including a washtub, during the New Jersey State Teen Arts Festival.

drama. The state festival includes workshops on subjects from electronic music to tap dancing to medical/scientific illustration. Two works of art from each county festival are selected by judges to be exhibited as part of a Visual Arts Touring Exhibit that travels statewide.

New Jersey Video and Film Festival [$]
Media Works, P.O. Box 1716, Newark 07101   201-690-5474
Held: annually and judged in June; showcase tour of twelve winning entries travels the state throughout the year.
Location: Symphony Hall, Newark, and at libraries, universities, and other locations throughout the state.

Sponsored by Media Works, the Newark-based media arts organization, this festival presents films that were made by New Jersey artists, are about New Jersey subjects, or were shot mainly in the state. The works are judged in June, and the twelve winning films are featured in showcase screenings at various locations around New Jersey.

New Jersey Young Film and Video Makers Festival $ 👤

Thomas A. Edison Media Arts Consortium, Main Street and Lakeside Avenue, West Orange 07052   201-736-0796
Held: annually in May
Location: galleries and auditoriums across the state.

Administered by the Thomas A. Edison Media Consortium, in collaboration with the New Jersey Institute of Technology, this festival showcases prize-winning entries by young, independent New Jersey film and video makers, and junior high, high school, and college students.

New Jersey Young Playwrights Festival $ 👤

c/o Playwrights Theatre of New Jersey, 33 Green Village Road, Madison 07940   201-514-1787
Held: annually in May
Location: State Theater, New Brunswick.

Cosponsored by the New Jersey State Teen Arts Program and the Playwrights Theatre of New Jersey, this festival features professionally staged readings of plays by young playwrights, ages thirteen through nineteen. Fifteen finalists and six winners are chosen from as many as two hundred entries in an annual statewide competition. Recent prize winners include *Donuts and Muffins: Or The State of the Adolescent Today,* stories about a young girl's efforts to "fit in," and *Old and New Reflections of Things Past,* a girl's recollections of her grandmother.

Newark Black Film Festival 👤

c/o The Newark Museum, P.O. Box 540, Newark 07101
201-596-6550
Held: annually during June and July
Location: Symphony Hall or the New Jersey Institute of Technology, Newark.

Every year The Newark Black Film Festival presents between eighteen and twenty films by black filmmakers or on black subjects. It is cosponsored by the Newark Museum, the New Jersey Institute of Technology, the Newark Public Library, Symphony Hall, and Rutgers, The State University, Newark. The festival, begun in 1974, shows new and old films, such as *Yeelen* by a filmmaker from Mali and *Princess Tam Tam*, a 1935 film starring the legendary entertainer Josephine Baker. The Paul Robeson Awards Competition, held every second year, awards prizes to young filmmakers.

Obon Festival
Seabrook Buddhist Temple, P.O. Box 5036, Seabrook 08302
609-455-5488 or 609-451-3427
Held: annually in July
Location: Seabrook Buddhist Temple.

Sponsored by the Seabrook Buddhist Temple, this festival features Japanese drummers, crafts demonstrations, and folk dancers in native costume.

Oktoberfest
New Brunswick Oktoberfest Committee,
P.O. Box 68, North Brunswick 08902   201-545-0026
Held: annually in October.
Location: Indoor and outdoor sites in New Brunswick.

An arts and ethnic celebration, the Oktoberfest has presented performances by Chinese and Hispanic dance troupes and by members of some of the state's best-known performing arts groups, including the Shoestring Players and the Princeton Ballet. In 1989, members of the ballet performed a jazz work commissioned by Oktoberfest Committee.

Onstage in New Jersey
The Carter G. Woodson Foundation, P.O. Box 1025, 69 Lincoln Park, Newark 07101   201-242-0500
Held: annually from April through May.
Location: theaters and community auditoriums in Newark, Camden, Trenton, Paterson, and Montclair.

Prominent black poets, essayists, vocalists, and dance and music ensembles perform during the series that make up Onstage in New Jersey, sponsored by the Carter G. Woodson Foundation.

Peters Valley Summer Craft Fair $ ⚘
Route 615, Layton 07851   201-948-5200
Held: annually in July.
Location: Peters Valley Crafts Center, Layton.

From Foreign Lands

New Jersey's arts scene has long been enriched by the contributions of people from foreign lands.

German singing groups thrived in the 1880s; in 1987, the United Singers, an association of amateur German-language singing groups, celebrated its one hundredth anniversary in Newark.

The state has spawned at least two Irish theater companies: the Celtic Theatre Company and the Gaelic Theatre Company.

Rutgers University's long ties to the Japanese (the first Japanese exchange students were graduated from that school in 1870) resulted in the founding of the International Center for Japonisme at the Jane Voorhees Zimmerli Art Museum, where scholars study the influence of Japanese art and culture on the Western world. In the southern New Jersey town of Seabrook, residents of Japanese descent annually host a Japanese arts showcase called the Obon Festival.

Mexican dancers and musicians perform every June in the Pine Barrens to commemorate the Mexican pilot Emilio Carranza, who crashed there during a goodwill flight from New York to Mexico City in 1922.

More than one-hundred-thirty craftspeople display their work during this juried exhibition and fair, held in a nineteenth-century village in the Delaware Water Gap Recreational Area.

Shore Festival of Classics [$][⚑][⚑]

Ocean Grove Camp Meeting Association, Ocean Grove 07756
201-775-0035
Held: annually in July
Location: Civic Auditorium.

This festival, set in a national historic site, encompasses classical and new music performed by the Festival Orchestra, a professional, union orchestra assembled for the festival, and guest artists. The festival also includes lecture/tours of local points of interest an hour before each performance. (Ocean Grove, a seaside community established as a Methodist summer tent community in 1869, is known for its Victorian architecture.) The festival also presents guest conductors and composers, who discuss their work with the audience during pre-concert "Meet the Composer" sessions.

FESTIVALS

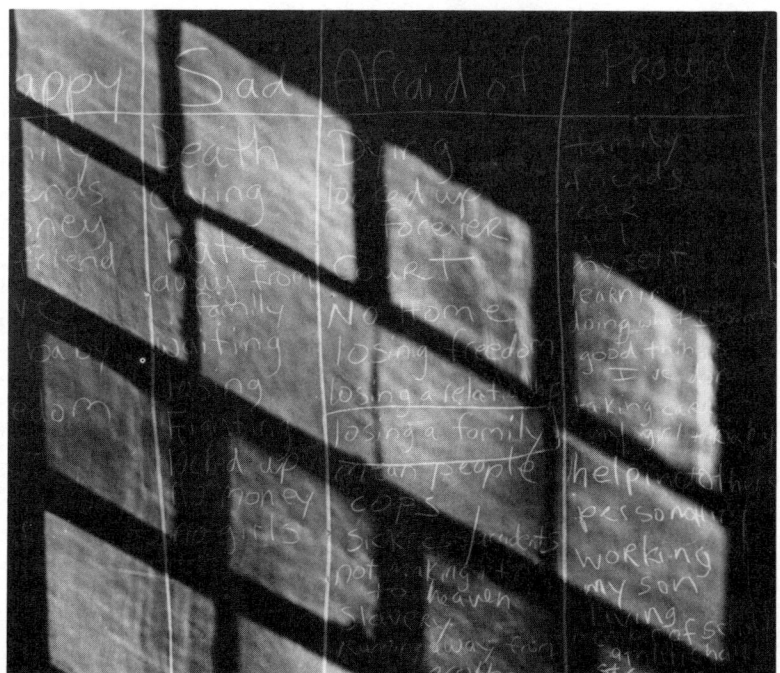

"What makes you ... happy, sad, afraid, proud?" Exploring the emotions through playwriting is one goal of the Playwrights Theatre of New Jersey's Special Needs Playwriting Festivals, which reach out to the disabled, prisoners, and substance abusers. Photo: Warren Salowe.

Special Needs Young Playwrights Festivals

Playwrights Theatre of New Jersey, 35 Green Village Road, Madison 07904   201-514-1787
Held: annually from September to June
Location: at Playwrights Theatre, Madison, and at various residential correctional facilities.

Sponsored by the Playwrights Theatre of New Jersey in association with the New Jersey Department of Corrections, Division of Juvenile Services, the festivals present plays written by juvenile offenders who are residents of correctional facilities and who have been appointed to the program by New Jersey Family Court judges. As many as ten to twelve plays are written for each festival, then presented in staged readings by professional directors, actors and actresses. Most readings are open, free of charge, to the public.

SummerFest $

Rutgers, The State University, University Arts Services, Mason Gross School of the Arts, New Brunswick 08903   201-932-7591
Held: annually in June, July, and August
Location: Rutgers New Brunswick campus.

One of the state's longest and most comprehensive summer festivals, SummerFest presents more than fifty performances of dance, music, and drama as well as visual arts exhibits, by New Jersey artists and companies and internationally known artists.

Super Mediamix U.S. 8 Contest and Film Festival $

c/o Mediamix, Inc., P.O. Box 1623, New Brunswick 08903
201-249-9623 or 201-249-1375
Held: annually
Location: tours the northwestern United States, with screenings at the Melody Cafe and Rutgers, New Brunswick.

Devoted to the dying art of the Super 8 millimeter film, this festival presents short (generally under thirty minutes), color or black and white, sound or silent works by experimental filmmakers from throughout the Northeast. The program features winning entries in Mediamix's contest, with such titles as "Flammable," "Avian Moves," "From Romance to Ritual," and "Italian Places." This touring festival is cosponsored by Mediamix of New Brunswick and the International Center for 8 Millimeter Film and Video of Somerville, Massachusetts.

Victorian Week $ 🎭
The Mid-Atlantic Center for the Arts
1048 Washington Street, P.O. Box 340, Cape May 08204
609-884-5404
Held: annually in October
Location: throughout Cape May.

Victorian Week, held in the national historic landmark town of Cape May, includes live Victorian theater and music, a stained glass tour, architectural and decorative arts exhibits, a costume ball, and vaudeville performances.

FESTIVALS

EQUITY SUMMER THEATER COMPANIES

Levin Theater Company
  Rutgers Arts Center, Rutgers, The State University, New Brunswick 08903   201-932-9892 (Rutgers Arts Ticket Office)

Stageworks/Summit
  Summer Theater, Kent Place School, Summit 07901   201-273-9383

Summerfun
  Weiss Arts Center, Montclair Kimberley Academy, Lloyd Road, Montclair 07042   201-256-0576

Theatrefest
  Montclair State College, Upper Montclair 07043   201-893-5112

Waterloo at Princeton $ 🎭
Waterloo Festival School of Music

Waterloo Foundation for the Arts, Inc., Village of Waterloo, Stanhope 07874   201-347-0900 (administration), 201-347-4700 (box office)
Held: annually during June and July
Location: Village of Waterloo, Stanhope, and Richardson Auditorium, Princeton University.

This June/July festival presents performances by the Waterloo Festival Orchestra and ensembles composed of fellows and faculty members from the Waterloo Festival School of Music. A six-week training program for young musicians aiming for professional careers (see Education and the Arts), the school is headquartered at Princeton University. Faculty chamber ensembles perform at the university's Richardson Auditorium on Friday nights, and the full orchestra performs every Saturday night at Waterloo Village. The programs often include performances by guest artists and soloists such as flutist Jean-Pierre Rampal. While chamber music concerts always open with the music of Bach, the orchestra performs works by American and rarely heard, prominent twentieth-century composers.

Waterloo Festival of the Arts $ 🎭

Waterloo Foundation for the Arts, Inc., Village of Waterloo, Stanhope 07874   201-347-0900 (administration), 201-347-4700 (box office)
Held: annually from June through September
Location: Waterloo Village.

FESTIVALS

The Waterloo Festival of the Arts is a summer-long event that encompasses Saturday night performances by the Waterloo Festival Orchestra (see Waterloo Festival School of Music—Education and the Arts) in addition to a popular music series featuring performances by folk, rock, jazz, and country stars such as Pete Seeger, Elvis Costello, James Taylor, and Willie Nelson.

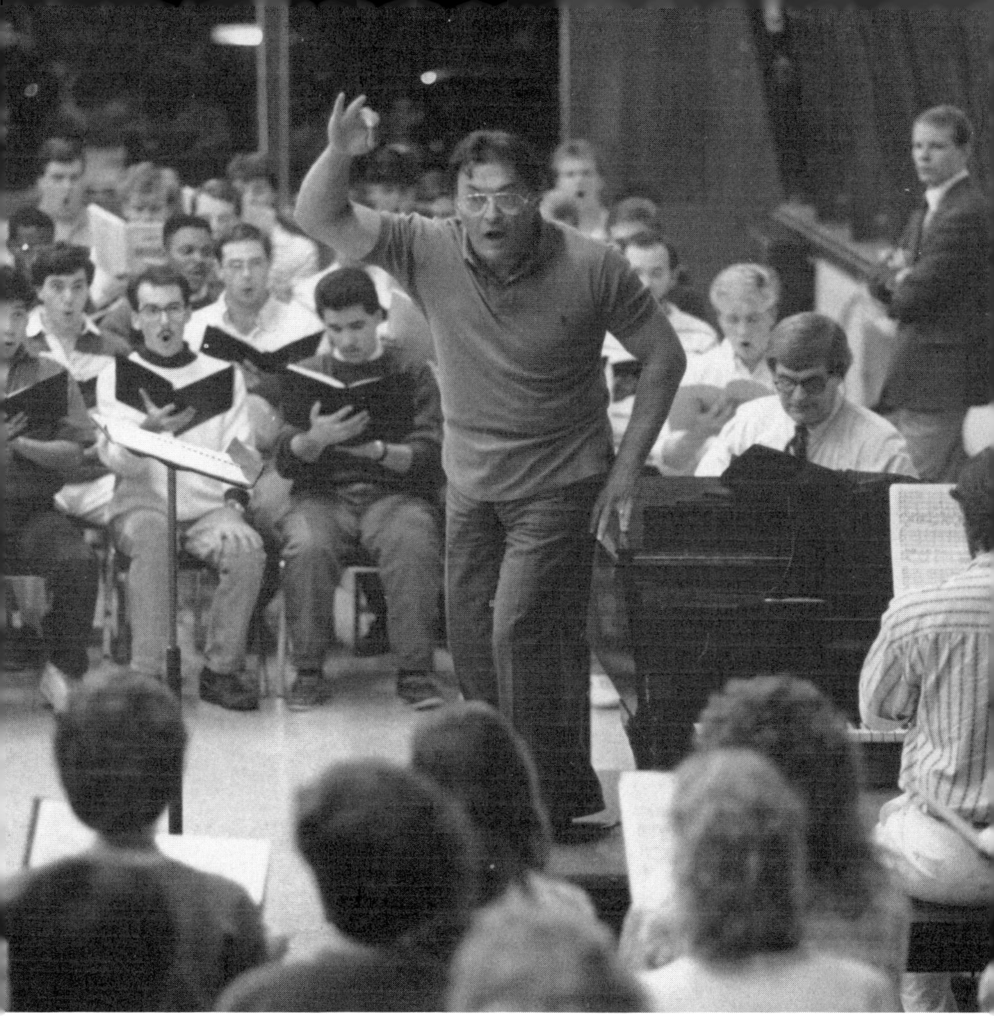

EDUCATION AND THE ARTS

Overleaf: Zubin Mehta, former music director of the New York Philharmonic, conducts the Westminster Symphonic Choir at Westminster Choir College during a rehearsal for a performance in honor of Leonard Bernstein's seventieth birthday at Carnegie Hall. Photo: Lawrence French.

EDUCATION AND THE ARTS

American Boychoir School (MIO, DAO 1988, 1989, 1990) 🚹
19 Lambert Drive, Princeton 08540   609-924-5858
Performance sites: The American Boychoir School and auditoriums on national and international tours.

The American Boychoir has performed and recorded in many of the world's most prestigious concert halls with leading conductors and orchestras. In 1988, for example, the choir performed at Carnegie Hall with Zubin Mehta and the New York Philharmonic, in honor of Leonard Bernstein's seventieth birthday. In addition to classics, the choir sings contemporary works commissioned for the choir from composers such as Ned Rorem and Milton Babbitt. American Boychoir soloists have appeared in productions of Andrew Lloyd Weber's *Requiem* and Bernstein's *Chichester Psalms*.

Inspired by the famous Vienna Boys' Choir School, the Kiwanis Club of Columbus, Ohio, founded the American Boychoir School under the name the Columbus Boychoir School in 1937. To be nearer to New York City, the school moved to Princeton in 1950, and in 1980, to reflect its national stature, changed its name and became American Boychoir School. The school enrolls boys ages seven to fourteen in its academic and performance programs.

Special Programs: □ Christmas performances in Princeton and Trenton; annual.

Educational Program: □ Albemarle, a summer music camp for boys and girls seven to fourteen.

Artist/Teacher Institute [$]
New Jersey State Council on the Arts, Four North Broad Street, CN 306, Trenton 08625   609-292-6130

The only residential program of its kind in the state, the ten-year-old Artist/Teacher Institute, sponsored by the New Jersey State Council on the Arts, brings teachers and members of the general public together with professional artists for ten days of arts workshops on subjects from poetry writing to opera, dance, and jazz. Open to anyone interested in the arts, this enrichment program is held annually at Stockton State College. Between one-hundred-thirty and one-hundred-fifty enroll in the institute, which includes daytime workshops with professional artists and evening performances by well-known performing artists from New Jersey and elsewhere.

"In 1988 The American Boychoir performed and recorded Charles Davidson's 'I Never Saw Another Butterfly' with the American Symphony Orchestra. A musical setting of poems written by children at the Terezin concentration camp, the work evokes the strength of the human spirit. After the choir finished rehearsal one afternoon, one young member pulled me aside and said, 'Mr. Litton, this could be the most important thing I've ever done in my life.'"—James Litton, Conductor, American Boychoir

Artists-in-Education
New Jersey State Council on the Arts, 109 West State Street, Trenton 08625   609-292-6130

A project of the State Council on the Arts, this program, which began more than twenty years ago, places working artists in classrooms (kindergarten through high school) in more than one hundred schools statewide. Dancers, architects, painters, storytellers, jazz musicians, and mime artists all work with teachers, helping students to understand a particular art form.

Arts-in-Education Showcase (see Festivals)

Arts Foundation of New Jersey
P.O. Box 352, New Brunswick 08903   201-463-3640

Founded in 1982 by Jacque Rubel, who also founded the New Jersey Teen Arts Program (see separate listing), the Arts Foundation presents programs that bring the public, teachers, and students together with professional artists to explore the arts. The foundation also sponsors conferences on arts-in-education issues. Its New Jersey Summer Arts Institute, held on Rutger's Livingston campus, enrolls students (selected through auditions) and offers them intensive training in one of several majors, including voice, instrumental, dance, visual arts, writing, theater, "interarts"—an examination of the creative process—and art and technology.

The foundation provides a service that matches clients with professional artists for performances and workshops in schools, corporate headquarters, malls, and festivals. In addition, it presents an annual performing arts series and sponsors two intensive arts training programs: the New Jersey Summer Arts Institute for middle and high school students and the Leonardo Teacher Institute.

Special Programs and Events: ☐ Professional artists placement program. ☐ Professional Artists Series, four-week performing arts series in July at Rutgers's Livingston campus.

Educational Programs and Events: ☐ Annual New Jersey Summer Arts Institute, a five-week, residential multidisciplinary program for middle and high school students. ☐ Leonardo Teacher Institute, a four-week, residential multidisciplinary fellowship program for teachers, conducted by Rutgers faculty members; annual.

ArtsPower $&♿♀

P.O. Box 9123, Paramus 07653   201-368-8486
Performance sites: on tour in eastern, southern, and midwestern school, theater, and community auditoriums.

Founded in 1985 by twin brothers and musicians Mark and Gary Blackman, ArtsPower develops theatrical and musical programs for school audiences. Its production *Four Score and Seven Years Ago* is a one-hour original musical based on the battle of Gettysburg and performed by an Equity company. ArtsPower also presents a number of performing arts ensembles in schools and community centers, such as Horns O'Plenty, a brass quartet, Journey into Jazz, a jazz quartet, Growin' up Drummin', a percussion trio, and Asian Dance Garden, a Chinese/modern dance troupe. ArtsPower study guides suggest discussion subjects, activities, recordings, and other resources for teachers. The organization gives between two hundred and three hundred performances annually.

Special Programs and Events: ☐ Interactive programs geared toward the disabled.

Educational Programs and Events: ☐ Band and choral clinic. ☐ Creative dramatics workshops. ☐ Instrumental and vocal workshops.

Artworks (see Visual Arts)

Cameo Productions, Ltd. $&♿♀

24 Lakeview Road, Sparta 07871   201-729-5524
Performance sites: schools in Sussex and Warren counties and on nationwide tours.

EDUCATION AND THE ARTS

Cameo Productions produces programs that are educational, not only for students but also for general audiences. For instance, it recently re-created the 1796 play *The Archers* by eighteenth-century New Jersey playwright and theater historian William Dunlop. Dedicated to reviving great moments in musical theater from all eras and both sides of the Atlantic, Cameo Productions repertoire includes *Musical Brittania,* a look at more than three hundred years of British musical theater history, and *Musical America,* a review of legendary American theater works and performers.

Special Program: □ Performances for the disabled and aged at the Garden State Arts Center.

Educational Programs and Events: □ In-school performances. □ Master classes.

> "Art has always flourished only where it is asked to flourish, and if we wish for a renaissance of art in America, we must be students and patrons."—John Cotton Dana, founder and director of the Newark Museum and one of the nation's leading proponents of arts education, speaking in 1914

Camerata Opera Theater $ 🏛

1006 Kingston Drive, Cherry Hill 08034   609-428-7999
Performance sites: in schools and senior citizens centers throughout New Jersey and eastern Pennsylvania.

The Camerata Opera Theater was founded in 1973 by Rita Dreyfus, a mezzo-soprano who trained at the New England Conservatory and wanted to bring more opera opportunities—for singers and audiences—to New Jersey. It travels to sites all over the state, giving as many as sixty-five performances of six productions during its October-through-June season. It considers itself a training company for young singers from some of the major music schools in New York and Philadelphia. All performances are in English and have been cut to fifty minutes to hold the attention of young and old audiences. Camerata's repertoire includes classics such as Puccini's *Madam Butterfly,* Bizet's *Carmen,* and Humperdinck's *Hansel and Gretel.* In addition, there is *Opera Antipasto,* sing-along opera revue, composed of well-known arias. The company recently staged a world premiere of *Joringel and the Songflower* by the New Jersey-born composer Margaret Garwood. Camerata takes a traditional but spare approach to opera; singers are accompanied by a pianist. The company tries to include students in each performance. Between five and eight professional singers appear in each production.

Educational Programs and Events: ☐ Lectures on opera, voice, and production in connection with performances. ☐ Opportunities for schoolchildren to participate by appearing on stage as gypsies, shepherds, and other extras.

Carter G. Woodson Foundation

P.O. Box 1025, 69 Lincoln Park, Newark 07101   201-242-0500
Performance sites: elementary and secondary schools, theaters, and community auditoriums throughout the state.

A resource for general audiences and school audiences, the Carter G. Woodson Foundation presents Afro-American performers and produces educational programs on Afro-American culture and history. In addition to its Artists-in-the-Schools program, it sponsors a national touring program for black performing arts soloists and ensembles, poets, writers, and speakers and an annual performing arts series featuring black artists (see Onstage in New Jersey—Festivals). This organization takes a multidisciplinary approach; for instance, its Artists-in-the-Schools program begins by placing two books on a given subject, such as Paul Robeson, in a school library for study. A related essay contest, musical performance, or film or slide show may follow. The foundation also arranges for black artists to perform during assembly programs.

Special Programs and Events: ☐ Black Culture on Tour in America, a national program presenting African-American artists, from writers like Amiri Baraka to the a cappella group Sweet Honey in the Rock, usually in university and college auditoriums. ☐ Onstage in New Jersey (see Festivals).

Educational Programs and Events: ☐ Study programs on Paul Robeson, Langston Hughes, and African music, folktales, and crafts. ☐ Artists-in-the-Schools (see above). ☐ Jazz residency.

Children's Theatre Center of New Jersey, Inc.

289 Maitland Avenue, Teaneck 07666   201-837-9029
Performance sites: theaters, schools, temples, churches, and community auditoriums statewide.

ARTS RESOURCES FOR THE DISABLED

New Jersey law requires that newly constructed public facilities and substantial renovations of existing public facilities be barrier free. Among the leaders statewide in handicapped access to the performing arts are McCarter Theatre Center for the Performing Arts and the Paper Mill Playhouse. However, an increasing number of facilities are wheelchair accessible, if not completely accessible (with access for the disabled to bathrooms, non-segregated seating, and special equipment for the visually and hearing impaired). Recently some previously difficult, if not impossible, arts access situations have improved. For instance, the Crossroads Theatre Company, once located in an all but inaccessible second-floor theater, is completing a new theater that is barrier-free. Before visiting any theater or arts institution it is wise not only to call ahead but also to contact the local county office on the disabled for the most up-to-date information on accessibility and special services or facilities.

The following organizations provide an array of arts programs and services for the disabled:

Very Special Arts New Jersey
  841 Georges Road, North Brunswick 08902 201-745-3885 or 201-745-3724

Visual and performing arts programs and companies geared toward the disabled (from the annual "Very Special Arts Festival" to the Unlimited Potential Theater Company, and Visibility, an organization for disabled visual artists) operate under the auspices of this umbrella agency, an arm of the national Very Special Arts organization. VSANJ holds numerous arts events for disabled people, including a conference on dance for special populations, in conjunction with the National Dance Association and the Dance Department at Mason Gross School of the Arts, at Rutgers, The State University. Its resource clearinghouse offers information on arts programs, exhibits, and ac-

---

The Children's Theatre Center of New Jersey, Inc., is dedicated to creating a strong regional theater for young audiences. Its first production, in 1987, was a parody titled *Flairy Tales*. Other works in its six-production repertoire include: *Theater Games, A Wish on a Golden Fish, Once Upon a Purim,* and *America in Song and Story,* a revue of American ballads and work and blues songs. All the works are original, created for the company by its directors, Sandra Johnson and Ofer Ben-Dor. The company plays from September through May, usually presenting about ten performances a month. It adds at least two works to its reper-

EDUCATION AND THE ARTS

cessibility. VSANJ also publishes a newsletter, *Access to the Arts,* and a yearly calendar.

Musical Interludes for the Ill and Homebound
Camden County Cultural and Heritage Commission
250 South Park Drive, Haddon Township 08108   609-858-0040
This program presents in-home performances by members of the Haddonfield Symphony Orchestra.

New Jersey Commission for the Blind and Visually Impaired
110 Raymond Boulevard, Newark 07102   201-648-3333
The commission owns and displays collections of works by blind and visually impaired artists.

New Jersey State Council on the Arts
Four North Broad Street, CN 306, Trenton 08625   609-292-6130
The council provides funding and information on disabled programs, organizations, and events.

Sharing
A Newsletter for and by the Handicapped of New Jersey
1422 Springfield Avenue, New Providence 07974   201-464-7790
Sharing publishes articles on all subjects, including theater arts, visual arts, book reviews, and poetry.

Special Audiences
75 Ferry Street, Newark 07105   201-465-5893
Special Audiences presents programs for special populations, including the physically and emotionally disabled, often at Symphony Hall, Newark. About ten performances by prominent solo artists and music, dance, and theater ensembles are given during the September-through-June season. Special Audiences sponsors a Newark Jazz Festival every Christmas. In addition, it distributes free tickets through more than three hundred social service and other agencies.

---

toire each year. Between two and four actors and actresses appear in each production.

Special Program: ☐ Nationwide children's playwriting contest.

Creative Theatre $ & ♿

102 Witherspoon Street, Princeton 08540   609-924-3489
Performance sites: in schools, churches, and community facilities

An Art Apart

In 1984, executives at New Jersey Commission for the Blind and Visually Impaired decided to demonstrate the range and professionalism of blind artists by establishing a collection of works by the visually impaired.

Today, twenty-six pieces are displayed in the commission's Newark headquarters: weavings, sculpture, photographs, etchings, and paintings, by artists from all over the United States, including four works by New Jersey artists: *One of Thirteen Episodes* and *Time Surfer and the Winds of Change,* both pencil drawings by C. Crist Delmonico of Morristown, and *Dog* and *Apeman* sculptures by Robert I. Isakower of Morris Plains. *Pool Table* (right), a work by Carmelo C. Ganello, draws on the dark, circular spots that plague the visually impaired artist.

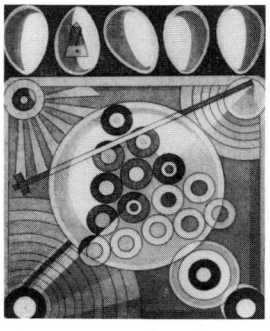

The Margot Studer Memorial Collection of works by blind artists was introduced to the public in an October 1984 opening at the Jane Voorhees Zimmerli Museum at Rutgers.

Another collection of works by the visually impaired is hung at the Library for the Blind and Handicapped in Trenton. Both collections are open to the public by appointment.

The Joseph Kohn Rehabilitation Center for the Blind and Visually Impaired in New Brunswick recently hung a wall bas-relief, designed for the blind by a New York sculptor Wopo Holup, which tells the story of Pegasus and is positioned at the height convenient for people seated in wheelchairs.

---

throughout New Jersey, regularly at the State Museum, Trenton, and on out-of-state tours.

Creative Theatre was founded under the auspices of the McCarter Theater in 1969 by Arthur Lithgow (father of film and stage actor John Lithgow) and Sharon Bown. Originally a children's creative dramatics school, it became a professional acting company in 1975. Today, it employs a resident company of five actors (all also trained drama teachers). The company tours four or five productions during its October-through-May season; some productions are original, others are fairy and folk tale adaptations.

EDUCATION AND THE ARTS

Creative Theatre encourages children to participate in its productions. The company sometimes holds workshops before performances, during which actors explain to students what their roles will be. For instance, during the play *The Legend of Sleepy Hollow* children help prepare dinner by cutting vegetables and mixing pie fillings at one character's house.

Special Programs and Events: □ Annual holiday production. □ Workshops and residencies in schools for the disabled.

Educational Programs and Events: □ Drama workshops for students and teachers. □ Classes in creative dramatics, acting, and video production. □ Residencies in school systems statewide. □ School of Creative Acting and Drama for children ages four to eighteen.

Festival of Music (DAO 1988) $ ⚕

P.O. Box 938, Englewood Cliffs 07632 (located at the Upper School, Charlotte Place, Englewood Cliffs) 201-567-1766
Performance sites: in schools and community centers throughout New Jersey, New York, Connecticut, and Pennsylvania.

Festival of Music brings professional actors, singers, and musicians to schoolchildren in hundreds of assembly programs each year. During one recent season, festival performers made more than eight hundred East Coast school appearances.

> "Having my artwork included is an honor. I'm deaf and blind in one eye, so it means a great deal to me that someone else appreciates something I have done, by myself."— Teen Arts Program Participant, Michael Uriando, M. Katzenbach School for the Deaf

Festival of Music was created in 1978 by John Devol, a professional trumpet player and former music teacher. The organization dispatches individual performers and ensembles to schools throughout the state, offering more than twenty different forty-five-minute programs for student audiences. Some programs highlight families of instruments;

EDUCATION AND THE ARTS

others songs or music history. "Sonic Boom" presents electronic music, "Road to the Isles," English and Gaelic tunes, and "Festival Brass," the sounds of a variety of horns. Programs such as "African Festival," "Japanese Festival," and "Salsa Festival" present music from different cultures. The festival season coincides with the school year.

Special Program: ☐ Festival of Music Showcase, an annual performance by several musical groups comprising the Festival of Music.

Educational Programs and Events: ☐ Artist-in-Residence programs. ☐ In-school performances. ☐ Instrumental clinics, instrument making, and teacher workshops.

Johnson Atelier (see Extension Gallery/Johnson Atelier—Visual Arts)

New Jersey State Teen Arts Program (see also Festivals)
841 Georges Road, North Brunswick 08902   201-745-3898

The Teen Arts program was founded in 1969 to encourage teenagers to learn about the arts by creating art themselves. It showcases teen works and sponsors workshops in music, dance, theater, creative writing, and the visual arts. The Teen Arts Community Performance Project sends New Jersey student performers into schools, libraries, corporations, and museums to demonstrate their talents.

Special Programs and Events: ☐ Community Performance Project. ☐ Statewide Visual Art Touring Exhibit. ☐ New Jersey Teen Arts Festival (see Festivals). ☐ New Jersey Young Playwrights Festival (see Festivals).

Educational Programs and Events: ☐ Master classes. ☐ Teacher and student workshops conducted by artists. ☐ Workshops in creative writing, dance, music, theater, visual arts, film, and video. ☐ Young Playwrights Residencies.

New Jersey Youth Symphony (DAO 1988, 1989)
P.O. Box 477, Summit 07901   201-522-0365
Performance sites: in civic, high school, and college auditoriums, and parks throughout the state and various halls on European tours.

Under the directorship of George Maull, the New Jersey Youth Symphony, founded in 1979, trains aspiring young New Jersey musicians. It consists of three orchestral groups: the New Jersey Youth Symphony Orchestra, based in Summit and made up of advanced musicians; the

EDUCATION AND THE ARTS

Preparatory Orchestra (less advanced musicians), also in Summit; and the Orchestral String Training Ensemble, based in Watchung. A recent concert program by the orchestra included Gabriel Fauré's *Pélleas et Mélisande,* Max Bruch's *Violin Concerto in G Minor,* and Ottorino Respighi's *The Pines of Rome.* The orchestras and ensemble present more than thirty concerts statewide during the season, which runs from September through May. Tuition-paying members audition for positions with the group, which includes more than two hundred young people from sixty-three New Jersey municipalities.

Special Program: ☐ Annual Play-A-Thon, during which the orchestra, preparatory orchestra and orchestral string training ensemble perform for the public at the Woodbridge Mall.

Educational Programs and Events: ☐ "Meet the Orchestra" series at Suburban Community Music Center, Madison; annual. ☐ Outreach school tours.

"As I lost my sight, I lost the ability to continue to work or enjoy the work of others. Sculpture . . . allows me to continue to 'see' my work and that of others with my hands and fingers."—Robert I. Isakower, whose *Dog* and *Apeman* hang in the Margot Studer Memorial Collection of Works by Blind Artists at the Newark offices of the Commission for the Blind and Visually Impaired.

The New School for the Arts/The New Jersey Opera Institute 💲♿🎵🎭

176 North Fullerton Avenue, Montclair 07042   201-746-4596
Performance sites: at the school and at the First United Methodist Church, Montclair, and school and community auditoriums throughout northern New Jersey.

Founded in 1975, the New School for the Arts offers classes not only in Montclair but also at five Newark locations and one in New York City. Performances by students and faculty are open to the public. The school, in addition to giving music, dance, voice lessons and performances, sponsors the New Jersey Opera Institute, which trains young singers for professional careers. In recent years, the opera institute has presented Verdi's *Un Ballo in Maschera,* conducted by artistic director Michael Trimble, and *Tosca,* starring George Shirley, who founded the program.

EDUCATION AND THE ARTS

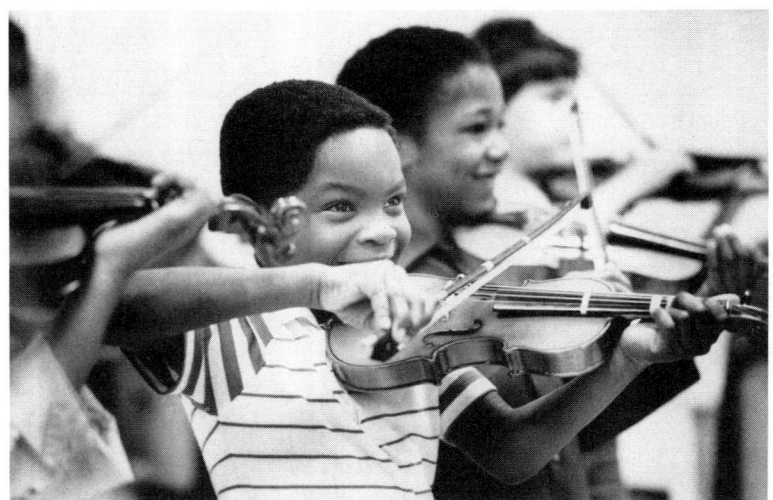

Classes in the arts, from Suzuki violin to recording techniques, are offered at the Newark Community School of the Arts, New Jersey's largest community arts school.

Special Programs and Events: □ New Jersey Opera Institute performances and New Jersey Concert Opera Series.

Educational Programs and Events: □ Music, dance, vocal, and other classes, including Kinderdance for children ages four and up.

Newark Boys Chorus School 🚹
1016 Broad Street, Newark 07102   201-621-8900
Performance sites: schools, corporate headquarters, and concert halls in the greater metropolitan area and on international tours every three to four years.

The Newark Boys Chorus School, an academic and choral institution, enrolls boys from this state's inner cities; many singers are minority students from East Orange and Newark. A number of the students continue their education at preparatory schools, often on scholarship. Most concerts are open to the public free of charge. The chorus performs classics, spirituals, and pop numbers by artists as different as Mahler and Whitney Huston. The Newark Boys Chorus is really two choruses:

an apprentice chorus for fifth and sixth graders and a concert chorus for older singers in the seventh and eighth grades. The concert chorus toured Japan in the spring of 1989. The school registers about seventy boys, grades four through eight, annually.

Newark Community School of the Arts (DAO 1987, 1989; GAA 1986) ♿ ♪ ♚

89 Lincoln Park, Newark 07102   201-642-0133
Performance sites: at the school, its two Newark branches, and annually at Symphony Hall.

The Newark Community School of the Arts offers a wide range of courses in dance, drama, music, and the visual arts to nearly all age groups and categories of students from preschoolers to senior citizens. Faculty members are working artists; some have performed in Broadway shows and written film scores. The school is New Jersey's largest arts school and presents nearly one hundred performances annually. It regularly highlights faculty and student talent, and recently produced a world premiere ballet, *And Still the Snowflakes Fall,* inspired by the Japanese arts of haiku and bonsai. The score was written by Randall Svane, then conductor of the Newark Boys Chorus, and performed with the Cathedral Symphony (see Music) at Symphony Hall. Most recitals and concerts (there are more than eighty annually) are free of charge to the public; there is a fee for the annual Symphony Hall Concert. Founded in 1968 by two Newark teachers, the student body of the NCSA originally numbered seventy-five. Today, it enrolls just under two thousand students. Professional companies in residence have included the Alvin Ailey Repertory Ensemble and The Ensemble Theatre Company (see Theater).

Special Programs and Events: □ Black History Program featuring accomplished black performers; annual. □ Cultural Festivals that highlight the artistic achievements of the Hispanic, Philippine, and other communities; annual. □ Gifted Students Concert; annual. □ Suzuki Festival; annual. □ Symphony Hall concert; annual.

Educational Programs and Events: □ Arts/business classes in such areas as recording, song writing, and artistic management. □ Master classes. □ Music, dance, drama, and visual arts classes for adults and children. □ Special classes for the gifted, disabled, and senior citizens.

"People in taxicabs, limos, airplanes, bicycles, roller skates, wheelchairs, crutches . . . they are coming, working, having fun, dancing, singing and conversing (in at least six languages) . . . so nourishing and so full of promise."—Newark Community School of the Arts staff member

Opera/Music Theatre International Inc. $◨

1016–18 Broad Street, Newark 07102   201-596-0087
Performance sites: Symphony Hall, Newark (2,800 seats), and in libraries, museums, recital halls, and private homes.

Founded in 1987 by Metropolitan Opera star Jerome Hines, who serves as general manager and artistic director, the Opera/Music Theatre International (formerly Opera/Music Theatre Institute of New Jersey) trains young singers, helping them to develop their careers and showcase their work. Hines has recruited his faculty from among his opera colleagues. Institute productions are always open to the public; one recent production of Mozart's *Magic Flute* starred Hines and members of the institute's company of fellows. Stage direction was by faculty member Frank Corsaro of the New York City Opera and sets by children's book writer and illustrator Maurice Sendak. Another recent production, on New Year's Eve 1989, starred mezzo-soprano Marilyn Horne. In one recent year, nineteen singers were chosen from twelve hundred who auditioned for admission to the institute. Fellows spend a year in intensive classes on such subjects as voice and languages; during that time they perform regularly for general audiences and occasionally, by special request, at private homes.

Special Event: ☐ New Year's Eve production; annual.

Educational Programs and Events: ☐ Classes, master classes, and seminars in voice, coaching, acting, foreign languages, and musical career development.

Project Impact (DAO 1989, 1990) $♿☤

Arts-in-Education Foundation, 41 East Center Street, Midland Park 07432   201-444-5753
Performance sites: on tours of New Jersey schools, community centers, and corporations.

EDUCATION AND THE ARTS

Project Impact produces and presents programs in nearly every arts discipline, from theater and dance to visual arts and music. All programs feature professional artists. The organization emphasizes arts programs for underserved students, from the gifted and talented to the disabled and preschoolers and to disadvantaged youngsters in urban schools.

Special Programs and Events: ☐ Artwork on loan, free of charge. ☐ Free outdoor musical performances in Bergen County parks; summer.

Educational Programs and Events: ☐ Artist-in-the-Classroom workshops. ☐ Performing arts assembly series. ☐ Teacher-training workshops.

Pushcart Players

197 Bloomfield Avenue, Verona 07044   201-857-1115
Performance sites: schools in New York, New Jersey, Pennsylvania.

The company's first production was based on an Armenian folktale. Today, the group offers original, fully-mounted musicals on diverse subjects such as physical and psychological wellness (*Who Cares, I'm Okay; You're Okay*) and the nation's bicentennial (*A More Perfect Union*). *Betwixt 'n Between,* a program on decision making, was based on five stories by classic authors such as Tolstoy. Since its founding in 1974, the Pushcart Players has developed programs called "mini-series," short, light-hearted presentations and workshops on serious subjects. One mini-series production, *Singing and Signing,* tells three stories about hearing-impaired children aimed at making hearing schoolchildren more sensitive to their disabled peers. Another, *The Lightest Baggage of All,* is designed to stimulate an interest in reading by dramatizing folktales from around the world. Study guides help teachers and/or parents prepare students for performances. Pushcart presents two original productions during its two seasons, one from September through December; the other from February through June. Its four actors and actresses, many of whom have been with the company for several years, present more than one hundred seventy-five performances annually.

Educational Programs and Events: ☐ Acting classes for junior high school and high school students. ☐ Creative dramatics classes for ages five through eight.

EDUCATION AND THE ARTS

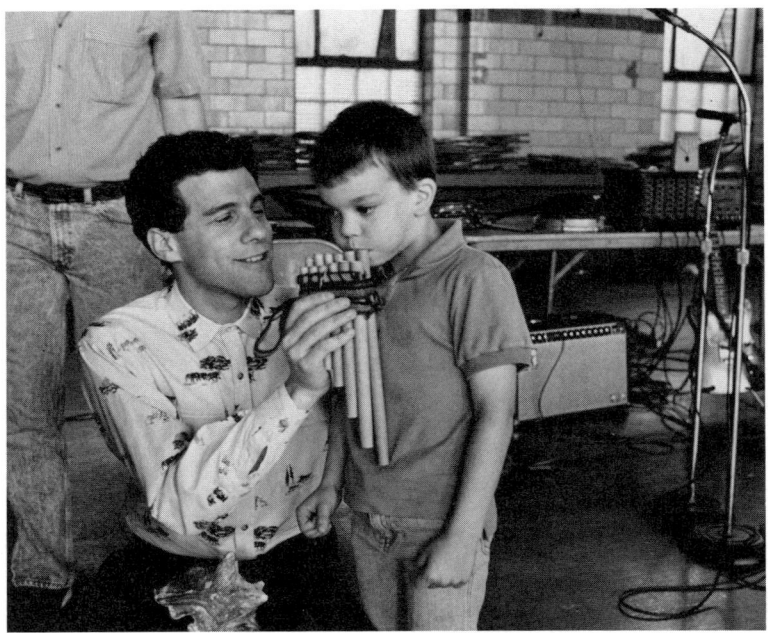

A child learns to play the pan pipes as part of a performance sponsored by Project Impact, during which students are guided by professional musicians.

Shakespeare for Schools 🐞 $ 👤
41 Madeline Avenue, Clifton 07011   201-546-0624
Performance sites: schools in New York, New Jersey, and Connecticut.

The company was founded in 1987 by Janet Villas, who sings in the New York City Opera chorus. Conceived as the "ultimate English resource" by Villas, a former teacher, Shakespeare for Schools helps students understand Shakespeare by performing the plays they are studying. A recent original production called *Shakespeare's Women* examined the playwright's attitudes toward women through monologues by and scenes involving Lady Macbeth, The Witches, Ophelia, Juliet, and others. The company performs about fifty times a year. It has nine one-half-hour shows in its repertoire, each featuring five scenes from a Shakespearean play.

Special Program: ☐ Shakespeare's Birthday performances in April.

EDUCATION AND THE ARTS

The Shoestring Players $ ♿ ⚕

Carriage House, Room 109, Douglass College, New Brunswick
08903   201-932-9772
Performance sites: State Theater, New Brunswick; schools and auditoriums on nationwide tours.

Founded in 1980 at Rutgers as a student theater group, Shoestring is now a professional company that sends its ensemble performances nationwide. The company produces works inspired by folktales and folk traditions from around the world. In 1987, it performed at the International Children's Festival at Wolf Trap Park outside Washington, D.C. Its production of *The People Who Could Fly,* based on six folktales, one about black culture and slavery, ran Off Broadway in 1989. Shoestring presents more than three hundred performances of one original production annually, casting an average of nine actors and actresses. Its season generally runs from September through May, and the company tours a revival of a previous production during the summer. Most productions combine dramatic and comic stories. Shoestring emphasizes theater basics; its actors use few or no props and minimal sets.

Special Program: ◻ Free performances for special populations at area hospitals and schools.

Educational Programs and Events: ◻ Post-performance workshops in group theatrics. ◻ Shoestring Plus, a program led by young professionals that teaches dramatics, playwriting, and rehearsal techniques to children in grades kindergarten through high school and special populations, including hearing and visually impaired.

Waterloo Festival School of Music (see also Festivals) $ ⚕

Waterloo Foundation for the Arts, Inc., Village of Waterloo,
Stanhope 07874   201-273-6883
Performance sites: Richardson Auditorium, Princeton University (1,000 seats), in the Waterloo Village tent, Stanhope (capacity 1,500), and other sites statewide.

Running through June and July, the Waterloo Festival School of Music (in residence at Princeton University) auditions musicians for six-week fellowships. Students dedicated to professional careers and faculty members perform for the public in a series of solo and chamber music concerts during the school's session. In addition to performing in Young Artists concerts, the fellows play at Waterloo Village with the full Waterloo Festival Orchestra during the annual summer-long Waterloo Festival (see Festivals).

EDUCATION AND THE ARTS

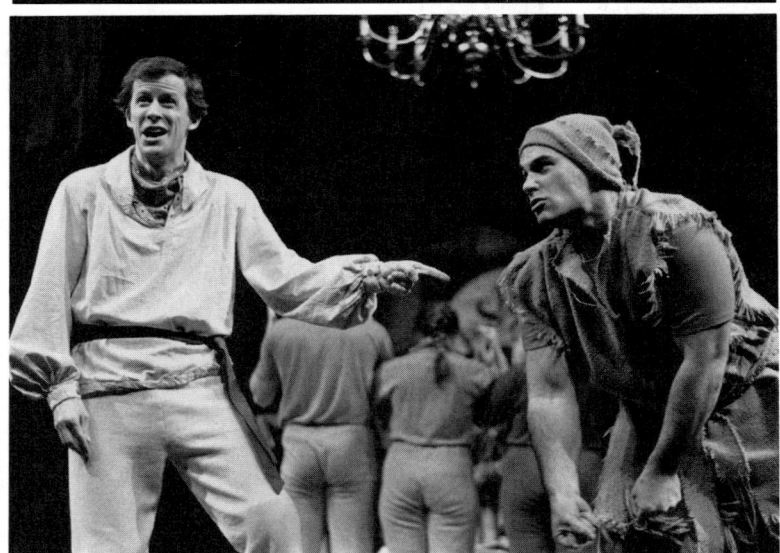

Using minimal props and costumes, the Shoestring Players present plays based on international folktales and traditions, in productions such as this one, titled *Molly Whuppie & Other Folktales from around the World*.

Westminster Choir College (DAO 1987) $ 🎵 ♿

Hamilton at Walnut, Princeton 08540   609-921-7100
Performance sites: Bristol Chapel and The Playhouse, Westminster Choir College Campus, Princeton, and on national and international tours.

Westminster choirs have apppeared all over the country with major orchestras and conductors. The largest choir, the Westminster Symphonic Choir, composed of two hundred members, performs regularly with the New York Philharmonic, the New Jersey Symphony Orchestra, and the Philadelphia Orchestra. (It recently performed Leonard Bernstein's *Chichester Psalms,* conducted by the composer, with the New York Philharmonic at Carnegie Hall.) The select Westminster Choir, made up of forty members, tours nationally and internationally and is chorus-in-residence at Spoleto festivals in Charleston, South Carolina, and Italy. Both the Symphonic and Westminster choirs are reserved for upperclassmen and graduate students; freshmen at Westminster sing in the Chapel Choir. In addition, the college has a Bell Choir (which performs on the world's largest set of handbells) and a popular music ensemble, The Westminster Singers, which performs show tunes, jazz songs, and holiday favorites.

Founded in Ohio in 1926, as a program of a Dayton Presbyterian church, the choir moved to Ithaca College before relocating to Princeton in 1932, in order to be closer to New York City concert halls. The college is a rich entertainment and educational resource not only for students enrolled, but also for the community; it sponsors numerous performances and recitals, and its Conservatory and Continuing Education Program offers classes for the general public. Westminster's Talbott Library in one of the country's largest music libraries, and it maintains an extensive collection not only of scores and recorded music but also of information on organs, including books on organs and organ building and original documents belonging to some of the world's greatest organists and organ builders.

Special Programs and Events: ◻ Choir Gala Spring Concert. ◻ Children's concert series. ◻ Christmas at Westminster, a three-week festival of holiday music featuring the college's performing ensembles and soloists. ◻ Faculty recital series from September to May. ◻ Spring Musicale conservatory faculty recital; annual. ◻ Student recitals, free of charge.

Educational Programs and Events: ◻ Continuing Education Program, college and graduate level courses in such subjects as music, music history, and voice. ◻ Saturday Seminars, one-day courses. ◻ Summer Sessions, continuing education programs. ◻ Professional Symposia: for example, "Church Music: The Future" gathered organ builders, organists, and other church musicians from around the country. ◻ Westminster Conservatory of Music, instrumental classes for children and adults, open to the community.

Young Audiences of New Jersey $|⛾|

245 Nassau Street, Princeton 08540   609-683-7966
Performance sites: in schools, libraries, and community centers statewide.

A chapter of the national Young Audiences organization, this group sends dozens of professional individual artists and ensembles, from harpists to puppeteers, into New Jersey classrooms and assemblies. Young Audiences presents more than one thousand performances and workshops during each academic year. Performances feature not only

EDUCATION AND THE ARTS

COMMUNITY ARTS SCHOOLS

Center for More Than Dance Education
(formerly Center for Modern Dance Education)
  84 Euclid Avenue, Hackensack 07601   201-342-2989

Garden State Academy of Music
  88 Park Avenue, P.O. Box 7699, Rutherford 07070   201-933-5454

Haddonfield School of Creative and Performing Arts
  P.O. Box 383, Haddonfield 08033   609-429-9327

Long Hill Chapel Music Center
  525 Shunpike Road, Chatham 07928   201-665-9721

Monmouth Conservatory of Music
  Two Cross Street, Little Silver 07739   201-741-8880

Montclair State College
Music Preparatory Division
  Upper Montclair 07043   201-256-8487

Neighborhood House School of the Arts
  12 Flagler Street, Morristown 07960   201-538-1229

New School for the Arts
  176 North Fullerton Avenue, Montclair 07042   201-746-4596

Newark Community School of the Arts (see main listing)

Suburban Community Music Center
  Madison Area YMCA, One Ralph Stoddard Drive, Madison 07940
  201-377-6200

Thurnauer School of Music
  J.C.C. on the Palisades, 411 East Clinton Avenue, Tenafly 07670
  201-569-7900

Westminster Conservatory of Music (see main listing)

---

artists and ensembles created for Young Audiences, but also existing New Jersey performing arts organizations, such as Gallman's Dance Theater of Newark and the Mount Laurel Ballet. Assembly performances and study guides cover music, dance, and other disciplines, often emphasizing cultural traditions. For instance, the 1989–1990 season offered *Dance España,* performances by the American Spanish Dance Theatre, and *String Encounters* by the Laurentian String Quartet.

Special Programs and Events: □ Black History Month program; annual.
□ Showcase of Young Audiences performers; annual.

EDUCATION AND THE ARTS

Educational Programs and Events: ☐ In-school artist residencies and workshops. ☐ Master classes in music, dance, and theater. ☐ Teacher workshops.

Youth Theatre of New Jersey [$][👤]
39 Newton-Sparta Road, Newton 07860   201-579-5734
Performance sites: St. Mary's Episcopal Church, Sparta (120 seats); The Garris Center, Branchville (70 seats); The Lyceum, Franklin (120 seats); and the Police Athletic League, Newark (200–250 seats) and other places on tours of northern New Jersey.

"When two twelve-year-old performers did an improvisation about a tie shop where one kept trying to convince the other that various rubber fish, toilet plungers, etc. were really the latest style in neckware, we witnessed near-pandemonium, the audience was so convulsed with laughter."—Robert Nersesian, Managing Director, Youth Theatre of New Jersey

---

Founded in 1984 as the All Kids Theatre of Sussex County by actress/director Allyn Sitjar, this company produces new dramatic plays and musicals about young people performed by actors ages seven through eighteen. In May 1988, it produced *Taking The Bait,* a "message musical" about drinking and driving. The company has produced more than thirty original plays and musicals about children's issues. The Youth Theatre introduces several new plays each season, including works written by members of the company. It offers classes year-round and presents six to eight productions (six performances of each) during the school year. Almost all productions are original and new each season; occasionally the group revives old favorites. Ten to fifteen young actors appear in each production. The company recently completed a tour of England.

Special Programs and Events: ☐ Summer Theatre Camp during July and August. ☐ Young Playwrights Festival in November.

Educational Programs and Events: ☐ Classes in acting, stage combat, mime, and voice and play-writing workshops. ☐ Play-writing competition and festival for writers ages seven to eighteen; the company produces the winning entries.

Appendixes

New Jersey County and Area Arts Agencies

These organizations provide a host of information, services, facilities, and state, county, and local monies to artists, arts organizations, and the public. In addition to coordinating local arts activities, certain agencies allocate state and county funds. They can provide information on local art leagues and co-ops, friends' groups, municipal arts councils and committees, service organizations, and cultural outlets of all kinds.

Typically, arts agencies publish cultural calendars, newsletters, and brochures listing and explaining the arts events and organizations in the areas they cover. They also sponsor shows and festivals featuring local artists and arts groups and arts-in-education programs for area schools. Some maintain permanent collections of works by area artists.

Many agencies provide arts and arts-therapy programs for disabled persons such as a choir for retarded citizens (Sussex County Arts Council) or a visual arts group for the disabled (Visibility, sponsored by Very Special Arts New Jersey and the Middlesex County Cultural and Heritage Commission). The Camden County Cultural and Heritage Commission program "Musical Interludes" sends performers into the homes of the seriously ill and disabled.

These organizations also sponsor technical assistance workshops and seminars, which assist artists, arts organizations, and community groups in developing skills in fund-raising, publicity, grants applications, and other areas.

The state umbrella agency, the New Jersey State Council on the Arts, channels funding and coordinates arts programs for individual artists and arts organizations statewide.

The New Jersey State Council on the Arts
Department of State, 4 North Broad Street, CN 306, Trenton 08625
609-292-6130

Arts Council of the Essex Area
Montclair State College, Valley Road, Upper Montclair 07043
201-744-1717

NEW JERSEY COUNTY AND AREA ARTS AGENCIES

Arts Council of the Morris Area
Embury Hall, Drew University, Madison 07940   201-377-6622

Atlantic County Office of Cultural and Heritage Affairs
1333 Atlantic Avenue, Atlantic City 08401   609-345-6700 x 2243

Bergen County Division of Cultural and Historic Affairs
Court Plaza South, Administration Building, 21 Main Street, Room 203 W, Hackensack 07601-7000   201-646-2778

Burlington County Cultural and Heritage Commission
49 Rancocas Road, Mt. Holly 08060   609-265-5068

Camden County Cultural and Heritage Commission
Hopkins House, 250 South Park Drive, Haddon Township 08108
609-858-0040

Cape May County Cultural and Heritage Commission
DN-101, Library Office Building, Cape May Court House 08210
609-465-1005

Cumberland County Cultural and Heritage Commission
50 East Broad Street, Bridgeton 08802   609-451-4802

Essex County Division of Cultural and Historic Affairs
22 Fairview Avenue, Cedar Grove 07009   201-857-5290

Gloucester County Cultural and Heritage Commission
c/o Doris Rink, 406 Swedesboro Road, Gibbstown 08027
609-423-0916/848-9149

Hudson County Division of Cultural and Heritage Affairs
114 Clifton Place, Murdock Hall, Jersey City 07304   201-915-1212

Hunterdon County Cultural and Heritage Commission
Administration Building, Flemington 08820   201-788-1256

Mercer County Cultural and Heritage Commission
640 South Broad Street, Trenton 08650   609-989-6701

Middlesex County Arts and Education Council
Hamilton Center, 16 Joyce Kilmer Avenue, New Brunswick 08901
201-249-5151 or -5158

Middlesex County Cultural and Heritage Commission (DAO 1989)
841 Georges Road, North Brunswick 08902   201-745-4489

NEW JERSEY COUNTY AND AREA ARTS AGENCIES

Monmouth County Arts Council
99 Monmouth Street, Red Bank 07701   201-842-9000

Ocean County Cultural and Heritage Commission
38 Hadley Avenue, Toms River 08753
201-244-2121 x 2200

Passaic County Cultural and Heritage Council
c/o Passaic County Community College, College Boulevard, Paterson 07509   201-684-6555

Salem County Cultural and Heritage Commission
Salem County College, P.O. Box 896, Salem 08079   609-678-7376

Somerset County Cultural and Heritage Commission
P.O. Box 3000, County Administration Building, Somerville 08876   201-231-7110

Southern New Jersey Advocates for the Arts
P.O. Box 158, Haddon Heights 08035   609-863-6587

Sussex County Arts Council
P.O. Box 502, Newton 07860   201-383-0027

Union County Office of Cultural and Heritage Affairs (DAO 1989)
633 Pearl Street, Elizabeth 07202   201-558-2550

Very Special Arts New Jersey (formerly Committee Arts for the Handicapped)
841 Georges Road, North Brunswick 08902   201-745-3885

Warren County Cultural and Heritage Commission
Warren County Court House, Belvidere 07823   201-475-5361

Grantmakers

Numerous organizations offer funding for artists and arts organizations nationwide. Following is a list of New Jersey-based or -oriented grantmakers, many of whom give priority to New Jersey artists, arts organizations, or projects. (See also New Jersey County and Area Arts Agencies Appendix).

Allied Corporation Foundation
P.O. Box 1057 R, Morristown 07960   201-455-2671

Allison Foundation
630 West Mt. Pleasant Avenue, Livingston 07039   201-992-3800

AT&T Foundation
550 Madison Avenue, 27th Floor, New York, New York 10022
212-605-6734

Frank and Lydia Bergen Foundation
c/o First Fidelity Bank, 55 Madison Avenue, Morristown 07960   201-829-7111
Prefers grants in the performing arts, primarily music; particular interest in opportunities for young conductors and educational activities

The Bunbury Company, Inc.
169 Nassau Street, Princeton 08542   609-683-1444

Campbell Soup Fund
Campbell Place, Camden 08103   609-342-4800

Capezio Ballet Makers Dance Foundation, Inc.
One Campus Road, Totowa 07512   201-595-9000
Prefers dance-oriented applicants

Community Foundation of New Jersey
Knox Hill Road, P.O. Box 317, Morristown 07963   201-267-5533
Prefers grants to grass-roots organizations with innovative programs

Crum and Forster Foundation
305 Madison Avenue, CN1932, Morristown 07960   201-285-7275

GRANTMAKERS

Geraldine R. Dodge Foundation Inc.
95 Madison Avenue, P.O. Box 1239, Morristown 07960
201-540-8442
Grants in all categories

Frelinghuysen Foundation
P.O. Box 726, Far Hills 07931   201-439-3499
Grants in all categories

Fund for the New Jersey Blind
1100 Raymond Boulevard, Room 108, Newark
07102   201-648-2324
Grants to visually impaired artists

Heritage Bank Foundation
P.O. Box 5470, Cherry Hill 08034   609-488-2516

Richard H. Holzer Memorial Foundation
120 Sylvan Avenue, Englewood Cliffs 07632   201-947-8810
Especially interested in grants in music

Hyde and Watson Foundation
437 Southern Boulevard, Chatham Township 07928   201-966-6024
Grants in all categories, generally within a fifty-mile radius of New York City

Grand Marnier Foundation
Glenpointe Centre West, Teaneck 07666   201-836-7799

Jacqueline Foundation
601 Ewing Street, Suite C-6, Princeton 08540   609-924-3210

Johnson & Johnson Family of Companies Contribution Fund
One Johnson & Johnson Plaza, New Brunswick 08933
201-524-0400
Grants in all categories, especially to New Brunswick artists and organizations

F. M. Kirby Foundation Inc.
c/o Delaware Trust Company, 17 De Hart Street, Morristown 07960
201-538-4800
Grants in all categories, especially to Morris County artists and organizations

GRANTMAKERS

Liz Claiborne Foundation
One Claiborne Avenue, North Bergen 07047   201-622-5000
Grants in all categories

Curtis W. McGraw Foundation
c/o Drinker, Biddle & Reath, P.O. Box 627, Princeton 08542
609-921-6336
Grants in all categories, especially to Princeton area artists and organizations

Merck Company Foundation
P.O. Box 2000, Rahway 07065   201-594-4375

Jay R. Monroe Memorial Foundation
44 Main Street, Millburn 07041   201-379-7730
Prefers grants in the performing arts

Mid-Atlantic Arts Foundation
11 East Chase Street, Suite 2A, Baltimore, MD 21202   301-539-6650
Grants for visual artists, performing arts tours, residencies, and technical assistance

Mutual Benefit Life Charitable Trust
520 Broad Street, Newark 07101   201-481-8107

Nabisco Foundation
Nabisco Brands Place, Parsippany 07098   201-682-7098
Grants in all categories

National Starch and Chemical Foundation Inc.
10 Finderne Avenue, Bridgewater 08807   201-685-5000
Grants in all categories

The New Jersey Committee for the Humanities
73 Easton Avenue, New Brunswick 08901   201-932-7726

The New Jersey State Council on the Arts
Department of State, 4 North Broad Street, CN 306, Trenton 08625
609-292-6130

Probably the largest patron of the arts in New Jersey, the State Council gave more than $18 million in grants in the year ending in June 1990. Grant categories to individual artists and arts organizations include: Artistic Focus Grants for important arts organizations aiming for national and international recognition; Challenge Grants; and Excellence Initiative Grants. The council is also administering $40 million in grants for capital improvements to cultural centers throughout the state, financed by a bond issue.

Charles E. and Joyce Pettinos Foundation Inc.
437 Southern Boulevard, Chatham Township 07928   201-966-6024
Prefers grants for a capital need, within a fifty-mile radius of Chatham Township

Prudential Foundation Inc.
15 Prudential Plaza, Newark 07101   201-802-7355
Prefers grants to aid underserved arts audiences; to explore the role of culture in economic development; to individuals and organizations in areas where Prudential offices are located: Newark, Florham Park, Roseland, Woodbridge, Plainfield, and Millville

Lilian P. Schenck Charitable Trust
Englewood Trust Office, One Engle Street, Englewood 07631   201-894-4824
Grants in all categories

Schering Plough Foundation
One Giralda Farms, Madison 07940   201-822-7407
Grants in all categories, especially to artists and organizations in areas where Schering Plough offices are located: Madison, Kenilworth, Union Township, Bloomfield, and Lafayette

Schultz Foundation
Suite 207, 1037 Route 46 East, Clifton 07013   201-614-8880

Seton Foundation
c/o Seton Company, 849 Broadway, Newark 07104   201-485-4800
Grants in all categories

William E. Simon Foundation
310 South Street, Morristown 07960   201-898-0293
Grants in all categories

Silver Mountain Foundation for the Arts
310 South Street, Morristown 07960   201-898-0293

South Branch Foundation
P.O. Box 477, Somerville 08876   201-722-6400

GRANTMAKERS

Subaru of America Foundation Inc.
Subaru Plaza, P.O. Box 6000, Cherry Hill 08034   609-488-5099
Grants in all categories in areas where Subaru facilities are located: Cherry Hill, Camden, and Gloucester and Burlington counties

Thomas and Betts Charitable Trust
920 Route 202, Raritan 08869   201-685-1600
Prefers grants to major state arts organizations

Victoria Foundation, Inc.
40 South Fullerton Avenue, Montclair 07042   201-783-4450
Prefers grants for arts education programs

Visceglia-Summit Associates Foundation
Raritan Plaza II, Raritan Center, Edison 08818   201-225-2900

Warner Lambert Charitable Foundation
201 Tabor Road, Morris Plains 07950   201-540-2150
Grants in all categories